WHAT YOU DIDN'T LEARN IN LAW SCHOOL ABOUT TRIAL PRACTICE

Charles Bruess

First published by Dog Ear Publishing
4010 W. 86th Street, Ste H
Indianapolis, IN 46268
www.dogearpublishing.net

ISBN: 978-159858-619-0

This book is printed on acid-free paper.

Printed in the United States of America

ACKNOWLEDGEMENTS

This book, as well as my entire legal career, have only been made possible by the dedication, support and encouragement from Jean, my wife of forty-five years.

I express my appreciation to Judge David F. Hamilton of the United States District Court for the Southern District of Indiana for providing me the privilege to serve as his courtroom deputy. Serving in this capacity provided me with a wealth of information that has been included in this book.

I want to acknowledge the contributions of Linda Carmichael and Fred Pratt, with whom I have worked at the United States District Court, for their support as well as for their typing the original manuscript of this book.

CONTENTS

1

INTRODUCTION

During my years as a law student, there were no trial practice or techniques courses.

Upon completion of law school, I reported for duty as a lawyer with the Judge Advocate General Corps of the United States Navy. Although I was required to attend Naval Justice School, this course provided no training in trial practice or techniques. Within days of reporting to my first permanent duty station, I was assigned to represent a defendant in a court martial. Without ever having seen a court martial, and without any courtroom training, there I was, making an opening statement, examining witnesses, interposing objections, and making a closing argument. Thereafter, I tried many more cases, both as a prosecutor and as defense counsel, with nothing but on-the-job training to guide me.

When I started in private practice, my law firm provided no formal training for litigators. No continuing legal education courses were even available. My law firm must have considered that the Navy made me sufficiently experienced as a trial lawyer, for within a month after starting as an associate, I was assigned to try a civil jury action alone. Other than attending four depositions and participating in three trials with more senior lawyers during my early years of practice, I was on my own for litigated matters. During my thirty years of private practice, I was responsible for litigation in nine different states, almost exclusively in the federal courts.

As a trial lawyer, my experiences included actions ranging between the following extremes:

- A trial in which the witnesses were not even interviewed prior to trial and an action in which one witness was deposed for 22 days.
- A trial lasting two hours and trials lasting 30 days.
- Actions with actual damages ranging from $100 to $345,000,000.

Starting in 1999, after I retired from private practice, I began serving as a courtroom deputy for Judge David F. Hamilton of the United States District Court for the Southern District of Indiana. As a courtroom deputy, I have witnessed, as a neutral observer, more than eighty trials and contested evidentiary hearings, as well as many arguments on motions. I also have had the opportunity to speak with jurors at the conclusion of trials.

While observing trials, I have seen examples of superior trial skills. I also have observed what I consider to be inadequate trial practices from lawyers who otherwise impressed me with their understanding of substantive law. I concluded that these inadequate trial skills were the result of lack of training, not lack of competence.

In my opinion, this lack of trial skills results from several factors:

- Many law schools still are not providing an opportunity for students to learn litigation skills.
- Only a very small percentage of actions filed actually results in trials. Lawyers have limited opportunities to develop and practice trial skills, especially in complex actions.
- Years ago, younger lawyers were able to attend depositions and trials with more senior lawyers. Now, because of high hourly rates, many clients will pay for the services of only the lawyers directly involved in the depositions and trials; therefore, younger lawyers do not have the opportunity to observe or practice trial skills under the tutelage of more experienced lawyers. When younger lawyers do observe trials or depositions, some of what they observe may be inadequate or even improper. After one trial, I met with a young lawyer to discuss what I considered to be problematic questioning techniques. The lawyer told me that her form of questions was patterned after a more senior lawyer whom she had assisted in a trial; she assumed that the questioning style was proper and effective. After I explained to her the problems with her style, she told me that she understood why what she was doing could be a problem and that she would thereafter change her form of questions.
- There is much pressure for younger lawyers, especially those in larger firms, to amass hours for billing purposes. These lawyers do not want to substitute time observing depositions or trials for billable hours.

When I was still in private practice, I shared my experiences with the younger lawyers in my firm. My hope was to assist them in avoiding some of the mistakes I had made because of lack of adequate training and to teach them some of the positive trial skills I had observed. I shared these experiences during formal presentations or more informally by providing a "lesson of the day" when an unusual, noteworthy experience occurred.

I believe that these presentations and lessons of the day were beneficial for the younger lawyers. Now that I have retired from the practice of law and as a courtroom deputy, I decided to make an effort to share these experiences with more lawyers, especially because serving as a courtroom deputy provided me with additional material to impart, including information obtained from jurors at the conclusion of trials. I also believe that my varied experiences as a Navy lawyer for three years, as a trial lawyer in private practice for thirty years, and as a courtroom deputy for almost ten years provide a unique perspective on trial skills.

This book is not written to promote myself as a litigator. My litigating days are over. I am not even proposing that lawyers adopt every suggestion contained in this book. There are different styles. There are different techniques. Instead, the purpose of this book is merely to compile examples of trial practices, both good and questionable, for lawyers to consider. Hopefully, these examples will assist lawyers in making decisions on how they will try cases based on a greater amount of information.

2

THE QUINTESSENTIAL LESSON OF THE DAY

Each juror comes to the courtroom with biases, prejudices, ideas, attitudes, likes, and dislikes. It is impossible to leave these outside the courthouse. Some of these may be revealed during voir dire; some may not. Some are not even susceptible to being disclosed during voir dire. For example, some jurors may be offended by flashy jewelry, demeanor of counsel, conduct or appearance of parties or witnesses, or wasting of time on irrelevant matters. Even if these matters were the subject of questions during voir dire, it is unlikely that any juror would admit to them.

Although the facts and the law should determine the result of a trial, these attitudes, biases, and so on, of jurors may affect the outcome of a trial. As evidence is being presented, this baggage of the jurors may cause them to disbelieve certain witnesses or evidence, or not accept the law as instructed, or more readily believe certain witnesses or evidence, or accept the law as instructed. What you or your clients or witnesses do or say during the trial may affect the jury's perception and ultimate decision, especially in a close case. It is necessary to do everything conceivable to have the jurors want to find for the party you represent and to avoid doing things that will lead the jurors to rule against that party. This idea is comparable to the lowest common denominator in mathematics.

Some of the comments included in this book are from jurors, albeit not always a large percentage. These comments should at least be considered by trial lawyers.

Some of the comments in this book are individualistic to me and may be idiosyncratic. When I have shared these comments with law clerks with whom I have worked, they say I am out of touch with reality. Nevertheless, you must realize that there will be jurors as old as I am and as idiosyncratic as I am.

Therefore, the quintessential lesson of the day is this: Avoid doing anything that may offend any juror and, instead, do everything you can to cause each juror to want to rule for the party you represent.

3

SUCCESSFUL TRIAL PRACTICE DEMANDS A WORKING KNOWLEDGE OF APPLICABLE STATUTES AND RULES

Every trial lawyer must have a familiarity with applicablc:

- Statutes.
- Rules of civil/criminal procedure.
- Rules of evidence.
- Local court rules.
- Particular judge's rules.

There are lawyers who believe that because they have graduated from law school and passed a bar examination, they no longer need to do research or review fundamental statutes and rules. This could be true for some lawyers, but there are other lawyers whose written work product and trial skills suggest a need to review statutes and rules. The following examples support this opinion.

Failure to Be Aware of Applicable Jurisdictional Requirements May Result in a Dismissal of the Action

Before filing in or removing any action to any court, be certain that the court has jurisdiction and that the requisite jurisdictional elements are pleaded.

One failure that occurs too often in federal court is a failure to allege diversity of citizenship. 28 U.S.C. 1332 states that "[t]he district courts shall have original jurisdiction of all civil actions where the matter in controversy exceeds the sum or value of $75,000, exclusive of interest and costs, <u>and</u> is between - (1) <u>citizens</u> of different states. . . ." (emphasis added).

Seeking to invoke diversity jurisdiction, either as an original action or as a removal, some counsel allege only "residency." Although residency and citizenship are usually the same, there remains a difference for purposes of diversity jurisdiction. A person who has a winter home in Florida may be residing in Florida but could be a citizen of Indiana. See *Guarantee Nat'l Title Co., Inc. v. J. E. G. Assocs.*, 101 F.3d 57, 59 (7th Cir. 1996). ("When the parties allege residence but not citizenship, the court must dismiss the suit.")

Another frequent error is the failure to allege properly the citizenship of a corporate party. For the purposes of 28 U.S.C. 1332(c), "a corporation shall be deemed to be a citizen of any State by which it has been incorporated <u>and of the State where it has its principal place of business</u>. . . ." (emphasis added). At times, there is an allegation of the state of incorporation, but no allegation of the state in which that corporation has its principal place of business. Jurisdiction has, therefore, not been established.

When a partnership is involved, there is often a failure to allege the citizenship of each of the partners. See *Guarantee Nat'l Title Co., Inc. v. J. E. G. Assocs.*, 101 F.3d 57 (7th Cir. 1996). Likewise, at least for actions filed in district courts in the 7th Circuit, a limited liability company is treated like a partnership so that all of its members and their citizenships must be pleaded. See *Cosgrove v. Bartolotta*, 150 F.3d 729, 731 (7th Cir. 1998).

Consider the following calamity for one set of lawyers. At 3:00 p.m. on a Friday afternoon, counsel filed a verified complaint and request for a temporary restraining order. The court, however, refused to consider the request because plaintiff failed properly to invoke federal diversity jurisdiction. More specifically, plaintiff failed to allege the citizenship of the individual defendant, alleging residence instead; plaintiff failed to allege the members and citizenships of the LLC defendant; and plaintiff failed to allege that there was $75,000.00 in controversy.

If you fail properly to allege jurisdiction, you may be fortunate enough to have the opportunity to cure the defect. In case of a removal, if you cannot cure and the action is remanded to state court, the awarding of costs and fees is a possibility.

There is an interesting decision in which, on appeal, the Seventh Circuit Court of Appeals ascertained that there was no diversity jurisdiction. Vacating the judgment, the Seventh Circuit said, "The costs of a doomed foray into federal court should fall on the lawyers who failed to do their homework, not on the hapless clients." The court ordered the lawyers to "perform, without additional fees, any further services that are necessary to bring this suit to a conclusion in state court or via settlement." See *Belleville Catering Co. v. Champaign Market Place, L.L.C.*, 350 F.3d 691, 694 (7th Cir. 2003).

Failure to Be Aware of Applicable Rules of Procedure May Result in Malpractice

Rule 36(a)(3) of the Federal Rules of Civil Procedure, Requests for Admission, provides that any matter for which an admission is requested:

> A matter is admitted unless, within 30 days after being served, the party to whom the request is directed serves on the requesting party a written answer or objection addressed to the matter and signed by the party or its attorney. A shorter or longer time for responding may be stipulated to under Rule 29 or be ordered by the court.

Failure to respond timely to a request to admit may result in an inability to present certain evidence or even a dismissal of the action and, hence, a basis for a malpractice action.

Likewise, unless extended by the court for cause, a plaintiff has only 120 days from the filing of a complaint to serve the summons and complaint. Failure to do so may result in dismissal of the action. [Rule 4(m), Federal Rules of Civil Procedure].

Failure to Be Aware of Rules of Evidence May Result in the Admission of Prejudicial Evidence or the Inability to Present Certain Evidence

When in federal court, you should be familiar totally with the Federal Rules of Evidence in the event that you need to object to the admission of certain evidence or respond to an objection made by opposing counsel. Too many lawyers do not understand the basic rules of evidence. Some lawyers, for example, do not understand that to introduce records of regularly conducted activities (business records) Rule 803(6) of the Federal Rules of Evidence requires a two-part foundation. First, the record must be "kept in the course of a regularly conducted business activity. . . ." Second, it must have been "the regular practice of that business activity to make the. . . record. . . ." Sometimes, lawyers forget the second part of the foundation and, upon objection, either have to be told by the judge to ask the second question or have the exhibit rejected.

Some lawyers still try to introduce evidence of settlement discussions despite the general prohibition of Rule 408 of the Federal Rules of Evidence. Other lawyers do not know how to utilize refreshing recollection. It was embarrassing for one lawyer who, when trying to refresh recollection, displayed the document on the courtroom monitors and the judge said to remove it; then, the lawyer tried to read the pertinent statement, but the judge instructed the lawyer to stop.

To the extent that the Federal Rules of Civil Procedure and Federal Rules of Evidence were not thoroughly digested for the purposes of bar examination, I recommend that newer lawyers adopt a schedule of studying a new rule each week. Doing so will assist these lawyers to become familiar with these rules in order properly to represent parties in court proceedings.

Failure to Be Aware of Local Court Rules May Quickly Establish Incompetency

Various courts promulgate rules governing practice in their courts. For the Southern District of Indiana, see www.insd.uscourts.gov. One of the most embarrassing results of a failure to know local rules is when a party files a brief exceeding the page limitation promulgated by a local rule and the entire brief, or the excess pages, are ordered stricken.

The most frequent failure of not reading local rules in the Southern District of Indiana involves enlargements of time. Rule 6.1 authorizes the filing of a notice of a first enlargement of time to respond to a pleading or to discovery. Counsel is supposed to contact opposing counsel and ascertain opposing counsel's position on the enlargement. The party seeking the enlargement then merely files a notice of the enlargement of time. Often, counsel files a motion that is denied, so counsel then has to file a notice. Second, this rule applies only to pleadings and discovery. A pleading is a term defined by Rule 7 of the Federal Rules of Civil Procedure as a complaint, answer, answer to counterclaim, answer to a cross claim, third-party complaint, and third-party answer. A motion or brief is not a pleading. Notice of an enlargement of time to respond or reply to a motion is inappropriate.

Failure to Be Aware of a Particular Judge's Rules May Lead to Embarrassment In Front of the Jury

Most judges have their own rules and preferences for how trials will be conducted in their courts. Be aware of them. For example, Judge Hamilton has certain rules to be followed in trials in his court. These rules, which can be found at www.insd.uscourts.gov, include the following:

- Stand when making an objection.
- If plaintiff intends to suggest a damages number to the jury, that number must be stated in the opening segment of plaintiff's

closing argument so that defendant has an opportunity to respond.

- Counsel may establish qualification of experts. The court will not declare a witness to be an expert.

Thus, before incorporating any suggestion contained in this book into your trial practice, be sure to verify that any suggestion you choose to adopt will be compatible with the particular judge's trial practices.

Be Prepared to React to What May Be Idiosyncratic Practices

In an action pending in a United States District Court before the requirement for initial disclosures, I served a request for production of documents and interrogatories, received the documents and answers to the interrogatories, and deposed the plaintiffs. One day, I received a call from the judge's clerk informing me that the case would be tried in two weeks. I said that there had never been a pretrial conference, initial or final; also, there had been no order requiring the exchange or filing of witness or exhibit lists. The clerk said, "So, what difference does that make?" I then called plaintiffs' counsel to propose exchanging witness and exhibit lists. He refused. When I arrived for the first day of the trial, there were fifteen to twenty people in the courtroom whom I did not recognize. I thought that surely these people would be testifying against the party I was representing. As it turned out, they did not testify. They were parties and counsel from related cases against the same defendant pending in other states. Nevertheless, I was quite nervous and thought that I might have committed malpractice by not preparing for the testimony of these unidentified persons.

Next, in their case-in-chief, plaintiffs called the defense's key witness. When plaintiffs' counsel finished his examination, I stood up to ask some clarifying questions, as well as, I hoped, ask some additional questions. The judge asked me what I was doing. I explained. He said I had to wait until plaintiffs rested. I stated that whenever a witness testified, opposing counsel should have an opportunity to do "cross-examination." The judge said that was not allowed. Plaintiffs rested shortly thereafter. I then called the witness back to the stand and asked my questions.

Later, the judge stated that the plaintiffs wanted to argue at the conclusion of the evidence. The judge asked whether I wanted to argue. I said, "Yes." The judge told me to go to the lectern and argue. I said that I represented the defendant and, typically, plaintiffs argued first. The judge said plaintiffs waived the initial part of the closing argument and wanted only to argue in rebuttal. I said that if I were in Indiana and plaintiffs waived final argument and defendant then waived the final argument, there would be no argument. The judge said, "You are not in Indiana. If defendant wants to argue, do it now." This was very unusual.

I do not know how to prepare for these idiosyncrasies, other than to ask as many questions as necessary of local counsel or court staff to be sure that you are prepared.

4

PREPARATION COMBINED WITH SKILL, AND NOT SKILL ALONE, ARE ESSENTIAL FOR A SUCCESSFUL TRIAL PRACTICE

Great trial skills alone certainly can lead to successful outcomes. Trial skills, coupled with preparation, will result in even more successful outcomes. The key is preparation, preparation, and more preparation.

Successful trial practice demands preparation starting with the time the potential cause of action, or the actual lawsuit, comes into the office and continuing thereafter through the last day of the trial. According to Judge Rosenbaum of the United States District Court for the District of Minnesota, "If you don't know where you are going, any road will get you there."

After you have been engaged to prosecute or defend a lawsuit, you must first do an evaluation to decide whether you can properly initiate a lawsuit or to determine whether the action can be successfully defended. At the outset of the employment and before doing any formal discovery, do as much factual investigation as is reasonable for the action. Do not accumulate $10,000 in fees for a $3,000 action. Interview key witnesses, such as the client, employees of the client, and non-parties who might have facts relating to the action; assemble and study documents obtained from the client. If you have obtained documents from non-parties (for example, police report, governmental filing), study those. Visit the client's place of business or the scene of the accident or other location that may be involved in the action.

Go to a law library to determine the law applicable to the cause of action. Again, according to Judge Rosenbaum, "To get where you want to go, start there. Know the law; start with the instructions, and go from there."

More important, this early investigation of the facts and the law may lead you to a determination (1) that there is no viable lawsuit, thereby saving time, money, and embarrassment and possible sanctions; or (2) that there is a very small chance of successfully prosecuting or defending the lawsuit, allowing you to explore settlement at an early stage of the litigation and before much time or money has been invested; or (3) what you need to do successfully to prosecute or defend the lawsuit.

Before starting formal discovery, but basing your assessment on the facts and law ascertained so far, determine what you have to do to win the lawsuit. Each form of discovery thereafter, whether interrogatories or requests for production of documents or depositions, should be approached with the objective of what you have to do to win the lawsuit. Each form of discovery should have a purpose. In other words, do not simply serve a standard set of interrogatories or request for production of documents; make them case sensitive. Do not take a deposition simply with the purpose of learning what the deponent may know.

Two examples make this point. The first involved an age discrimination action. If it could have been established that the employer posted certain Equal Employment Opportunity Commission–issued posters on the employer's premises, the statute of limitations would bar the action. In meeting with the company's representatives, before starting discovery, I asked to see, and was shown, the appropriate posters that had been posted. One had been posted in the cafeteria along the line that employees, including plaintiff, would use while waiting to obtain food. I requested an 8 inch by 10 inch photograph of the applicable poster. At the plaintiff's deposition, I asked if he ate in the company cafeteria. When he said, "Yes," I asked him whether he ever read any posters while he was waiting in line. He said, "Yes." I then showed him the picture of the applicable EEOC poster and asked him if he had ever read that poster. He said, "Yes." This answer ended the litigation.

The second example, demonstrating the value of early preparation, involved an action in which I represented a supplier of medical products that was sued by a distributor. The distributor, believing it had a long term contract with the supplier, filed suit alleging a wrongful termination of the "contract." Researching the law disclosed an appellate opinion stating that a "subjective expectancy" of a contract would be insufficient to establish a binding agreement. At the deposition, after having the distributor's president describe what he thought the contract was, I asked whether what he described was really only a "subjective expectancy." He said, "Yes." The result was summary judgment for the supplier.

On the other hand, failure to undertake proper factual preparation can be detrimental. In an action in which the parties believed that providing or not providing charitable services was essential to winning the litigation, plaintiff had completed a pro forma balance sheet that showed zero dollars for charitable purposes. Defendant argued in its pretrial brief that the zero dollar entry established plaintiff would not be providing charitable services and, therefore, plaintiff could not win the litigation. Defendant assumed that the zero entry meant that no charitable services were going to be provided and did not establish this belief during discovery. At the trial, plaintiff's witness testified that the amount estimated for charitable services had been subtracted from plaintiff's proposed gross income shown on another line on the pro forma balance sheet. Directing this witness's attention first to the defendant's assertion in the pre-trial brief and then having the witness contradict the assertion was very detrimental to defendant's theory of the case.

As discovery is being conducted and continuing during trial preparation, and even during the trial, you need continually to reevaluate what you need to do to establish, or prevent the establishment of; and determine how you will accomplish this. To do this, you will need to review all documents obtained from any source, all depositions, notes of all interviews, any trial testimony, as well as the law. Each witness examination and cross-examination, including the introduction of exhibits, planned objections to exhibits, and motions in limine, should be prepared with your established objectives in mind.

5

LITIGATING COUNSEL SHOULD ASCERTAIN PERTINENT INFORMATION ABOUT THE COURT BEFORE WHICH THE ACTION MAY BE OR IS PENDING

Because my experience has been almost exclusively with the federal courts, the comments in this chapter are more applicable to federal courts. Many of these items should also be appropriate for state court actions.

If the Court Has Divisions, Determine if There Are Any Rules or Practices That May Govern the Filing and Future Course of the Action

- What are the divisions (for example, Evansville, Indianapolis, New Albany, Terre Haute)?
- Does each division have a separate office?
- Are the judges assigned to one division or to all the divisions?
- Can a civil action be filed in any division?
- Can an action be transferred to another division by motion of a party or on the court's own motion?
- Can hearings or a trial be held in another division at the court's discretion or upon request of a party?

Learn How Actions Are Assigned

- Are actions assigned to the judges by random draw or some other way?
- If magistrate judges are assigned, how are they assigned?

- How are the responsibilities divided between the district judge and the magistrate judge? (For example, in the Southern District of Indiana, the district judge rules upon dispositive motions, conducts the final pretrial conference, and conducts the trial; generally, the magistrate judge handles all other pretrial proceedings, including the initial pretrial conference, discovery disputes, and settlement conferences.)

Identification of Key Personnel Is a Necessity

- Who is the Article III judge assigned to the action?
- Who is the magistrate assigned to the action, if one is assigned?
- Who are the members of the judge's staff, principally, the courtroom deputy and the case administrator?
- Who is the court reporter who will be assigned for hearings and trial?

Understand the Responsibilities of a Motions Judge

A motions judge is generally a judge assigned to handle miscellaneous filings, for example, a subpoena for a witness for a deposition in an action pending in other federal district courts or an emergency matter if the assigned judge is unavailable. If a temporary restraining order or emergency relief is sought, that request should be directed to the assigned judge; it will be taken to the motions judge only if there is an emergency and the assigned judge is not available.

All Court Filings Should Conform to Established Procedures

- Does the court require electronic filing ("an ECF Court") and, if so:
  1. How does counsel become registered?
  2. Are courtesy copies required, and, if so, when?
- If not an ECF court:
  1. What are the hours when filing is permissible?
  2. Is there a requirement for the form of paper, such as:
     a. Color?
     b. Size?
     c. Hole punched?
  3. How many copies must be filed?
  4. Are facsimile copies are allowed?
  5. Are courtesy copies to chambers expected or appreciated?

- How are motions for leave to file another document to be filed?
  1. Non ECF court - Attach copy of proposed document to the motion.
  2. ECF court - Attach proposed document to the electronically filed motion.

All Court Filings Must Bear the Proper Cause Number

Every action receives a cause number. In the Southern District of Indiana, a number such as 1:07-cv-0169-DFH-TAB means the following:

- "1" is Indianapolis Division.
- "07" is the year the action was filed.
- "cv" is for civil; ("cr" is for criminal).
- "0169" is the number of that case for the year 2007.
- "DFH" stands for the initials of the district judge.
- "TAB" stands for the initials of the magistrate judge.

Using the wrong number can result in unexpected action taken in your case if the court is unaware of a critical document filed in the wrong case.

On occasion, actions are reassigned from one judge to another. These changing assignments can result in a change of the part of the cause number that identifies the judge and magistrate judge. Make these changes internally in your files. Failure to do so can result in papers not being properly routed to the assigned judge. In one action, a hearing was scheduled for 2:00 p.m. At 1:00 p.m., a party filed papers relating to that hearing but used the initials of the wrong judge. Because that judge was out of the office, the paper bearing the initials of the wrong judge was processed routinely. When the 2:00 p.m. hearing started, the filing party referred to the recently filed paper. The judge assigned to the case did not have it. The proceedings were then delayed.

6

EVERY ACTION REQUIRES SOME DISCOVERY

Do Not Rely on Initial Disclosure as a Substitute for Discovery

Rule 26(a)(1) of the Federal Rules of Civil Procedure, Initial Disclosures, requires the disclosure of only persons "that the disclosing party may use to support its claims or defenses. . . . and documents "that the disclosing party may use to support its claims or defenses. . . ." (emphasis added). There is no requirement to disclose witnesses or documents that may defeat the claims of the disclosing party. Thus, do not rely on initial disclosures as a substitute for discovery. Some discovery is a necessity.

Interrogatories Are of Limited Value and Should Be Used Sparingly

Too often, hours of billable time are spent drafting comprehensive interrogatories seeking to narrow the issues and obtain helpful information and even admissions. In most instances, the responses, drafted by lawyers, consist of objections or evasive answers that are useless; thus, the time spent drafting the interrogatories is a waste of time and money. Remember, if an opponent submits an evasive or ambiguous response or objection, you need to pursue with a letter, a conference, and a motion to compel, if necessary.

A better practice, with limited exceptions, is to use depositions instead. It is amazing how much more information can be obtained in a deposition when the witness may have no idea of the questions to be asked, and, especially so, when the deponent has not been properly prepared for the deposition by the deponent's counsel. Once, I scheduled depositions of five plaintiffs at one-hour intervals. The information being sought was similar for each deposition. As one deposition was concluded, we immediately started the next one. Because of the way the depositions were scheduled, plaintiffs' counsel was not able to prepare subsequent plaintiffs for their depositions based on what had occurred at the prior deposition or depositions. The result was summary judgment.

Exceptions that merit consideration for the use of interrogatories are to request opposing parties to identify persons who may have knowledge of facts relating to the litigation, to identify documents germane to the litigation, or to request a defendant to state the bases for any affirmative defenses. Seeking such information at a deposition will generally not result in as thorough an answer as should be received through interrogatories.

It is also essential to submit interrogatories to opposing parties to request that they identify facts known to, or opinions held by, experts retained but not expected to testify at trial. See, Federal Rules of Civil Procedure 26(b)(4)(B). Another possible use of interrogatories is to seek purely statistical information or uncontroverted facts such as the nature and amount of medical expenses, sales figures, or number of employees.

Requests to Produce Documents and Things Are a Necessity

First of all, without a request to produce, you may never obtain documents or other things helpful to your case. Second, even if some documents are identified in initial disclosures or exhibit lists, you need to obtain copies of all documents and production of other things that you consider necessary to prepare for trial, including documents or things that are not required to be disclosed by your opponent's initial disclosures and that could be prejudicial to your opponent's case.

If an opponent does respond to a request for production of documents with an evasive or ambiguous answer, or an objection, you must follow up with a letter, a conference and a motion to compel, if necessary. In one action, plaintiff asserted that a certain device used by defendant was an illegal decrypting device. Defendant said it was not. Plaintiff, by a Request to Produce, requested production of the device. Defendant's formal response to the Request was that the device would be made available and that plaintiff's counsel should contact defendant's counsel to make the necessary arrangements. Plaintiff never followed up to inspect the device. At the trial, defendant said that he no longer had the device. The failure of defendant to retain the item would not support a spoliation instruction because plaintiff never responded to defendant's offer to make the device available for inspection.

Requests for Admissions Should Ordinarily Be Limited to Authenticity and Admissibility of Documents and Only Those Facts That Are Truly Uncontroverted

The earlier you can establish authenticity of documents, the better. If you can establish authenticity of documents prior to the start of depositions, you can save time during depositions or you may even eliminate the need to take certain depositions, for example, depositions of record custodians.

You may also want to utilize requests to admit to establish certain uncontroverted facts, such as dates of employment, dates and amounts of medical treatment, amount of product shipped, and so on. These admissions can expedite discovery and the trial. An advantage of using requests to admit is that if the opposing party denies the request and you need to take a deposition or call witnesses at trial to establish authenticity of these documents or to prove these facts, you may be able to recover the costs of taking the required depositions or bringing witnesses to trial. See Rule 37(c)(2), Federal Rules of Civil Procedure.

Requests for admissions ordinarily should not be used to seek admissions that will destroy the opposing party's case. As with interrogatories, the responses will be drafted by lawyers who will certainly deny or at most provide ambiguous or evasive answers. On the other hand, if you submit requests for admissions that essentially destroy or weaken all or a portion of an opponent's case, there are instances where opposing counsel may be lazy or incompetent and not respond as required by Rule 36 of the Federal Rules of Civil Procedure. Then, the matters should be deemed admitted, pursuant to Rule 36, and the action conceivably won.

Respond to Discovery Requests Promptly and Properly

Responding falsely to an interrogatory or not producing documents that have been requested can result in the imposition of costs, as well as an adverse ruling or even dismissal of the action. In one trademark action in which plaintiff alleged that defendant had infringed plaintiff's name, plaintiff was requested, prior to trial, to produce all documents relating to consumers' perceptions of the plaintiff. Despite being in possession of a report by an outside consultant on precisely that subject that had been provided to plaintiff's Board of Directors, plaintiff did not produce this report. Plaintiff recovered a large jury verdict. During discovery allowed during post-trial motions, the defendant learned of the existence of this report, which supported the defense's theory. The result was the granting of a new trial and the assessment of fees and costs.

Filing Discovery with the Court Is the Exception

Rule 5(d) of the Federal Rules of Civil Procedure states:

> the following discovery requests and responses must not be filed until they are used in the proceeding or the court orders filing: depositions, interrogatories, requests for documents or to permit entry upon land, and requests for admission. (emphasis added).

7

EFFECTIVE CONTROL AND USE OF EXHIBITS CONTRIBUTE TO AN EFFICIENT AND SUCCESSFUL TRIAL

Efficient Control and Use of Exhibits Requires the Implementation of an Effective System for Marking of Exhibits

The ability to find a specific exhibit when you want to use it, to utilize effectively an exhibit when you want to use it, and to share an exhibit with the jury or judge at the appropriate time are all critical to successful trial practice.

To use exhibits at trial, traditionally counsel took a document to the court reporter, requested the court reporter to mark the document as an exhibit, distributed a copy or otherwise identified the exhibit to other counsel, and then took the exhibit to the witness for identification. If admitted into evidence, sometimes the document was passed to the jury. When the witness was finished with the exhibit, the exhibit might stay at the witness chair or be placed on the court reporter's table or elsewhere. Frequently, the exhibit was difficult to find when needed for the next witness, or even on cross-examination of the same witness.

The traditional system not only extended trial time but also was irritating to jurors. Many jurors do not like to be away from their daily lives in the first place. They resent wasting time with exhibits. Imagine the reaction by one jury when, after counsel fumbled trying to find exhibits and then to mark them, the court directed the jury to retire while counsel located, sorted, and marked exhibits.

It is important to implement an alternative method to speed the time of trial and to ensure the accuracy of the record. Many courts now require parties to pre-mark exhibits for trial and even for depositions and direct that copies be provided to the other parties in advance of the trial or deposition.

Confusion Reigns When the Same Exhibit Bears a Different Identification Number or Letter at Different Depositions, Between Depositions and Trial, and Even at Trial

Nothing is more ridiculous than having the same exhibit, such as the contract to build the power plant at issue in the case, marked during depositions as:

Deposition	Exhibit Number
Carlson	Deposition Exhibit 2
Benson	Plaintiff's Exhibit 4
Olsen	Olsen Exhibit C

It is also confusing if, at Benson's deposition, an exhibit is marked as Plaintiff's Exhibit 10, yet that very same document had a notation written on it as Carlson Deposition Exhibit 14. It is even more confusing if the same document bears one or more deposition numbers and then a "new" exhibit number for trial.

Traditionally, many lawyers have used, and some courts have required, a system of letters for plaintiff and numbers for defendant or Plaintiff's Exhibit 1, 2, and so on, and Defendant's Exhibit 1, 2, and so on. Needless duplication can result when a separate marking system and a separate set of documents are used for plaintiff and a separate marking system and a separate set of documents are used for defendant. Often, both plaintiff and defendant will plan to use and do use some of the same documents.

Having both plaintiff and defendant use their own marking system and set of documents can also create confusion. In a breach of contract case involving the sale and purchase of a coal mine, the contract was pre-marked by plaintiff as Plaintiff's Exhibit A and pre-marked by defendant as Defendant's Exhibit 1. The parties stipulated to the admissibility of each other's exhibits. It was confusing when plaintiff questioned its witnesses by referring to the contract as Exhibit A and then defendant later questioned its witnesses by referring to the contract as Exhibit 1. Finding the appropriate number or letter to state, for the record, when the same document bears different exhibit numbers or letters is difficult. In the pressure of the trial, it could be very easy to select the wrong number or letter when there are so many options.

An extreme example of confusion for a jury is the use of Plaintiff's Exhibit 1 and Defendant's Exhibit 1 for different documents. When this has happened, on occasion, both counsel referred in questions merely to Exhibit

1. This also definitely complicates drafting of opinions by a judge in a bench trial, creates havoc in preparing appellate briefs and can create confusion for appellate judges.

Additional confusion results when letters are used and there are more than 26 documents. Start using AAA and AAAA several times and you will understand what I mean. That is why I prefer numbers rather than letters. If you are required to list exhibits by letter, and there are many exhibits, a better system is to use A through Z; then AA, AB, and AC through AZ; then, BA, BB, BC through BZ rather than A through Z, AA, BB through ZZ, and AAA through ZZZ.

Also, at trial it can be confusing if a document bears a designation of Deposition Exhibit 9 and a designation as Trial Exhibit 15. The jurors, most of whom have no idea what a deposition is, can be confused as to the difference between a Deposition Exhibit and a Trial Exhibit. This can be a problem, for example, when deposition testimony of an expert is used at the trial and the deposition testimony refers to the expert's report as Deposition Exhibit 9 but the trial testimony refers to the report as Exhibit 15. Also, it is easy for counsel during the stress of trial to refer to the wrong number if an exhibit bears both a deposition number and a trial exhibit number.

In one action, plaintiff used photographs as trial exhibits. Each photograph had a label — Plaintiff's Exhibit B-13, Plaintiff's Exhibit B-14, etc. — as a result of marking at a deposition. At trial, all these photographs were grouped together as Exhibit 38 and identified and admitted into evidence as Exhibit 38. None of the photographs had any marking of Exhibit 38. During examination of plaintiff, counsel carelessly referred to Exhibit 13 (not even B-13) and Exhibit B-14; counsel did not refer to Trial Exhibit 38. This created confusion for the jury, as well as a poor record for appeal.

Counsel Should Confer and Agree from the Commencement of Discovery on an Identification System that Will Avoid Confusion and Duplication of Exhibits both at Deposition and Trial

No one system can ensure success in achieving effective control and use of exhibits for all depositions and trials. Moreover, no one system works for all lawyers. I even used different systems in different cases.

Before adopting any system, determine whether there is a court order generally or specifically for the particular case detailing how to mark exhibits, whether for deposition or for trial, or both. If there is, abide by that rule or order or obtain permission to use some other system. I never had a judge refuse to accept an identification system on which opposing counsel and I had agreed.

Identifying All Exhibits with Consecutive Numbers Only, Beginning with the First Exhibit at the First Deposition, Is the Most Efficient System for Marking Exhibits

The system I recommend is one in which the first document used at the first deposition is marked as Exhibit 1, rather than Johnson Deposition Exhibit 1 or Plaintiff's Exhibit 1. This way, the same exhibit, for example, the contract for the sale and purchase of the coal mine, will have only one identifying number and can be used and referred to as Exhibit 1 throughout all depositions, pretrial motions, and trial. This certainly eliminates a source of confusion.

Some lawyers argue that consecutive numbering during depositions will not work when multiple depositions are taken on the same day or in different cities on consecutive days. This problem is solved by assigning blocks of numbers. If the last deposition finished with number 1215, one of the next depositions could start with 1216. An estimate can be made of how many exhibits might be used at this deposition. If the estimate is 30, the other deposition could start with 1300. The fact that this could result in a gap in the numbers is of no consequence.

For those lawyers concerned about having the record show which party introduced which exhibits, designating exhibits Plaintiff's Exhibit or Defendant's Exhibit, or by letters and numbers, does make that determination easier; but, the record will always show which party introduced which exhibit, if that really is an issue, but this rarely occurs.

There Are Additional Advantages by Having the Same Document Bear the Same Exhibit Number Throughout the Litigation.

- **Using the Same Numbers for Both Deposition and Trial Exhibits Simplifies the Use of Depositions at Trial**

In one action, nine days before trial, plaintiff took a video deposition of a doctor. At the deposition, plaintiff marked as Exhibits 1 and 2 certain medical records from the doctor's file. These same two exhibits were later marked as Exhibits 5 and 6 at the trial. As the video deposition was being shown during the trial, counsel did not tell the jury that Deposition Exhibits 1 and 2 were the same as Trial Exhibits 5 and 6. The jury was not able to relate the medical records in evidence to the doctor's testimony. If a proper numbering system had been used, this problem would not have arisen.

A similar problem occurs if a deposition is being read to a jury or if the transcript is provided for the court's review and the trial exhibit number is not the same as the deposition exhibit number.

If the numbers of the exhibits from the depositions are not the same as the trial exhibit numbers, prepare and have signed a stipulation to show the cross-reference — probably a double list — deposition number to trial number and trial number to deposition number. If you have this stipulation, be sure to pencil the changes in the copies of the transcript to be used by the witness, the person reading the transcript, and the judge. This way, you will not flounder while using the transcript during the trial and the judge and jurors can more readily coordinate deposition testimony with trial exhibits. Then, if counsel objects as you read the transcript testimony, either as evidence or impeachment, you can counter that objection by stating that the new numbers being read were stipulated and counsel knew this. This way, opposing counsel will appear to be the obstructionist.

- **Using the Same Exhibit Number for the Same Exhibit Throughout the Discovery Process and for Trial Is Essential for Effective Impeachment**

Consider the situation that results when a witness testifies at trial differently than at deposition with respect to a critical exhibit, and if the exhibit was marked as Deposition Exhibit 4 at the deposition but as Exhibit 16 for trial. If you start to impeach, you can either:

1. Substitute the trial exhibit number when reading from the deposition transcript. Doing so could result in an objection from opposing counsel, who might say that what you are reading is not what the transcript says, or counsel might suggest that you wait while counsel compares the deposition exhibit with the trial exhibit.
2. Stop reading the transcript and ask whether opposing counsel will stipulate that the different numbers refer to the same document. Counsel will undoubtedly ask for time to study the two documents.

In either situation, you will look unprepared in front of the jury. More important, you will be giving the witness a chance to realize that the witness has testified inconsistently and provide the witness time to gather his thoughts to explain the inconsistency.

There is an additional problem when the exhibit numbers from a video deposition are not the same as the trial exhibit numbers. As the video is being displayed, you can stand up and state what the trial exhibit number is; or you can stop the video when the exhibit is first mentioned and state what the trial exhibit number is; or you can investigate whether the tape, CD, or DVD can be edited to convert the deposition exhibit number to the trial exhibit number; or, if possible, superimpose the new number on the tape, CD, or DVD. Of course, you should seek an agreement from opposing counsel or permission from the court to do either of the last two options so that you are not met with an objection during the trial.

The potential use of video depositions at trial is reason enough to adopt an identification system whereby the deposition exhibit numbers are the same as the trial exhibit numbers.

- **Using the Same Exhibit Number for the Same Document Throughout the Discovery Process Simplifies Brief Writing**

In an action seeking severance benefits following the sale of a business, the six named plaintiffs contended they were never told that if they were offered a job with the new company they would not qualify for severance benefits. The defendant's position was that this condition was spelled out in a letter sent to all employees before the sale. During their depositions, each of the plaintiffs was shown the letter in question and each time the letter was marked Exhibit 3. Because receipt of this letter by each plaintiff was crucial if summary judgment were to be granted, the brief quoted the letter, marked as Exhibit 3. Then, direct deposition testimony from each of the plaintiffs was included in the brief in which each plaintiff acknowledged receiving Exhibit 3. Arguably, the brief could have stated that all the plaintiffs received the letter and cited to the appropriate page of each transcript; however, direct testimony on critical points is more effective. Having the brief use the same exhibit number for all plaintiffs avoided the need to explain that the same letter was involved; only the fact that the numbers were different. Plus, the Appendix had to include only one letter, not six.

- **Using the Same Number for the Same Document Throughout the Litigation Simplifies Trial Preparation**

In preparing for trial, it is important to know what all deposed persons said about a certain exhibit. If there are twenty depositions, some of which had discussions of an exhibit, each transcript can be reviewed to provide a page and line for each reference. The task becomes much simpler if all transcripts can be reviewed for references to Exhibit 10, rather than simply for the letter of, say, January 10, 2007.

Using the same number for all depositions also aids in understanding of the case. If a significant letter, for example, the letter sent to all employees discussed above, is always Exhibit 3, lawyers become used to that designation. In reviewing a transcript that refers to Exhibit 3, a lawyer may understand the significance of the exhibit more readily than if the exhibit is referred to as Exhibit 2 in one deposition and Exhibit 10 in another deposition.

- **Using the Same Exhibit Number for the Same Document Throughout the Litigation Process Simplifies the Preparation and Use of Exhibit Lists**

Typically, any trial will require the preparation and filing of exhibit lists. Having each separate document bear only one number makes it simpler to prepare a master list of exhibits and thus easier to determine duplicate exhibits as well as easier to determine what exhibits all other parties may seek to introduce into evidence at trial.

A master list also enables the court to determine the volume of exhibits instead of having to review two or more lists and then try to determine whether any duplicates exist.

More important, using the same number for the same exhibit makes the task of pretrial argument about, and rulings on, objections easier. All counsel and the judge can work from this one numbered list and will not have to study two or more lists to discover if the documents for which objections are being made are also on another party's exhibit list. The use of the one master list, therefore, allows objections to be more easily addressed.

In one large case, the parties jointly tendered one exhibit list consisting of 700 exhibits. The parties then submitted their objections to certain exhibits. By having the master exhibit list, as well as having the documents themselves at the final pretrial conference, all counsel and the court were able to address and resolve the objections much easier. Without such a list, both parties would have worked with different lists and it would have been more difficult to address specific objections.

In contrast, in another action, for which there were objections to proposed exhibits to be addressed at a pretrial conference, plaintiff submitted an exhibit list:

E0780 - E0985 Correspondence
E1061 - E1087 Payroll information
E1327 - E1331 Certificate of Insurance
008718 - 008723 Existing liens
008738 - 008740 Line of Credit Note

Defendant, on the other hand, prepared its exhibit list which included many of the same documents as were included on plaintiff's list, but identified the exhibits as Defendant's Exhibit 1, 2, etc. It was difficult to address objections since the opposing parties did not have these exhibits with the same designations.

- **Suggestions for Preparation of One Master Exhibit List**

Having one master set of exhibits not only avoids confusion at the trial and with the trial transcript, one master set of exhibits with one master exhibit list makes it simpler to keep track of what exhibits are offered into evidence during the trial and whether or not the exhibits were admitted.

After discovery had been concluded, I approached the other side, usually the plaintiff's counsel, and asked plaintiff's counsel to provide me with a list of all documents plaintiff *might* use at trial. Based on that designation, I then told plaintiff's counsel any additional documents defendant *might* use and, based on my designation, allowed plaintiff to add to the list. If plaintiff added more, then I might have chosen to add more, and so on. After the list was completed, I then collected and organized all documents that either party *might* use at trial.

If you have a prior agreement that the trial exhibits will bear the same numbers as used for those exhibits at deposition, use those numbers. It is not a problem if all deposition exhibits are not utilized at trial. Trial exhibits might only be 5, 7, 8, 21, and 75. If other exhibits are to be utilized at trial that were not deposition exhibits, assign them a new block of numbers. If the last deposition exhibit was 49, start any new exhibits with 101 or let plaintiff start with 101 and defendant start with 201.

If, by chance, when you are preparing for trial, there has been no agreement as to marking of exhibits and the numbers are chaotic from the depositions, contact opposing counsel and attempt to agree on one numbering system for all documents that the parties indicate might be used at trial. If this happened, I preferred to organize the documents chronologically and then to mark them consecutively starting with number one, or arranging them by year and marked specifically in this manner:

2005 documents	1–23
2006 documents	101–137
2007 documents	201–207
2008 documents	301–316

or

Contract Documents	1–14
Repair Documents	101–122
Damage Documents	201–215
Tax Returns	301–309

You will then need to create a stipulation cross-referencing deposition exhibit numbers to trial exhibit numbers.

- **Using the Same Exhibit Number for the Same Document Expedites Depositions and Saves Copying Costs**

I did not like to waste time at depositions. In preparing for a deposition, I had all the documents assembled that I might use at the deposition with appropriate copies. Having a copy of the exhibits for each lawyer who attended the deposition as well as the official copy to be shown to the deponent also expedited the deposition by avoiding wasted time if counsel representing the deponent requested to review the documents before the witness was questioned about the documents and then the witness reviewed the documents before testifying. If I thought I might use fifteen exhibits at the first deposition, I premarked them as Exhibits 1–15. Pre-marking the exhibits saved time by not having to stop while the court reporter marked each exhibit and all other counsel marked their individual copy. If by chance I decided not to ask any question about the document I pre-marked as Exhibit 8, I did not, and there was a gap in the numbers; but the transcript showed the gap. Sometimes, I stated that there was no Exhibit 8, or I marked another document as No. 8 in a future deposition.

For the next deposition, I referred to any of the Exhibit Nos. 1–15 used at the first deposition about which I wanted to question this second witness and marked any new exhibits about which I wanted to question this witness starting with number 16.

Marking the same document with a different number in two or more depositions creates needless waste and confusion. If you provide a copy of the document to accompany the transcript and for each counsel attending the deposition, the same document is copied innumerable times. It is easier if each separate document is marked with one distinct number the first time it is shown to a witness at a deposition. Thereafter, each party can keep a folder or notebook of deposition exhibits. It can be agreed that each party should bring these prior deposition exhibits to further depositions; or you can agree to bring copies for other lawyers.

- **Having all Exhibits Pre-marked with One Set of Numbers, as Opposed to a Plaintiff's Set and a Defendant's Set, Allows You to Include the Exhibit Number in Your Prepared Trial Questions Because You Will Know What the Trial Exhibit Number Will Be**

For record purposes, it is better to include in your trial question "referring to Exhibit 1610" than "referring to this letter." If separate systems are used, you will not know whether the document will be introduced as Exhibit A or Exhibit 1.

Any Time There Are Documents, Whether as Attachments to a Pleading, Motion, or Brief or as a Deposition or Trial Exhibit, Each Page of Each Document Should Be Separately Marked

Marking only the front page of a document is not as efficient as marking each page. When questioning a witness, either at deposition or at trial, it is better, if you are trying to make a point with respect to a specific part of a document, to direct the attention of the witness to the exact page on which that specific part is located. If the document has many pages that are not individually numbered, you often waste time by directing the witness to the 12th page from the back or the page that has "2007 Strategy" at the top. Or worse, counsel might have to approach a witness to assist in locating the appropriate page. This is distracting and can be avoided by the numbering of individual pages. Jurors have complained about exhibits that are not individually marked on each page; they could not always find the pages about which the witnesses were being examined.

Consider the following example. Plaintiff introduced into evidence materials sent to members of a Board of Directors prior to their upcoming meeting. The exhibit consisted of a four-page cover letter with separate pagination, to which were attached an offering circular with ten pages having its separate pagination and a financial report with sixteen pages having its separate pagination. There was no consecutive pagination for the entire exhibit of thirty pages. It was slow and difficult for the witnesses and the jurors to find the particular pages about which the witnesses were being asked questions. Marking each page as Exhibit 10, p. 1, Exhibit 10, p. 2, and so on would have expedited the trial and made counsel look more organized.

Sometimes, multi-page exhibits already have their own internal numbering. This could be used in lieu of having each page marked again. Without having the exhibit number on each page, though, counsel or the witness may just refer to Page 3 — but of what exhibit? Frequently, the exhibit number is initially mentioned, and then there is some intervening testimony, and then there is a return to questions about the exhibit. If counsel or the witness refers only to Page 3,which is easy to do if the exhibit number is not shown on the page, it could take some study of the record to link the exhibit to the testimony.

It is acceptable to use Bates' numbers for internal pagination numbers, if that system was used during discovery, but you still need to have the exhibit number on each page and refer to the exhibit number in your question. Be careful, though, in using both Bates' numbers and marking each exhibit with a separate trial exhibit number. For example, in one action, the parties pre-marked their trial exhibits starting with 1 and going through 4000. Each document had internal numbering from a Bates' numbering system used in production of documents during discovery in which each page had a number, as well as some alpha characters. Here is the problem:

Counsel used, for example, the following trial exhibit numbers:

2961
2848
3581
3724

Then, when using Exhibit 3581, counsel directed the witness look at "2845", and the numbers "2845" apparently were the last four digits of the Bates' numbering system. Because "Page" 2845 is close in number to "Exhibit" 2848, a question arose as to whether counsel was referring to a page or an exhibit, especially when counsel referred only to "2845."

It is possible, if there are no duplicate numbers, to use the Bates' numbers as the exhibit numbers for all depositions and trial. When this has happened, counsel usually agree that the exhibit number for a particular document will be the Bates' number shown on the first page of the document.

Caveat: In one construction case, the parties marked an 80-page set of building specifications using a decimal system, for example, Exhibit 1272.1.3.1, Exhibit 970.50.1.5, etc. This was a very difficult system to use to identify documents and for the court reporter to record the testimony.

Whatever system is used, all numbering should be placed in the lower-right corner of the document. The numbering should be high enough and far enough away from the right margin so that all or part of the numbers are not cut off during the copying process. On some pages, the numbers could be placed higher up or further to the left of the lower-right corner. Every page should be marked in a place where it can be seen after the document is copied.

Whether by hand, sticker, or machine, the documents should be marked so that when copied the numbers are legible. If you are marking with a pen, use dark ink. Once, I used blue ink to mark exhibit numbers. The coping of several hundred pages had to be redone as the numbers on the copies were illegible. It is acceptable to write the exhibit numbers on the documents. Exhibit stickers are not necessary unless so directed by the court. Some copy service companies will mark each document or page, if you prefer, with a number pursuant to your instructions.

One lawyer was quite creative in marking exhibits. In an action involving alleged illegal drugs, counsel had a medical treatise marked as an exhibit and referred to portions of the treatise as part of the defense to establish the drugs were not illegal. Counsel placed red sticky tabs on those pages considered important. Counsel reviewed each tabbed page with the witness, who pointed out what was important on that page. When the treatise was provided to the jurors during deliberations, the jurors did not have to rely on their memories; they could go right to the tabbed pages. This method not only assisted in deliberations, it also expedited the deliberations.

Photographs, Diagrams, Maps and Charts, Even if Used Just for Demonstrative Purposes, Can Aid in Understanding the Action

Remember the adage, "A picture is worth a thousand words." In certain actions, pictures can more easily establish what needs to be proved or understood. Before the advent of video cameras, an employer during a strike hired a photographer to document violent activities. During an arbitration proceeding addressing the discharge of certain employees, who allegedly participated in violent activities, one employee denied throwing rocks at the administration building. When shown a picture of the employee facing the administration building with a rock in his hand, the employee acknowledged that the picture was accurate but stated that he did not throw the rock. Later, when asked whether he participated in the beating of strike breakers, the employee said, "If you have a picture that shows that I did, I did. If you do not have a picture, I did not participate."

In a wrongful discharge action, the employer's defense was that plaintiff had been terminated for violating various company rules and policies. One company policy allegedly violated was one that prohibited smoking on the premises. To help establish plaintiff's knowledge of the policy, a company witness testified there was a big "No Smoking" sign at the entrance to the company's premises to remind employees that the premises were "smoke free." No picture of the sign was introduced into evidence at the trial. Having a picture of the sign would have helped to establish the incredibility of plaintiff's testimony that he was not aware of the policy.

If photographs are to be used, they require special marking. To document its allegations that the defendant tenant vacated the premises in an unsatisfactory condition, plaintiff introduced pictures of the premises before the lease started, during the term of the lease, and after the tenant vacated the premises. The pictures were numbered but not identified by date. It was not possible by looking at the pictures to determine when the pictures were taken. There was testimony by a witness as to "approximately" when each picture was taken. Worse yet, the questioning was sloppy in that the questions referred to "this picture" or "these pictures" without a specific reference to the exhibit number of the pictures. A juror commented after the trial that the jury was confused during deliberations because the pictures had no dates. As to another set of pictures, a juror said, "At least they put dates on those."

When authenticating pictures, in addition to establishing that the pictures are an accurate depiction, establish when they were taken and by whom. In one action, a witness testified that a picture was taken in 2003. The processing date stamp on the back of the picture stated 2004. The discrepancy in dates should have been explained to the jury.

The bottom line on pictures: Place the date taken on the front or back of each picture and include in your question the exhibit number of each picture about which a witness is being questioned.

In certain trials, especially in criminal trials involving drugs, guns, and money, photographs are substituted for the actual exhibits and only the photographs, not the actual exhibits, accompany the jury for deliberations. The best system that I have seen was used in a trial in which a defendant was charged as a felon in possession of fifteen guns. There was a separate exhibit tag on each gun with the serial number of the gun written on the tag; each tag was marked separately, as in, "Exhibit 49"; a picture was taken showing the gun and the exhibit tag showing the exhibit number; the picture was marked "Exhibit 49-A."

Diagrams can also be helpful. Typically, in actions involving accidents, a diagram of the scene rather than just an oral description results in a better understanding of how the accident occurred.

Diagrams are helpful in technical cases. In an action involving the alleged theft of satellite television signals, plaintiff used a diagram to depict the path of a television signal from its place of origin to a customer's house.

Then there are times when diagrams were not used but should have been. In an action involving alleged excessive force, there was testimony about a building, an alley, a truck, the route plaintiff took when he first arrived on the scene, his confrontation with the police, and a take-down of plaintiff to the ground by the police. A diagram would have helped explain the whole episode, but none was used.

Demonstrative exhibits are also very helpful, especially in patent cases. To demonstrate how a defribillator worked, one party presented an animated video of a heart showing the pumping mode normally; it then showed the ventricular chambers beating faster, but not the atria; then how shocks were sent to the heart by the defibrillator, followed by the ventricular chambers returning to normal beating.

When used, demonstrative exhibits should be appropriately marked with an exhibit number. This was particularly helpful in one action in which each party had several demonstrative exhibits that were shown to different witnesses. At first, the exhibits were not identified by number. Time was wasted in finding the appropriate exhibit to show to subsequent witnesses. After the exhibits were marked, little time was lost in directing a witness to the correct exhibit. Comparing testimony about demonstrative exhibits for purposes of closing argument or appeal might be difficult if there are several demonstrative exhibits none of which are marked. Start the numbering of demonstrative exhibits with a new series, such as 1001 or 6001.

In one criminal action, the government used as a demonstrative exhibit a floor plan of the defendant's residence, marked as Exhibit No. 30. The government had different police witnesses describe where they found the various guns and various quantities of drugs. Government counsel requested each witness to place, on the floor plan, differently colored sticky notes, one color for guns and another color for drugs. As the trial progressed, the sticky notes fell off. Prior to the use of the sticky notes, I suggested that the police officers mark on the floor plan the location of the guns and drugs with differently colored pens. When a witness testified as to where a shotgun was found, the witness could have marked that spot with a red pen, using the number 30-10 to correspond to the shotgun that was marked as Exhibit 10. When a witness testified as to where drugs were found, the witness could have marked that spot with a blue pen, using the number 30-24, to correspond to the drugs that were marked Exhibit 24. This way, all the locations would have been visible during the whole trial. As it was, the demonstrative exhibit failed to depict accurately, throughout the trial, the locations where all the drugs and guns were found because some of the sticky notes fell off.

When maps, diagrams, pictures, or similar materials are being used as exhibits, and when locations or features on such documents are being pointed out by witnesses or counsel, such locations should be indicated by appropriate markings on the documents if they are not readily apparent from the exhibits themselves. Unnecessary markings should be avoided. Marking on exhibits should be made only after considering the views of opposing counsel and only after receiving the court's permission. Counsel should then describe the markings for the record. It is also possible to use a copy of the exhibit, e.g. Exhibit 60, on which the markings can be made, and the copy can be marked as a separate exhibit, e.g. Exhibit 60A. Exhibits with overlays or with movable parts have been very useful

Four Ways to Show Exhibits to a Jury or Judge

Keep in mind that the goal in using exhibits is to inform and educate the jury as a foundation for persuasion.

There are at least four ways, or combinations of ways, to show exhibits to a jury or judge:

1. Wait until the evidence is concluded so that the jury sees the exhibits for the first time during deliberations or the judge sees the exhibits while drafting an opinion. (This is absurd.)
2. Pass the exhibits to the jury or judge after each exhibit has been admitted into evidence. (This is very time consuming.)
3. Display the exhibits using the Video Evidence Presentation System ("VEPS").
4. Provide a copy of each document for each juror and the judge. (This is the best way to inform the judge and jury.)

It is acceptable to use a combination of methods, such as providing jurors or judge with some of the exhibits but displaying others using the VEPS, or passing others to the jury or judge.

Discussion of the options follows.

1. Waiting to provide exhibits to the jury or judge until the evidence is concluded is the least acceptable method. If all you do is discuss exhibits with witnesses and do not display the exhibits on the monitors using the VEPS, do not provide each juror and the judge with their own copies, or do not pass exhibits to the jury and judge, and thereby wait until jury deliberations begin or the judge starts working on a decision, you may lessen your chances of educating the jury and the judge. It is too much to expect jurors and the judge to comprehend satisfactorily the contents of documents or other exhibits that are merely discussed with witnesses.

   When exhibits were not provided to the jurors and counsel failed to display the exhibits on the monitors for the jurors to see, one court instructed counsel to place the exhibits under the document camera.
2. Passing of exhibits to the jury as the exhibits are received into evidence is not recommended, although it probably could be done for the judge in bench trials. Passing the exhibits does expose the jury to the exhibits, but considerable time is wasted while the exhibits are passed from juror to juror. Some jurors

and judges resent this time delay, especially if they are aware of another system used by an opposing party to show exhibits.

Although passing exhibits is generally not recommended, physical evidence such as confiscated money, guns, drugs, and inventions in dispute should be passed to the jurors. Doing so helps involve the jurors. In a drug trafficking case, it was very effective to pass to the jurors the actual drugs introduced into evidence — properly packaged, of course. Most jurors will have never seen, or handled, illegal drugs, at least not in such quantities. By providing the jurors the opportunity to see the drugs, the jury will have some "ownership" in the case. Not only should the drugs be passed to the jury, but an appropriate witness should state the quantity and the street value. Mentioning the street value will emphasize how terrible drug trafficking is.

In another drug case, in which $65,000.00 in cash was seized at the time of the arrest and admitted into evidence, the money, in a sealed plastic bag, was passed to the jury. The jurors were fascinated with this opportunity to see close up the cash confiscated during the arrest.

Passing guns to the jury also can be effective; however, some jurors do not want anything to do with guns. In one action in which guns were involved, even though the prosecutor said the weapons were inoperative, one juror said she did not appreciate having the guns pointed in the direction of the jury when the guns were placed on the exhibit table. Another juror did not appreciate the government's lawyer handling the guns. The comment was that counsel was waving the guns around like a "madman." The fear was that the guns would discharge. Handle the exhibits as if they were dangerous. Doing so respects the jury.

In certain actions, such as patent infringement and product liability, bring the devices, if small enough, to the courtroom and ask permission to pass them to the jury. It is poor practice to have a witness identify a product and not pass it to the jury. In one patent action involving medical devices, plaintiff did not show the devices to the jury during opening statement; defendant did. During its case-in-chief, plaintiff did not show any devices to the witnesses or jury. In defendant's case, defendant passed some of the devices to the jury. The difference in procedure was noticeable.

Another effective instance of passing objects to a jury was an action in which plaintiff's expert testified that plaintiff's loss of a part of his thumb during a sawing procedure resulted from the saw being .005 of an inch out of tolerance. There was testimony that .005 of an inch was about the thickness of two sheets of paper. Defendant brought calipers to court to demonstrate how small .005 of an inch was and passed the calipers to the jury. This demonstration was very dramatic in a defense verdict case.

3. The use of VEPS must be given strong consideration for the display of exhibits, including demonstrative exhibits. Pictures, diagrams, maps, and charts, unless too large in size (if using only the document camera), can be displayed on the VEPS. The advantage of using VEPS is that once displayed, the exhibit can be manipulated.

In a bank robbery trial, the government's first witness was a teller who identified a diagram of the interior of the bank. The diagram was then placed on the document camera and displayed on the monitors. On the touch screen at the witness chair, the teller placed an arrow to show her work station and an arrow to show the front door of the bank. Then, using her finger, she drew the route of the robber from the time he entered the bank until the time he left.

In an arson case, counsel displayed photographs of the interior of the destroyed home on the monitors. Using the touch screen, the expert witness placed arrows on the monitor next to significant matters such as the gasoline can and the burned hole in the floor; he also drew lines and circles to show the jury the burn pattern.

In an action involving a police chase after a drug purchase, an area map was displayed on the monitors. The witness marked the site of the purchase, and then drew the route the police and defendants took during the subsequent chase through the streets of Indianapolis. In another action involving a defendant who tried to flee from the police, counsel displayed on the monitors a map of the city streets involved in the chase. The police officer then drew on the touch screen the defendant's route in blue and the officer's route in yellow.

On the other hand, in trying to show where a latent fingerprint was found on a gun, counsel stood thirty feet from the jury but next to the witness who pointed to the place on the gun where the fingerprint was found. This was too far away. The gun should have been placed under the document camera and the witness could have touched the monitor to show the location of the fingerprint.

4. The best way to utilize exhibits is to provide all potential exhibits to the judge and individual copies to each juror of all, or at least the most critical documents, once they are admitted into evidence. Trial lawyers live with their cases and know the documents. Counsel believe that the information contained in documents shown to witnesses or displayed on the monitors is obvious and establishes what counsel seek to prove. Remember, though, that the jurors and judge do not have the same long involvement and do not comprehend immediately the significance of the documents.

   In a bench trial, you will need to provide all exhibits to the judge at some point. Do this at the start of the trial. Either the documents will have been stipulated into evidence or the judge will need to see them anyway to inspect them before ruling on admissibility.

If jurors have their own copy of the exhibits, the jurors can place their own marks and comments on the exhibits as the exhibits are being discussed by the witnesses during the trial. Whenever copies are provided to the jurors, many, but not all, jurors write on their copies, or underline or highlight certain lines or words. They make their own comments, or they may mirror comments made by the witnesses or counsel while each exhibit is discussed in open court. Also, a judge frequently writes on documents during testimony to assist later in the preparation of an opinion or order.

Comments written by jurors on documents provided to them include:

- "Not as consistent as prior visit."
- "Never received report — they were requested."
- On Exhibit 41, a juror wrote, "vs. Exhibit 20."
- On Exhibit 58, a juror wrote, "refer to Ex. 81."
- Opposite the words, "tests will establish" on one document, a juror wrote, "not done."
- "Never received response from this letter."

Notes on copies of pictures include:

- "acid on floor"
- "tears in insulation"
- "hole in foundation"
- "wall pushed out at bottom"
- "after floor was cleaned — still shows signs of acid spills"
- "When taken?"

If each juror has a copy of the exhibits, each juror can study the exhibits during deliberations. Jurors probably will not remember what was displayed on the monitors or passed to them during the trial, even if counsel thinks the documents were significant; and, likewise, the jurors probably will not remember the documents during deliberations. Deliberations will be expedited and improved if each juror has his or her own copy of the exhibits instead of depending on one juror to describe the exhibits or having to wait until the exhibits are passed around to all jurors. In fact, jurors state that having their own copy of the exhibits shortens the time of deliberations and assists them in their deliberations.

Some lawyers prefer to use a combination of distributing hard copies of exhibits and displaying the same exhibits on the monitors. That is, all exhibits, once admitted, are given to jurors. As critical documents are being discussed, they are displayed on the monitors using VEPS; then, counsel or the witness marks on the touch screen monitor to emphasize certain parts of the exhibits.

In cases with a large amount of documents, it may be too cumbersome to provide each juror with an individual set of exhibits. In these circumstances, using the VEPS instead of passing the exhibits to the jurors will speed the trial; however, you should consider passing or distributing individual copies of at least critical documents to the jurors. In a bank fraud trial involving thirty-one loans, each loan file containing many documents was introduced into evidence. Counsel then prepared and introduced a five-page exhibit summarizing the critical terms of each loan and provided each juror with a copy of the summary. This summary made it easier to comprehend testimony of the witnesses when discussing the various loans.

In an action with a joint exhibit list comprising over 600 exhibits it took nine notebooks, each 5 inches thick, to hold the exhibits. These notebooks were used by the witnesses but not by the jurors during the trial. It was very cumbersome and inefficient for the witnesses to keep switching notebooks when the questioning skipped around from exhibit 5 to 170, 20, 320, 97, 510, and 640. It would have been more efficient if the parties had used the VEPS, provided that counsel had the documents ready in the order they were going to be used, or if the documents had been loaded onto a CD, DVD, or hard drive of a computer. Likewise, in a case of this magnitude, it would not have been practical to pass the exhibits to the jury or provide each juror with an individual copy. Displaying the documents using the VEPS was the only sensible choice.

A dilemma arises when only one party has documents loaded onto a computer. In one action, plaintiff did not want to use notebooks because so many documents were involved. Plaintiff opted to use VEPS to display documents using a computer and appropriate software. Defendant had a small number of documents and was not able to display them using a computer. Defendant had the option of placing documents under the document camera. However, during cross-examination of plaintiff's witnesses, defendant's counsel asked plaintiff's technician to put documents on the monitors using the computer. Be prepared for this possibility.

Use of Notebooks Results in Better Control of Exhibits and a More Efficient Trial

After the potential trial exhibits have been determined, consideration should be given to using notebooks to control better these exhibits. Use of notebooks may not always be feasible especially when exhibits are too numerous.

If notebooks are to be used for a bench trial, one notebook for each party, one for the witness, one for the judge, and one for the court reporter is recommended. For jury trials, a notebook for each juror should also be used.

Using notebooks saves time by eliminating:

- Counsel's distributing a copy of each exhibit to opposing counsel.
- Counsel's handing an exhibit to the witness and hovering over the witness while asking questions about the exhibit.
- Looking around the courtroom to find exhibits when needed. Sometimes, without notebooks, one counsel will use an exhibit or take it to counsel table when finished questioning the witness, or a witness may take an exhibit after testifying. Delays can result from having to locate exhibits thereafter. In one action, an exhibit was missing. Counsel who last used the exhibit denied having the exhibit. The trial was stopped while a search was conducted. The jurors stayed in their seats. Then, in front of the jury, the counsel who denied having the exhibit produced it. In another action, one counsel, by inadvertence, took an exhibit home at night, mixed in with his file for the closing argument.
- Handing a copy to the judge when an inspection of the document is required for a ruling on an objection or when the judge needs to see the exhibit for some other reason.
- Passing exhibits to the jury.

Keeping the exhibits in notebooks in numerical order also helps the jurors more quickly to find the exhibits to follow along with the testimony, aids the court reporter in preparing a record, and helps the judge in making various rulings, especially in bench trials, and in post-trial motions.

Starting a trial with empty notebooks is not recommended. It is better to have exhibits already in notebooks prior to the start of the trial. In one action, defense counsel chose to give the judge, jurors, and the first witness only an empty notebook. When an exhibit was introduced into evidence, counsel distributed a copy of the exhibit and asked the witness, judge, and jurors to place the exhibit in their notebooks. Counsel said this system was used so that the witness would not know what was coming next. Even if the notebook given to the witness had all the documents in the notebook, there is no way that a witness on the witness stand can testify and read ahead in the notebook. Conceivably, counsel may not want to give a notebook containing all of the exhibits that might be used to opposing counsel, who can study the documents at breaks; but it is better to place all the exhibits in the notebooks for the witness chair, the judge, and jurors. More important, the witnesses put the documents into the notebook in the order used and not in numerical order. Delays resulted when subsequent witnesses tried to find exhibits. This system was very inefficient because time was wasted in distributing the exhibits, opening the notebooks, attempting to find the right place, closing the notebooks, and then finding the exhibits with subsequent witnesses.

When jurors have been asked to place exhibits in notebooks, three things have happened:

1. Some jurors do not insert the exhibits in their notebooks.
2. Some jurors place the exhibits in the notebooks in an improper sequence, so they have difficulty finding the exhibits later.
3. Jurors complain about having to open and close the notebooks; they prefer having everything provided for them so that they do not have to do any organizing. They especially complain when they are given notebooks with some exhibits and later are asked to insert others. They wonder why all the exhibits were not in the notebooks from the beginning.

In conclusion, it is better to have as many exhibits as possible in the notebooks at the start of the trial.

Prior to the start of a trial, a joint exhibit list or a separate exhibit list for each party will typically be prepared. Thus, all parties should know which exhibits potentially could be sought to be introduced into evidence at the trial. Furthermore, prior to the start of the trial, counsel should meet and enter into stipulations as to the admissibility of some, if not all, of the documents, or at least a stipulation as to authenticity. Thus, these documents could be placed into the notebooks.

For a bench trial, the notebooks should contain all the potential exhibits, even those for which there will be objections. For a jury trial, the notebooks should contain at a minimum all the exhibits to which admissibility has been stipulated. If there have been no stipulations, then the notebooks will probably have to be empty.

It is possible for the notebooks to contain all the potential exhibits, including those whose admissibility or authenticity may be contested. This requires special instructions from the judge for each juror, until the conclusion of the evidence, to look only at the exhibits about which the witnesses are being questioned and to leave the notebooks in the jury box during recesses.

If there are documents that may be highly controversial or prejudicial and whose admissibility has not been stipulated, it is better not to place them in the notebooks even with an instruction to the jurors that they are only to look at documents about which a witness is being questioned and not to "read ahead."

In one action, in which admissibility of ninety percent of the exhibits had been stipulated, counsel placed into the notebooks numerous highly controversial exhibits for which there had been no stipulation as to admissibility and for which there were going to be objections. When this situation was discovered, the court told the jury not to look at any of these exhibits and sternly instructed counsel to remove the disputed exhibits from the notebooks at the next break.

If a party believes that it will seek to introduce into evidence a document that had not been stipulated, that party should have available in the courtroom sufficient copies of that exhibit, properly marked, and properly punched. This way, if the document, following a proper foundation, is admitted into evidence, the document can be distributed to the jurors and placed by them into their notebooks at that time, hopefully in the proper place.

When admissibility of exhibits has been stipulated, counsel could move to have all of the stipulated exhibits, stating the numbers of the exhibits; e.g., 2, 10, 16, 27, 110, admitted at the start of the trial in order to streamline the admission process. On the other hand, the judge could state for the record that exhibits 2, 10, 16, 27, and 110 are admitted into evidence.

What frequently happens, though, if a blanket admission of exhibits occurs at the start of the trial, is that not all the exhibits included in the stipulation are actually discussed with a witness. The record then contains more exhibits than were actually used. The jurors ask why they were provided more exhibits than those actually addressed by the witnesses. Judges may also wonder about appellate review of their decisions based on exhibits not addressed or even explained in any testimony.

A modified procedure is to place all the potential exhibits for which admissibility has been stipulated into the notebooks and then utilize a further stipulation that provides that, if any exhibit included in the stipulation is referred to in open court during the examination of a witness, that exhibit is deemed admitted into evidence. At the conclusion of the evidence, the nonadmitted exhibits can be removed from the notebooks.

Using a separate notebook for each party is another option. In one action, there was a joint exhibit list. Plaintiff placed the exhibits that plaintiff wanted to use in one notebook, and defendant placed the exhibits defendant wanted to use in a separate notebook.

If separate notebooks are used for each party, a different-colored notebook for each party is recommended.

In another action, without any prior agreement, plaintiff provided a black notebook for each juror containing exhibits that plaintiff planned to use for its case. When defendant presented its case, defendant assembled into a larger bright-red notebook all the exhibits in plaintiff's black notebook, plus all the documents that defendant used during cross-examination in plaintiff's case and the additional documents that defendant would use in defendant's case. The defendant's intent was to convey to the jurors that plaintiff did not tell the whole story; and, therefore, plaintiff's evidence was unreliable.

In cases with many documents, two or more notebooks might be required. These can become difficult to handle. Some counsel prefer, in these circumstances, to use one notebook for each witness or just for certain key witnesses. If the parties agree which exhibits will be shown to a witness, one notebook per witness should suffice. What usually happens, though, is that counsel will not, in advance of trial, tell opposing counsel what exhibits will be used with which witnesses. Thus, the party calling a witness has a separate notebook for use on direct questioning and the opposing party has a separate notebook for use on cross-examination. Each of these notebooks is provided to each juror. Certainly, the same exhibits may be in several notebooks, but that is not a problem. These notebooks are collected at the end of each witness's testimony. At the end of the trial, the jury is then provided with a full set of the exhibits introduced into evidence at the trial, usually arranged in exhibit number order, and another set of exhibits in a separate notebook for each witness. In complicated actions, this method assists the jurors. If separate notebooks for each witness are used, it is probably better to organize the exhibits in numbered order rather than order of use.

In one construction delay case in which five notebooks would have been required to hold all the relevant documents, I used issue notebooks. That is, I determined what issues would be addressed at the trial, such as the electrical contractor delay and the strike delay, and placed all documents relevant to each particular issue in a separate notebook, in the order I would most likely use the exhibits at trial. Because there were fifteen issues, I obtained fifteen kinds of notebooks, differing by color or style. For each of the fifteen issues, there was one notebook for each juror, the witness, opposing counsel, the judge, and me. Because jurors learn by seeing as well as hearing, I wanted the jurors to see the particular documents being discussed with a particular witness. And, there was no VEPS system available. If I gave each juror a master set of exhibits, much time would have been wasted by having the jurors shuffle notebooks to find the appropriate exhibits. By organizing the documents by issue and in the order I would use the exhibits, the jurors had only to turn to the next tab each time I went to a new document. This method also assisted me in preparation for the direct and cross-examination of the witnesses.

Not only is it helpful to use notebooks containing pre-marked exhibits, but it is better to use **numbered tabs or dividers** to separate the exhibits. One plaintiff did prepare a notebook of exhibits, with the exhibits pre-marked, but did not use tabs. A witness claimed that he could not find the exhibits. The failure to use tabs resulted in wasted time looking for the proper exhibits.

The tabs should have labels on them. The tabs should coincide with the exhibit numbers. For example, there is potential confusion when you place exhibit 1213 into a tab marked 1; exhibit 799 in tab 2; and exhibit 1112 in tab 3.

Using tabs does not mean that you do not have to mark the exhibits separately. Some tabs are identified on only one side, so if the tab or divider is turned to the left, the witness or the jury may not be able to find the exhibit being discussed.

If exhibits, once admitted, are to be given to the jurors to put into notebooks, a tab for the new exhibit should also be provided. In one action, Exhibits 313 and 315 were in the juror notebooks with tabs. Then defendant later introduced Exhibit 314. The exhibit was given to the jurors, but without a tab. Thus, Exhibit 314 was placed in the notebooks by the jurors in various locations. It was difficult for the jurors to find Exhibit 314 later.

There is also a unique procedure available for use in actions with many documents. Prior to trial, both parties submitted a joint exhibit list. It started with number 1 and went to number 4980. There were gaps in the numbers, but there were potentially hundreds of exhibits. The parties attempted to stipulate in advance on admissibility. They even filed periodic updated lists with their stipulations and objections. Based on representations that the parties were making progress on stipulations, the court did not address the objections in advance of the trial.

Just before the start of the trial, the parties agreed that on each trial day, such as Monday, plaintiffs would tell defendants the witnesses and exhibits that plaintiffs planned to use the next day, such as Tuesday. Later on Monday, defendants would tell plaintiffs which exhibits that defendants would use with the designated witnesses for Tuesday. The parties then met at night to discuss any objections to the proposed exhibits. On each day of the trial, thirty minutes before the jury was to return to open court, the court held a hearing to address any objections. If there were no objections, it was agreed that an exhibit would be deemed admitted into evidence if mentioned during examination of a witness. Because all objections were addressed this way, no jury time was wasted while objections were made and argued, either in open court or outside the presence of the jury.

Irrespective of What System of Numbers or Letters or Any Combination Is Used, There Must Be One Master List of Exhibits That Will Be or May Be Introduced Into Evidence

To avoid contentiousness, this list should contain for each exhibit only one exhibit number or letter, a date (if possible), and a brief (nonargumentative) description such as "letter," "memorandum," or "photograph." Having columns for date offered, admitted, or denied are helpful. Thus, at the trial you can record the date when the exhibit was offered, which party offered it, whether an objection was made, and whether the document was admitted into evidence. In case the numbering system is not in date order, a separate list of the exhibits arranged chronologically is helpful.

A copy of this list should be given to the court reporter and the court prior to the start of the trial. Unless it is certain that all exhibits in the master list will be introduced into evidence, the list should not be given to the jurors at the start of the trial.

Exhibits Must Be Reviewed Before the Evidence Is Closed to Be Certain that All Exhibits You Want in the Record, or Thought Were in the Record, Are, in Fact, in the Record

After the evidence has concluded and before the exhibits are delivered to the jurors for their use in deliberations, you should meet with opposing counsel and court staff to verify that all the exhibits received into evidence, and only those exhibits, will be provided to the jurors.

It also is recommended that one counsel from each party sign a document enumerating all exhibits that will be provided to the jurors for their deliberation. This can save time and embarrassment at a critical point in the trial. In an action in which all counsel signed a paper acknowledging which exhibits were in evidence, plaintiff's counsel, in closing argument, referred to an exhibit not on the list. Instead of having a discussion concerning whether the exhibit was in evidence or having the court reporter search the transcript, a quick look at the signed list resolved the issue, and the court took corrective action in a timely fashion.

I was involved in one action in which the parties not only prepared a comprehensive list of the exhibits but also prepared and signed separate documents listing by number the exhibits introduced into evidence and the witnesses through whom the exhibits were introduced.

An Index of the Actual Exhibits Introduced Into Evidence Should Be Prepared and Given to the Judge and Jury for Their Use

This recommendation stems from a specific request made by one jury within minutes of the start of their deliberations. The note said, "May we receive a list of each exhibit and its description?" If at least one party has a master list of exhibits from the start of the trial and had this list on a computer, this request should be easy to accomplish by deleting from the master list any exhibits not admitted into evidence and adding any additional exhibits that were not on the list. Having this index enables the jury to find exhibits easier.

Miscellaneous Lessons on Exhibits

- All exhibits should be verified for accuracy, completeness and availability before being mentioned in trial.

In your trial preparation, you must review your witness outline and the actual exhibits so that you do not look unprepared in front of the jury. In other words, practice exactly what you will be doing during your examination with the exhibits, including looking at the actual exhibits and actual pages of the exhibits that will be shown to the witnesses and about which the witnesses will be questioned. Similarly, for cross-examination, review the actual exhibits and pages about which you will be asking questions.

If you are the lawyer in charge of the case or of questioning a witness, **you** are responsible for reviewing the proposed exhibits. Be sure to check, double check and triple check your exhibits to be sure you are not the victim of Murphy's Law. In one action, the pages of the exhibits were two-sided, but when copies were made for the court and jury, the exhibits were copied on only one side. There is no excuse for such an oversight. In another action, some of the exhibits were copied upside down, so the witnesses and the jurors had to turn the exhibit notebooks around. If copying errors happen, do **not** blame the paralegal or secretary.

In a bank robbery case, the government introduced into evidence a pair of pants worn by the defendant at the time of the robbery. No one checked the pockets of the pants. The foreperson of the jury gave the bailiff an old arrest warrant found in a pocket of the pants and stated, "We do not think we should have this."

In an action in which plaintiff sought damages for improper medical treatment while in jail, defendant offered Exhibit 51 into evidence and stated that these were plaintiff's medical records from the jail. The exhibit was admitted into evidence. Then, during examination of the witness, it was discovered that the exhibit also contained records from a hospital. Defendant then argued that the hospital records should be removed from the exhibit because they were inadmissible. It is inappropriate and poor trial skills to introduce an exhibit into evidence and then later argue that a portion of your own exhibit is inadmissible.

Be certain that an exhibit is available in the courtroom before directing the attention of the witness to the exhibit. One counsel sought to ask a witness about a document, thinking that it was in the notebooks. Counsel asked the witness to turn to the exhibit. The exhibit was not there, and counsel had no other copy available. One plaintiff called as a witness Mark Jones. During cross-examination, defendant used an affidavit of Mr. Jones for impeachment. On redirect, plaintiff's counsel, because he did not bring a copy of the affidavit to the trial, asked to borrow defendant's copy. This is inexcusable. A proper procedure is to have a folder for each witness and to place in that folder every document prepared by, or referring to, that witness.

Likewise, it is inexcusable for a lawyer to direct a witness to look at a certain document, such as the employment contract, and then not know the exhibit number. Not knowing the exhibit number and not having a copy at your fingertips detracts from your examination. Confusion resulted when a lawyer turned to a technician operating the VEPS equipment and requested a display of the "rejection letter" without an exhibit number, and the technician could not find it.

It is embarrassing for counsel to ask a witness to refer to Exhibit 15 when the correct exhibit was 18. Even worse is to ask the witness to refer to Exhibit 205 in the notebook, only to find that no Exhibit 205 exists. At one trial, counsel asked a witness to look at Exhibit 24. What counsel had marked as Exhibit 24 was not Exhibit 24 in the notebook of stipulated exhibits.

In another action, on several occasions, counsel asked the witness to look at a document and then, only, after a pause, said, "Wrong document." Once, a lawyer who was assisting the lead counsel had to go to the official set of exhibits, open the notebook, pull out an exhibit, and give it to lead counsel. Then lead counsel said, "Wrong document."

- Do not seek to introduce into evidence a document that had previously been withdrawn.
- Be certain that the first exhibit you offer into evidence will be admissible. It is not impressive when a jury sees you strike out with your first at-bat.
- Use of requests to admit authenticity of exhibits needs strong consideration.
- If necessary or possible, use opposing party at trial to authenticate an exhibit. Plaintiff was seeking damages from defendant for using an illegal encrypting device. Plaintiff struggled to have packing slips admitted into evidence that were not available at the defendant's deposition. Later, in defendant's case, defendant admitted to receipt of the packing slips. Plaintiff should have considered calling defendant to the stand in plaintiff's case to authenticate these packing slips. If defendant acknowledged receipt, proof would have been simple. If defendant denied receipt and when plaintiff ultimately established receipt by other means, defendant would have lost credibility.
- If you are trying to emphasize something contained in an exhibit, make sure that the judge and the jury have the exhibit in front of them, either in hard copy or on the monitors, and an opportunity to read it. Often, a lawyer knows the case well and reviews documents rapidly with witnesses because, to the lawyer, the evidence contained in the documents is obvious. But it is not obvious to the trier of fact, and the trier of fact gives up trying to read the exhibits. Sometimes, it may be a good idea to ask the judge or jurors whether he, she, or they have the particular exhibit being discussed with a witness, or need more time to review the exhibit.
- If an exhibit must be marked for identification in open court, counsel should state, for the record, what is being done and describe briefly the nature of the exhibit.

- Do not expect the court to provide exhibit labels, if required to be used.
- Ascertain where exhibits, once admitted into evidence, are retained during the trial. Typically, if the trial involves only documents and the documents are kept in notebooks, the "official" or "record" set of exhibits is kept at the witness chair in the notebook(s); but, if physical objects or single copies of exhibits are used, find out where they will be retained. Generally, each counsel is responsible to return exhibits taken from the storage point or witness stand.
- Consider, especially in a technical case, providing each juror with a notebook containing such things as the patents, preliminary instructions, and paper for notes. Something else to include is a glossary of technical terms, including, for example, tachycardia, bradycardia, acronyms, witness lists or a list of the major "players" in the action.
- If a foundation must be laid before an exhibit can be introduced into evidence, no questions about the content of the exhibit should be asked until the exhibit has been admitted into evidence.
- If opposing counsel asks a witness about the content of a document before it has been admitted, object immediately if you know that there may be a valid objection to the admissibility of the document. If you do not do so, inadmissible evidence may be presented to the jury.
- Do not wait until the conclusion of a particular witness's testimony or the conclusion of your case to offer exhibits into evidence. In one trial, plaintiff's counsel stated that he would refer to and probably identify exhibits during questioning of witnesses, but defer offering them until the end of plaintiff's case. The judge stated that doing so was not appropriate. Before a witness should be allowed to discuss a document, as opposed to questions necessary to establish authenticity or admissibility, it should be clear that the document has been admitted. More important, if counsel waits until the end of the witness's testimony or the end of the case to offer the document, it may be difficult for the judge to rule properly because the testimony about the document could have occurred hours or days earlier, or counsel may forget to offer the exhibit.

- Even though they are of limited value, interrogatory answers and responses to requests to admit generally may be used at trial. Rule 33(c) of the Federal Rules of Civil Procedure provides that interrogatory answers may be used at trial to the extent permitted by the rules of evidence. Responses to requests for admissions can also be used at trial. If made by a party, an answer to an interrogatory or response to a request to admit is evidence available to an opposing party. It is a rare event for parties to utilize interrogatory answers or responses to requests to admit as evidence. If utilized, they can be used in different ways:
  1. They may be read.
  2. A copy of the appropriate answer or response can be marked as an exhibit. This does not mean that the entire document comprising the answers or responses should be marked and introduced as an exhibit. What typically happens is that an exhibit is prepared consisting of the pages that contain the caption, title of the document, the page(s) with appropriate questions, answers or responses, the page with the signature and date, and, probably, the certificate of service. Without objection, the entire set of answers or responses could be introduced into evidence. Unless you are comfortable with this, then you must object to having the entire document being made an exhibit. In one action, when plaintiff's counsel read one interrogatory answer of defendant and then offered the entire set of answers into evidence, defendant should have objected and allowed only the one answer to be admitted into evidence, because these other answers were prejudicial to defendant.
  3. The responses could be displayed using the VEPS.
- Exhibits that have been offered, but not admitted, into evidence are part of the record and are generally retained by court personnel in the event of an appeal.

Provide a Copy or Show Demonstrative Exhibits to Opposing Counsel Before the Hearing or Trial

Whether for an oral argument or for trial, provide to opposing counsel a copy of any demonstrative exhibits you plan to use before the hearing or trial. If you do not, it could be devastating if you refer to demonstrative exhibits in front of a jury and the court will not allow their use. Remember the Golden Rule. Besides, you will appear to be unfair by attempting to spring something on the other side.

Demonstrative Exhibits Do Not Go with the Jury

Be careful. In one action, the jurors liked the demonstrative exhibits. They did not know that the demonstrative exhibits would not be available for deliberations. They said that if they had known that they would not see the exhibits again, they would have taken more notes. Consider telling, or requesting the judge to tell, the jurors at some time, during the early part of the trial, that they will not have the demonstrative exhibits available for deliberations.

Do Not Be Overly Aggressive with Preparation of Demonstrative Exhibits

In an action involving theft of television signals, plaintiff used a demonstrative exhibit to explain how a signal was sent to a satellite and then to a receiver and how a "hacker" could steal the signal. Plaintiff drew a picture of a seedy-looking character as the "hacker." This might have seemed clever to those on plaintiff's trial team, but some jurors thought that this was in poor taste and was too aggressive.

Creation of Demonstrative Exhibits During a Trial

Some lawyers create demonstrative exhibits during examination of witnesses. For example, they may use blank paper and write down key words, answers, dates, or a summary of what the witness has testified and then refer to these words or numbers later in the same examination to demonstrate inconsistencies or to emphasize certain points. Sometimes, counsel uses these papers with subsequent witnesses or during closing argument. In an action in which dates were important, counsel wrote on a piece of paper the important dates as testified to by a witness (e.g., a timeline) and then used this paper and dates with the same witness for other questions; also, this timeline was used with other witnesses to assist in understanding the case.

Another interesting example is from a drug case. There was an issue of how many kilograms of cocaine were delivered over a certain time period. As defense counsel was reviewing with a witness the various dates of delivery and the quantities of each delivery, counsel placed a blank piece of paper under the document camera and wrote down the alleged amount delivered on each date. At the end of the listing, the quantities were totaled and written on the paper. This was effective to discredit the quantities listed in the indictment.

Sometimes, what starts out as a demonstrative exhibit can become an exhibit. When a witness explained the various steps of the company's disciplinary procedure, counsel had the witness diagram the procedure on a page from a pad of paper. The page was then marked as an exhibit, and then offered and received into evidence.

In an employment discrimination action in which the defendant company maintained plaintiff was discharged for excessive absenteeism, an issue was what days plaintiff worked or did not work. Counsel brought large monthly calendars, placed them on an easel, and, as the witness testified as to the days worked or not worked, the dates were marked accordingly on the calendars. The calendars were marked as exhibits and were introduced into evidence.

In another action in which plaintiff's erroneous audits were an issue, counsel also used large calendars. Counsel asked a witness questions about the dates on which audits were done, how many deposits were received, how many of those deposits were late, and what percentage of deposit slips that were reviewed were late. The answers were written on the appropriate dates on the calendars. Because demonstrative exhibits, unless later marked as exhibits, do not go to the jury, after the statistics were finished, counsel should have marked these calendars as exhibits and sought to introduce them into evidence. Defendant also should have used VEPS, which makes it easier for jurors to see documents rather than small print on an easel several feet away.

Be Certain that Nondocument Exhibits Can Be Used in the Courtroom

If you have a large or unusual exhibit, either for demonstrative or evidentiary purposes, determine sufficiently in advance of the hearing or trial that the exhibit can fit through the courthouse doors, in elevators, or on stairways and that it can be brought through the courtroom doors.

On the morning of one trial, an exemplar of a section of an automobile barely fit through the courtroom doors. In another action, a video game machine would not fit through the courtroom doors. The judge, participants, and court reporter all had to move to the hallway for testimony regarding the machine. In contrast, in another action, defendant used two exhibits that were fifteen to twenty feet long. On the Friday before the start of trial, a paralegal brought the exhibits to the courtroom to determine how they could be used. Three easels were set up on which to display the exhibits. Waiting until the defendant wanted to use the exhibits during the trial would have been a disaster.

In a criminal case, the government prepared folding poster boards to display pictures of the many defendants; however, the boards would not stand up in the courtroom. Counsel tried numerous ways to get the boards to stand up, while the jury merely watched this frustrating endeavor.

Large Exhibits Can Be Dramatic

In an equal pay action, defendant announced it was closing Department T of its plant. Plaintiffs who worked at this department were given the opportunity to accept less desirable jobs in a newly created Department M at the plant when those jobs became available. Each time jobs became available in Department M, the jobs were first offered to plaintiffs. When plaintiffs refused to accept the jobs, employees with lower seniority than plaintiffs accepted the jobs or defendant hired new employees for Department M. Some plaintiffs refused as many as ten times to accept jobs in Department M. When Department T shut down, plaintiffs sought to displace the employees in Department M who accepted the jobs that plaintiffs previously rejected. All of plaintiffs' refusals were combined into one exhibit, two feet tall, and introduced into evidence. This exhibit stayed in the courtroom for the entire trial and was a stark reminder of the unfairness of plaintiffs refusing jobs and then trying to displace those employees who took the jobs plaintiffs previously had not wanted. The jury agreed.

Summary of Voluminous Records Should Be Considered

A very effective document is one that summarizes certain facts. Rule 1006 of the Federal Rules of Evidence provides:

> The contents of voluminous writings, recordings, or photographs which cannot conveniently be examined in court may be presented in the form of a chart, summary or calculation. The originals, or duplicates, shall be made available for examination or copying, or both, by other parties at reasonable time and place. The court may order that they may be produced in court.

In one action, plaintiffs wanted to emphasize the stock sales by various corporate employees over a period of several months. The actual documents reflecting the sales were several thousand pages and were marked as exhibits; however, plaintiffs prepared a ten-page summary reflecting the name of the executives, dates of sales, number of shares involved, option strike price, sales price, and profit. The presentation was quite dramatic in this form.

The underlying documents do not have to be introduced into evidence as long as they have previously been made available to opposing counsel. The underlying documents, however, need to be provided to opposing counsel sufficiently in advance of their use so that opposing counsel can verify the information. In fact, the summary document should be on the Final Exhibit List.

In one action, plaintiff's Final Exhibit List included a summary document, but none of the underlying documents had been provided to opposing counsel. The court, at the final pretrial conference the Friday before the trial, instructed the plaintiff to provide the summaries by noon on Saturday. This was not done. Instead, on the second day of trial, plaintiff sought to introduce the summary. The court sustained the defendant's objection to the use of the summary exhibit.

8

WHILE PREPARING FOR DEPOSITIONS AND TRIAL, CONSIDERATION SHOULD BE GIVEN TO THE USE OF STIPULATIONS

Most litigated matters involve some documents. Stipulations with respect to documents, as well as facts, can expedite both depositions and trials.

To streamline depositions, lawyers can stipulate to certain matters: all objections are preserved, thereby eliminating the need to make objections; all objections are preserved by merely stating "objection," thereby avoiding the need to specify a particular ground; or, unless an objection is made at the time a document is first shown to a witness, all foundational bases are waived.

Be aware of that to which you are stipulating. If confronted with a request to adopt the "usual stipulations," do not accept. Instead, say something like, "I am not sure to what you are referring, so please tell me;" or, "I prefer to have the stipulations listed on the record and then I can state if I agree to them."

Stipulations as to documents/exhibits are extremely helpful for trial purposes. Some jurisdictions have local rules requiring the submission of pretrial orders in which the parties are ordered to list the potential trial exhibits, stipulate to their admissibility, or list the reasons for objecting to the introduction of the listed exhibits.

It is a waste of time for the court, counsel, parties, and jury when one party takes time laying a foundation for the admissibility of a document only to learn that there is no objection. Stipulating to authenticity of documents not only saves trial time but also may save money and inconvenience to others by eliminating the need to call certain witnesses. If, for example, defense counsel stipulates to the authenticity of plaintiff's medical records, plaintiff will not need to call the custodian of those records.

Stipulations as to admissibility of exhibits allow preparation for trial to be more complete and certain because it will be known which exhibits will be admitted into evidence if any party chooses to use them. If approached sufficiently in advance of the trial, stipulations, or refusals to stipulate, as to admissibility or authenticity, may provide a preview of what further evidence will need to be introduced at trial and who will have to be called as witnesses.

Even without a court order, it still is prudent to approach opposing counsel to discuss stipulations with respect to exhibits. Failing to meet with counsel prior to trial to explore stipulations on authenticity or admissibility can result in intervention by the court. In one action, for which there had been no attempts to stipulate, the court ordered both parties to bring all potential exhibits to the courthouse three days before trial and, under the supervision of court staff, seek to reach as many stipulations as possible.

Although stipulating to admissibility as to all, or at least most, of the potential exhibits is desirable, sometimes the effort to negotiate with opposing counsel on admissibility may be a waste of time for the following reasons:

1. Lawyers should know which documents they may use or may not want the other side to use. But many lawyers do not make up their minds on these matters until just before trial. Although counsel may be willing to stipulate on authenticity before trial, they may be reluctant to stipulate on admissibility. Thus, the whole process of stipulating may break down.
2. Lawyers may not want to alert opposing counsel to exactly which documents they intend to use at the trial or to objections to documents that the opposing party may use at trial.
3. Precipitating arguments and confrontations over admissibility issues before trial often leads to hostile feelings and the inability to reach any stipulation.
4. A possible stipulation to use when the parties might not want to stipulate on admissibility, or even authenticity, but anticipate that at trial they will probably not object to the admissibility of documents, is the following:

> Any document listed on [a stipulated list] that is referred to by number during questioning of a witness in open court shall be deemed admitted into evidence unless objection is made to that document at the time the document is first referred to by number. Any objection made to a document will be addressed at the time the objection is first made.

This stipulation delays ascertaining which exhibits will be admitted, if offered, but it will expedite trial time if few objections are made at trial. If objections are made, the party seeking admission of the exhibits can lay the necessary foundation. This approach should force counsel to object only when there is a good faith belief in the objection. To object continually to the introduction of documents and have those objections overruled results in a quick loss of credibility with the jury.

If the parties can agree on stipulations as to authenticity or admissibility before the start of depositions, some depositions may be able to be eliminated.

Time can also be saved at depositions by using the following stipulation:

If, during depositions taken in this action, a document is marked as an exhibit, is shown to a witness during any deposition, and counsel for the witness states, "Stipulation," and no counsel for any other party objects to the stipulation, it is hereby stipulated and agreed that:

1. Except for any handwritten notations that may appear in the margins of any typewritten document, the document is a true and correct copy of the original document.
2. The document (including any attachments) was signed by or under the direction of each person whose signature appears on the document and was signed on or about the date indicated on the face of the document.
3. The document (including any attachments) was prepared by or under the direction of the person or persons so identified as responsible for its preparation.
4. If the document identifies the person transmitting the document to others, the document (including any attachments) was transmitted by that person to each person identified on the document as a recipient.
5. If the document identifies recipients, the document (including any attachments) was received at the address of each recipient identified on the document on the date indicated on the face of the document as a receipt date or, if there is no such receipt date indicated, within a reasonable time after the date of the document.
6. A document purporting to be minutes of a meeting is, in fact, minutes of the meeting referred to and the minutes were prepared by a person or persons having authority and responsibility for preparing such minutes.

7. A document purporting to be a report does constitute a report of such matters as are included in such document and the report was prepared by or under the direction of the person or entity identified on the document as being responsible for the preparation of the report.
8. A document purporting to be a memorandum, report, record, or data compilation of a regularly conducted activity such as acts, events, conditions, opinions, or diagnoses was made at or near the date or dates shown on the document from information transmitted by a person with knowledge, was kept in the course of a regularly conducted business activity, and it was the regular practice of that business activity to make the memorandum, report, record, or data compilation.

If there is no question about the authenticity of a document, it is ridiculous to waste time at depositions with foundational questions. If you, as the defending party, know that a document is authentic, state, "Stipulation" when the document is presented to the proper witness for identification. Counsel defending a deposition can control if there will be a stipulation. If you, as the counsel defending the deposition, know that the witness is not capable of authenticating the document or there is a question of authenticity, then, if you do not say, "Stipulation," you have committed to nothing, but you do allow the party taking the deposition the opportunity to try to authenticate the document.

If a witness is unable to authenticate the document, but you know that someone else can, you still may want to say, "Stipulation" and avoid having to depose another person. You can choose not to say, "Stipulation" at this deposition and wait until the proper witness is deposed. If the other side never deposes the proper witness and the proper witness does not appear at trial, then the document might never be used at trial.

Stipulations can expedite trials by eliminating the need to prove certain facts and boring evidence such as:

- Medical expenses
- Dates of various events such as dates of birth, employment, and termination, and dates absent from work
- Chemical analyses of drugs
- Dates of invoices
- Damages to property
- Amount of lost wages

In an ERISA case, the issue was whether the plaintiff would be entitled to recover medical expenses. During discovery, the medical bills were produced. Because the bills were not paid by plaintiff, the caregivers submitted multiple copies of the bills to plaintiff. Because defendant requested production of all medical bills for which reimbursement was being sought, plaintiff's counsel forwarded all of these multiple copies to defendant's counsel. Prior to trial, there was a stack of bills one foot high. Ultimately, I called plaintiff's counsel and requested that counsel review the bills and submit to me only one copy of those bills for which reimbursement was being requested. I then sent the bills identified by plaintiff's counsel to the claims administrator for the defendant, who advised that if liability were found, the plaintiff would be entitled to receive $23,546.97. The parties were then able to stipulate that if plaintiff were entitled to recover in the action, plaintiff would be entitled to recover $23,546.97. With a one-sentence stipulation, a large number of exhibits and the need to call witnesses to authenticate the bills were eliminated. This result benefited all concerned.

In another ERISA case, this one involving long-term disability coverage, the parties stipulated to the basic facts such as birth date, dates of injury, dates of claims, and the claims themselves. In fact, so much was stipulated that plaintiff's counsel had little to elicit from plaintiff at the trial.

9

DEPOSITIONS ARE THE MOST IMPORTANT FORM OF DISCOVERY; MOST CIVIL ACTIONS ARE WON, OR LOST, OR SETTLED, AS A RESULT OF TESTIMONY GIVEN, OR NOT GIVEN, AT DEPOSITIONS

When to Take Depositions

Although you need to be prepared to take a deposition (see Chapter 4), do not wait until any date established by the court to complete discovery is about to expire before taking depositions. Matters learned at one deposition may necessitate taking other depositions or doing some other form of discovery or conducting further investigation. If you wait until discovery is about to expire to take depositions, you may not be able to take further depositions without agreement of opposing counsel or permission from the court. In any event, you need to take depositions sufficiently in advance of trial to be sure that your discovery is complete and to be sure that you have sufficient time to utilize information learned from these depositions in trial preparation.

Be prepared to take depositions at odd times, for example, early in the morning, in the evening, or on weekends, if necessary. Arrange a schedule, if possible, that will aid in your strategy, such as not allowing sufficient time between depositions for opposing counsel to prepare for subsequent depositions, or taking one or more critical depositions before your opponent takes any depositions, or that will allow you to depose a witness who has other commitments.

Poor preparation makes for a poor deposition and can result in unnecessary time at trial. Failure to ask necessary questions at a deposition may require you to ask these questions during trial. Then, if, at trial, the witness does not know the answers anyway, the jurors will believe that you have wasted their time. In one action, plaintiff deposed defendant's president two times. At the trial, plaintiff's counsel asked questions of this president that should have been asked at deposition, but were not, and received many, "I don't know" answers. This wasted everyone's time; both the judge and jury were annoyed by this. Moreover, if you fail to ask an important question at a deposition and are foolish enough to ask it at trial, your case may suffer if you receive an answer you did not expect.

Where to Take Depositions

Too often, counsel notices a deposition for the noticing counsel's office. This is not recommended. As the first option, schedule depositions of opposing parties to take place at the office of opposing counsel. This is the polite action to take. It's also part of the old adage, "Turnabout is fair play." If, later, your client is deposed, opposing counsel may schedule the deposition in that counsel's office. Your client may be more comfortable being deposed in your office where the client has probably been several times earlier, rather than in opposing counsel's office. Going to opposing counsel's office for an opposing party's deposition also assisted me in another way. I represented a number of large corporations whose senior executives were not based in Indianapolis. I set the tone for requiring opposing counsel to go to the home office of these executives by saying, "We always went to your offices or your client's offices for your clients." Even so, where executives or employees came from outside Indiana to Indianapolis, it was better to have these people in my office rather than in opposing counsel's office because these executives and employees were more relaxed in my office; also, it was more convenient in the event that these witnesses needed to review documents that were in my office.

Another reason for going to opposing counsel's office for depositions of opposing parties is that, at times, a deponent will refer to a document not previously disclosed or produced in discovery. It is possible at that time to ask for the document to be produced; and, if it is, examination can then be conducted as to that document during the deposition instead of, perhaps, adjourning the deposition and possibly never concluding it by oversight, thereby never examining the deponent about this document.

A second option for a place to take a deposition, if the opposing party is a corporation, is the corporation's place of business. I have taken depositions in strange places such as a factory and a construction site. This again provides the opportunity to obtain documents, either by asking for them if identified during the deposition or even by happenstance. One time, in a construction delay case, a deposition was being taken at the contractor's office. The conference room where the deposition was being taken had a bulletin board on which was placed a timeline for the construction project in litigation; this timeline had not previously surfaced in discovery. Because this document was germane to the action, the timeline was removed from the bulletin board, marked as an exhibit, and identified at the deposition.

It is for this reason that I did not let opposing counsel into my client's place of business. The only exception to this rule was for senior executives of large, out-of-state corporations. When dealing with lower-level executives and employees, I always had them come to Indianapolis or local counsel's office. So, except for those senior executives, I did not want any opposing counsel in my client's place of business. When a deposition was held at the client's place of business, the offices were of an administrative type and were sanitized. I never allowed entrance to a manufacturing plant or sales office. Once, I had a request from opposing counsel to use a room in a manufacturing plant to take a deposition. Not wanting to take a chance on what the lawyer would see or do there, I refused and forced this counsel to rent a room at a motel.

Another option for a place to take a deposition is a court reporter's office. Most court reporters have conference rooms for this purpose. Although using a neutral place for depositions of your clients makes it easier to refuse any request to produce documents at that time, it is not as convenient if you or your witness want to check on something during a recess during the deposition, and probably is not as comfortable or relaxed for your witnesses.

Who Should Be Deposed

The following sections discuss some guidelines when making decisions about whom to depose.

Use Some Discretion in Deciding Whom to Depose

Do not start deposing every person whose name appears on initial disclosures, witness lists, or documents collected. Do not take a deposition just to ask what the witness might or might not know about the action. Do some investigation to decide why a deposition should be taken; for example, to learn certain essential facts, to commit a witness to certain facts, or to gather evidence needed to prepare for trial. Without such a purpose, you will be wasting time and money and perhaps preserving testimony for trial for the benefit of your opponent that otherwise may not be able to be introduced into evidence at the trial.

Client (Client Representatives)

Normally, you will not depose your own client, or, in the instance of a corporate client, that client's officers and employees. After all, why alert the opposition to what these persons will say? The opposing party will most likely depose these persons anyway.

There are several exceptions to this rule. If your client or client's employee, whose testimony is likely to be needed at trial, is diagnosed with a terminal illness, this witness's testimony needs to be preserved by deposition. A second exception arises if one of the key officers or employees of a client has announced a retirement or resignation or will be terminated in a reduction of force; in such an event, thought should be given to deposing this person. After this person leaves your client's employment, there is no guarantee that the person will be available for trial. If you rely on that person's commitment to come to trial, and the witness moves beyond the subpoena power of the court, that witness may later decide—because of starting a new job or for other reasons—not to come to trial voluntarily. Of course, if this happens after discovery is closed, you could seek permission from the court to depose this person. A third exception is best illustrated by an action I defended involving retirement plan benefits. Twenty years earlier, Ajax Corporation, that I represented, acquired Blackstone Company. All of the employees of Blackstone Company became employees of Ajax Corporation. Upon reaching retirement age, some of the former employees of Blackstone Company contended that they were entitled to additional benefits based on the terms of the contract pursuant to which Ajax Corporation purchased Blackstone Company. At the time that the lawsuit was filed, only one surviving person was still employed by Ajax Corporation who could provide certain facts with regard to how retirement benefits were affected by the acquisition. This person was sixty-eight years old. Without testimony from this witness, there was no way the action could be won, so I noticed and took this deposition.

Opposing Party/Opposing Party's Representatives

Deposing the opposing party or key employees or officers of the opposing party is a necessity. It is essential to learn what facts these persons know about the litigation as well as to get them committed to those facts. Not only will you be able to elicit facts about the action, which will enable you to do better at trial, this is also the best way to obtain admissions from a party opponent. At times, these witnesses will provide facts that are contrary to the position of the opposing party. On the other hand, sometimes all the relevant facts may not be known to your client. Deposition testimony from these adverse witnesses may provide facts, which may direct attention to settlement and avoid other expensive discovery and litigation. By way of example, I was defending a lawsuit seeking benefits from a long-term disability ("LTD") plan. For some unknown reason, plaintiff attached to the complaint a transcript of an *ex parte* deposition of a doctor. The doctor stated that, although the plaintiff could not do his particular job at the defendant's plant, the plaintiff could do any number of other jobs. This testimony disqualified plaintiff from long-term disability benefits based on the language of the plan. Upon being deposed, plaintiff revealed for the first time that he was receiving Social Security disability benefits. Upon learning this, I obtained the plaintiff's entire Social Security file and forwarded it to the client. The client, after reviewing the file, advised that this file, which did not contain any reports from the "deposed" doctor, did contain competent medical evidence that plaintiff was entitled to benefits under the LTD plan. I was instructed to advise plaintiff's counsel that plaintiff would be enrolled in the LTD plan. Thus, after only limited discovery, this action was settled with limited costs to the client.

Another reason to depose an opposing party and its witnesses is that the deposition testimony should be the foundation for the questions to be asked at trial.

Some lawyers who represent large or affluent clients believe that, if the opposing party is an individual of modest means or is represented by counsel who is not experienced, a lengthy and confrontational deposition may cause the opposing party to abandon the lawsuit or settle quickly for a nominal amount. Unquestionably, a thorough deposition can lead to a quick settlement, especially if the testimony establishes weaknesses of the opponent's action. For example, I defended a race and sexual employment discrimination lawsuit brought by an African-American woman. Her résumé was very impressive: high school education, welding school, welding certificates, and five years' prior welding experience at two previous employers. The company I was representing was so eager to employ an African-American female welder that the company did not verify plaintiff's information. At her deposition, rather than question the plaintiff about the items in her employment application, I asked her to relate in specific detail her educational and employment history. She had not graduated from high school, had no welding certificates, had no welding training, and had held no prior welding jobs. She fabricated all the information on her application in order to obtain the job. Her counsel did not even know of these fabrications. Needless to say, the lawsuit was quickly dismissed.

Although a thorough deposition can result in dismissal of a lawsuit, as described above, or establish the weakness of an opponent's case, taking a deposition solely to intimidate a party or counsel misses the point and could be an abuse of the legal system.

Of course, deposing the opposing party or its witnesses preserves their testimony. In one employment discrimination lawsuit, plaintiff died after filing the action and before his deposition was taken. His wife, as Administratrix of the Estate, succeeded as the plaintiff. Without the original plaintiff's testimony, it was a more difficult case to prove. In fact, the jury rendered a verdict for the defendant. If defendant had deposed the former employee before he died, a different result might have occurred.

Nevertheless, it is still necessary to depose an opposing party or its key officers, employees, and witnesses. You cannot rely on the fact that one of these people may die or otherwise become unavailable. How many of these people you depose depends on what you believe they may say. Remember, just as your client's key officers and employees may die, retire, or resign and move beyond the subpoena power of the court, so may key officers and employees of the opposing party. If you depose these persons and their testimony is harmful to your case, then their testimony is preserved.

Non-Parties

This section discusses several issues pertaining to depositions of non-parties.

Interview First

Before deposing non-parties who have been identified as having knowledge of the facts of the lawsuit, these persons should first be interviewed. Contact these witnesses in person, usually at home, not at their work. Trying to arrange an interview by phone will probably result in a refusal to meet. And, a witness may be reluctant or embarrassed if approached at work. After interviewing them, the information they provide at the time of interview should be reduced to a written statement at that time. Ask each person to review the statement and to sign it if it is correct. If the statement is not correct, ask the person to strike out the incorrect material and place their initials in the margin of the document next to any change. If the witness wants to add additional material, you should add the material. If you do not allow the witness to add the material, the statement is used at the trial, and the witness testifies you would not allow any additions, you will lose credibility. The value of having this statement is there is some means of impeaching the witness if the witness does come to trial and testifies differently and there was no deposition. If you return to your office and have a statement prepared, you will have to mail the statement or go back to the witness, who may not then be available or may refuse to sign a statement, especially if an opposing party has approached this witness.

One issue to consider is whether this written statement should be thorough. That is, consider if the statement should include all relevant facts, or just those facts helpful to your client. Also, some counsel purposely place incorrect information in the statement and encourage the witness to strike through the incorrect material. These lawyers opine that if this statement has to be used, the stricken material establishes that the witness read the statement before signing it. This is an unacceptable practice. First of all, there is a problem of what to do if the witness does not strike the erroneous material. How will it look to the trier of fact if the witness should testify at trial that after the witness was asked to sign the statement, you asked the witness to delete certain parts of the statement. Second, the trier of fact may simply conclude you were trying to trick the witness and cannot be trusted.

When you interview a non-party, consider taking with you another person who could be a witness at trial in case this non-party provides helpful evidence, will not sign a statement, and then testifies differently at trial. Without having this other person available, impeachment will not be possible.

A Witness Does Not Have to Consent to an Interview

There is absolutely no requirement that any witness, or potential witness, talk informally to a party or a party's counsel. The only way that a witness can be required to provide information prior to trial is pursuant to a subpoena for a deposition.

If you approach non-parties who then ask you whether they have to consent to an interview, you must tell them that the only way they can be required to provide information prior to trial is by a deposition preceded by a subpoena. Nevertheless, you should tell them that you would appreciate them talking to you at that time, if at all possible.

If Sally Smith, a witness who properly can be interviewed, has been asked first by an opposing party to be interviewed, and Ms. Smith asks you whether she should consent to the interview, you can properly tell her that she can refuse to talk to anyone, but she also can be subpoenaed and forced to testify at a deposition or at trial. Only the witness can make the decision about being interviewed. **Do not advise Ms. Smith what to do**. Do not even state your preference; however, you can advise that if a deposition is taken, you could be there to observe and ask questions if necessary. If Ms. Smith does consent to be interviewed by the other side, you can advise her that if the interview is recorded or if there is a written statement given to her to sign, she can request that she be given a copy of the recording or statement that was signed and that you would like the witness to provide you with a copy of it as well.

If you do advise a witness that the witness does not have to be interviewed by the opposing party and the witness refuses, that could create a concern with a jury. Potentially, all that the jury will learn is that the witness refused to be interviewed. The jury may not be told that it is acceptable to refuse to be interviewed and that a deposition provides a better record of what is said. The jury may believe that the witness is trying to inhibit the party seeking the interview. It can be worse if it is revealed that the witness refused to be interviewed based on your advice or after meeting with you.

Deciding Which Non-Parties Should Be Deposed Requires Some Thought

After preliminary investigation, you can decide which non-party witnesses you want to depose. If you think that the witnesses will provide only damaging information, think twice if you want to preserve this evidence, which in theory could be the only evidence against your client. Although it is helpful to have deposition testimony to use as a basis for questioning and impeachment, the same should be possible with a signed, written statement if the witnesses do, in fact, testify. If these people are the source of critical facts that you need to establish, you must decide whether you can be certain that they will be available at the time of trial. Again, the issue of potential death or unavailability is there; otherwise, if these people are within the subpoena power of the court, they can be asked to testify at trial but, as a precaution, they should be subpoenaed to testify. If you subsequently learn that these people will be out of the subpoena range at the time of the trial and discovery has been closed, you can contact the opposing side and request that depositions be taken. If no cooperation is received, relief could be sought from the court.

If critical witnesses are or will be beyond the subpoena power of the court at the time of the trial, these people should be deposed for at least two reasons. First, although they may at some time agree voluntarily to come to court, those commitments may change for various reasons. If so, you may not have this testimony available. Second, these witnesses may be volatile or not make good in-person witnesses. I once had a lawsuit for which testimony from a witness beyond the subpoena power of the court was critical if I was going to win the lawsuit. I took a deposition. My questioning went fine, and I obtained what I needed. On cross-examination, the witness, based on questions of plaintiff's counsel, became very defensive and agitated, stood up, and screamed at plaintiff's counsel. This conduct indicated that this person would not make a good witness in court. Despite the willingness of this witness to come to the trial, I elected to present this testimony by deposition only.

Another situation to consider is when information that is critical to your case is not asked at a deposition of a non-party witness being taken by your opponent. If you ask these questions to be assured that the record is made, you may alert the opposing side to the critical evidence, which the opposing party can prepare to rebut at trial. If you do not ask the questions, the information is not available from any other source, and the witness becomes unavailable, the evidence may never be introduced into the trial record.

In Most Instances an Opposing Party's Expert, But not Your Expert, Should Be Deposed

If the opposing party's expert is likely to testify, it is necessary that the expert be deposed. If the expert has submitted a report, an effective cross-examination of this witness at trial based on the expert's report, published materials or testimony in prior litigation is possible, but not likely.

There have been instances when no deposition of an expert was taken and the expert died. This resulted in nominal settlements, especially when the courts did not continue the trials or the clients did not want to employ other experts.

Generally, there is no reason to depose your own expert unless you are trying to intimidate the opposing party or perhaps to promote settlement. On the other hand, if your opponent does not depose your expert, the expert is critical, and there is some risk that the expert will be unavailable for trial, you probably should depose your own expert.

Rule 30(b)(6) Depositions Are a Valuable Discovery Technique

A procedure to consider if your opposing party is a corporation or other organization is a Rule 30(b)(6) deposition. This is not a substitute for deposing the officers and employees of a corporate party. It is simply easier to obtain admissions rather than have to depose different people or run the risk of your opponent arguing that the deponent was not authorized to make the admissions.

Establish Priority for Your Depositions, but Use Common Courtesies in Scheduling

Rule 30(b)(1) of the Federal Rules of Civil Procedure states,

> "A party who wants to depose a person by oral questions must give reasonable written notice to every other party."

Do not start sending notices for depositions that meet only your schedule. Remember the Golden Rule. It is easy to notice depositions when it is convenient for you. This may not be a convenient date for other counsel or for the deponents. If the time is inconvenient, other counsel may rearrange counsel's schedule. When this counsel notices depositions, the dates may not be convenient for you. If you request a change, counsel may say, "No, you did not consult me about dates for your depositions."

For most of my trial practice, I represented corporations who were named as defendants. My goal was to depose the plaintiff, or key employees of the plaintiff, before plaintiff's counsel took any depositions. Instead of sending notices for depositions, I sent a letter to opposing counsel identifying who I wanted to depose and requesting counsel to provide me with dates convenient to counsel and the designated witnesses.

Some lawyers opine that merely sending a letter rather than a notice will not accomplish the goal of priority in taking depositions if the opposing party later issues a notice. I disagree, although I never had to litigate the issue. One time, after I wrote a letter requesting dates for a plaintiff's deposition, opposing counsel issued a notice of deposition of an employee of my client for an earlier date. I told counsel either to cancel his notice or I would seek relief from the court. I argued how much more civil it was to explore dates with opposing counsel rather than arbitrarily picking dates. I further argued how unprofessional it was for counsel to ignore my request and then issue counsel's own notice. Counsel withdrew the notice.

It is not appropriate, either by letter or by notice, to demand that all your depositions be taken before any of those desired by the other side. Make the first request and then insist on one or more of your depositions proceeding first and then work with counsel on appropriate schedules for remaining depositions.

When scheduling or noticing a deposition, confirm first that the deponent will be available on the date selected. The date may be appropriate for all counsel to the litigation, but not for the witness. When a young lawyer noticed a deposition for a non-party witness, I called and asked for rescheduling because the date was not convenient for me. This young lawyer wanted to show me how aggressive he was and said, "No." I did some rearranging to accommodate the date. Then, this counsel called me to state that the deposition had to be continued after all, because the witness was out of the country and would not return until after the date of the scheduled deposition. Failure to check the deponent's availability can also be upsetting to the deponent. Irritating a non-party before the deposition may not make for a cooperative witness.

Also, agreeing to a date for depositions of people you represent without discussing dates with them will not endear them to you if the dates are inconvenient for them. And, you probably will frustrate opposing counsel if you later call to reschedule.

There Are Limits to the Number and Length of Depositions

Unless otherwise agreed or ordered by the court, Rule 30(a)(2)(A) of the Federal Rules of Civil Procedure allows only ten depositions to be taken, and Rule 30(d)(1) limits each deposition to one day of seven hours. So, if you anticipate needing to take more than ten depositions or one or more depositions of more than seven hours, first seek agreement from opposing counsel. In many cases your opponent will have similar needs and so agreement is usually reached. If opposing counsel will not agree, then you will need to seek relief from the court. If you seek permission from the court, be sure to identify which additional depositions are needed and why they are needed or state why the time limits need to be exceeded. Approval should not be difficult to obtain in complicated actions.

After Being Scheduled, All Depositions Should Be Noticed and Subpoenas Issued For Non-Party Depositions

After you have agreed with counsel and the deponent on the date for a deposition, you should (1) confirm this by letter and (2) issue a notice pursuant to Rule 30(b), Federal Rules of Civil Procedure. If no agreement has been reached, simply issue the notice. If the deponent is a party to the lawsuit, issuing a notice will provide you with a basis to seek expenses if the deponent or opposing counsel does not appear; doing so also protects you from having to pay reasonable expenses if the deponent or counsel does not appear but counsel for another party does appear. If the deposition may exceed one day, add to the notice after the date the words "and to be continued day-to-day thereafter until completed."

For non-party depositions, also use a subpoena. If the deponent is a non-party who does not appear, failure to serve a subpoena can result in the imposition on you of reasonable expenses of any party or counsel who did appear for the deposition.

I never used a subpoena for a deposition of a party opponent.

Combine a Request for Production of Documents with the Notice or Subpoena

In lawsuits for which the opposing party will not have many documents, consider including a request made in compliance with Rule 34, Federal Rules of Civil Procedure for production of documents to accompany the deposition notice rather than using an earlier request for production of documents. See Rule 30(b)(2), Federal Rules of Civil Procedure. The advantage of this procedure is that some counsel will fail to meet with their clients or deponents before their depositions. Counsel will merely forward the notice and any subpoena to the deponents and instruct the deponents to appear at the appointed time and place for the depositions with the requested documents. If that occurs, and it did for me, simply start the deposition by asking the witness to produce the documents requested. You either can take a few minutes to review them or have them all marked as exhibits and ask questions about them sometime during the deposition. You would be surprised at how effective this can be.

Be Familiar with the Requirements for Issuing and Serving Subpoenas

Rule 30(a)(1) of the Federal Rules of Civil Procedure provides that, "The deponent's attendance may be compelled by subpoena under Rule 45." When issuing a subpoena, be aware that there are certain requirements that, if not met, can be a source of embarrassment or the assessment of costs.

Issuing Court Limitations

Rule 45(a)(2) of the Federal Rules of Civil Procedure states that a subpoena for attendance at a trial must issue from the court for the district where the trial is to be held and a subpoena for attendance at a deposition must issue from the district court where the deposition is to be taken. If the subpoena is issued by the wrong court and the witness does not appear, then the imposition of expenses and fees on the party issuing the notice could be a possibility. To put this in perspective, I once defended a lawsuit pending in Indianapolis in which plaintiff sought to depose in Georgia a non-party who was a citizen of Georgia. Counsel served on the proposed deponent a subpoena issued by the District Court for the Southern District of Indiana. I did inform plaintiff's counsel of this error. I did not want to go to Georgia only to find that the deponent failed to appear. I could have sought fees and expenses if that had occurred, but doing so would be wasteful; besides, counsel appreciated this advice and, I believe, would have been receptive to helping me in a similar situation.

This is not the only time that I have seen this rule violated. This is more a matter of attention to detail than a deliberate flaunting of the rule.

Subpoena Range Is Limited

Rule 45(b)(2) of the Federal Rules of Civil Procedure states:

> a subpoena may be served at any place:
> (A) within the district of the issuing court;
> (B) outside that district but within 100 miles of the place specified for the deposition, hearing, trial, production, or inspection....

Some lawyers issue deposition subpoenas to persons who live outside the district that is issuing the subpoena and whose residence is beyond 100 miles of the place for the taking of the deposition. Query, is this air miles or road miles? Expenses and fees to noticing counsel can result when opposing counsel and parties appear at the noticed time and place but the witness does not.

Service Restrictions of a Subpoena

Counsel, but not a party, may serve a subpoena. Rule 45(b)(1) of the Federal Rules of Civil Procedure provides a subpoena may be served by any person who is not a party and who is at least 18 years old. One client inquired whether it could save money by serving subpoenas by its own field personnel. A young lawyer, obviously without reading this rule, approved. When this service was discovered to be ineffective, the client balked at paying for someone else to serve the subpoenas, taking the position that the time of the client's employees was valuable as well. The law firm had to stand the costs for the proper service of the subpoenas.

Tendering of Fees Required

Rule 45(b)(1) of the Federal Rules of Civil Procedure requires that at the time of service of the subpoena the witness be tendered fees for "1 day's attendance and the mileage allowed by law."

Confirm the amount authorized for mileage. You do not want to have a proposed deponent fail to appear for a deposition (or trial) because you paid one or two cents per mile less than the authorized rate. These rates change periodically. Do not assume that you know the rate from the last time you served subpoenas.

Do not be skimpy on the miles. If the proposed deponent advises of the mileage, use that mileage. If you do not ask, try to estimate as close as you can, but be certain that your estimate is not below the actual mileage. Determine the most accurate mileage and add five to ten miles to be sure. Again, is this air miles or road miles? Overestimate; do not underestimate. Of course, if you go over by 100 miles, you quickly will be accused of paying the witness to testify.

Know the daily rate allowed by law for the witness fee (see 28 USC § 1821). Currently, under federal law, $40.00 per day for each day's attendance is the proper amount.

Sometimes a witness asks to be paid for lost wages as a result of having to appear for a deposition or for trial. I always took the position, without doing research, that a witness could be reimbursed for lost wages as a result of being subpoenaed. I thought that no one should be out-of-pocket as a result of being subpoenaed. If the witness was earning $20.00 per hour and would be away from work for eight hours and would not be paid by the employer, I would pay $160.00 and the $40 fee. Obviously, paying $500.00 would be inappropriate. If a witness will not lose income from work, do not pay the witness beyond the witness fee. Use common sense and think about how it will look to the jury if these facts are disclosed.

The rule contemplates tendering the witness the fee for one day's attendance and mileage. If you are able to depose for a second day of deposition, be prepared. If the original subpoena only specified attendance for one day and if you did not previously pay the deponent for the second day of the deposition, have another subpoena and a check for the appropriate amount for the fees and mileage in your briefcase, and serve it upon the deponent before the deponent leaves at the end of the first day. This admonition also applies to witnesses subpoenaed for trial testimony.

What to Do If Opposing Counsel Does Not Appear for a Deposition

If the deposition is local, the witness appears and opposing counsel does not, the proper action, although not required, is to contact opposing counsel to ascertain whether opposing counsel was delayed, ill, or for some other valid reason was unable to be there. If so, you will have to decide whether to wait if counsel is in route or reschedule the deposition. If you need to reschedule the deposition, you have to decide whether to seek to recover fees and expenses as a result of counsel's failure to appear. A more difficult question is what to do if the deposition is not local, the deponent, a non-party, does appear and opposing counsel does not appear. If you call and counsel asks you to reschedule, you will have to decide whether you will do so. If you reschedule, you should extract a commitment at that time to be reimbursed for all fees and expenses as a result of the cancellation in order to make it easier to recover these items later. This commitment should be put on the record with the court reporter. On the other hand, you are entitled to go forward with the deposition in the absence of opposing counsel. That is what I did in the only instance when this occurred. I received no objection from opposing counsel and used the deposition during the trial. If counsel will not agree to reimburse you for the fees and expenses, strong consideration should be given to proceeding with the deposition.

Witnesses Rarely Should Take Notes to a Deposition

Do not allow your witness to bring documents or notes to a deposition unless you have first reviewed them. If there are many uncontroverted facts, such as dates, having a list should not affect the credibility of the witness, other than opposing counsel perhaps establishing that the witness has no independent memory. If you are the one who prepared the list or notes, this may affect the credibility of the witness.

There is another exception for allowing a witness to have notes when testifying, although this exception involves a trial. A newspaper printed an article about a woman's change of name proceeding. The critical parts of the article were taken from one of three court records documenting the proceedings. Plaintiff sued for libel and invasion of privacy. Basing an article on a public court record would provide a defense to the newspaper on the libel count. Plaintiff's counsel had obtained a copy of only two of the three court records, which would not support the defense of public record. So, for the trial, I copied the third court record and had the publisher place it in his pocket. Trying to establish that the newspaper had no adequate defense of public record, plaintiff's counsel asked the publisher if the article was based on the first court record. The publisher said, "No, but counsel did not have the correct record." Counsel then asked if the article was based on the second court record. The publisher said, "No, but counsel did not have the correct record." Counsel asked if there was another record. The publisher said there was and then produced the third court record. After plaintiff's counsel spent a few minutes examining the third court record, the record was marked as an exhibit and shown to the jury. Subsequently, there was a defense verdict on both causes of action.

If a Witness Refers to Documents or Notes at a Deposition in Order to Answer a Question, Opposing Counsel Is Entitled to Inspect Those Notes and May Have Them Marked as an Exhibit

Be careful. A record must be made to establish that the witness did refer to documents or notes. If you are asking questions, and the witness refers to documents or notes prior to answering questions, you can ask the witness whether the witness referred to documents or notes prior to answering every time the witness does so. You can also wait until the end of the deposition by asking the witness whether the witness referred to documents or notes prior to answering questions. The better approach is to ask each time that a witness refers to documents or notes and then follow up with a summary at the end of the deposition, confirming that the witness periodically referred to documents or notes during the deposition. One counsel, who, weeks after a deposition was concluded, sought to obtain notes referred to by the witness during a deposition, was unsuccessful because no record existed of what happened at the deposition. Without a record, it will be difficult, if not impossible, to get production of these notes.

If opposing counsel is deposing and the witness refers to documents or notes, you should interrupt and state on the record each time that the witness refers to documents or notes.

In both instances, wait until you or all other counsel are done asking questions before asking for the documents or notes to be produced. If you ask for the documents or notes to be produced the first time to which they are referred, opposing counsel may get smart and not have the witness refer to documents or notes anymore. Obtaining one note listing prior addresses or job history may not be very helpful. If a witness refers to documents or notes, you can hope that the witness will refer to them many times so that you can get all of them at the conclusion of the deposition.

Be prepared with legal authority if you seek to have produced any documents or notes referred to at a deposition or referred to in preparation for the deposition that opposing counsel argues are covered by the attorney-client or work product privileges. If you are met with such an objection, and the notes or documents are not produced at that time, be sure that the documents or notes are sufficiently described on the record in case you need to pursue a motion to compel production of the notes or documents.

Request Production of Documents During a Deposition If You Are Taking the Deposition, but Decline to Produce Documents If You Are Defending a Deposition

Frequently at a deposition, after a witness identifies documents not previously produced, the witness is asked by deposing counsel to produce those documents at that time or sometime in the future. Do not let any witness you represent make any commitment to produce any documents at the deposition or in the future. It is necessary for you to inspect any documents before providing them to an opposing party. The documents may not have to be produced, or parts of the documents may properly be redacted.

In the event that a witness commits to producing documents subsequent to the conclusion of the deposition and the documents are not required to be produced or not produced in their entirety, you will be sure to hear about this commitment if you later object to production of the documents. Opposing counsel will undoubtedly argue that the witness waived any objection. The correct position to take, if a witness you are representing is requested to produce documents during a deposition, is to intervene and say that the production of documents is governed by Rule 34 of the Federal Rules of Civil Procedure. If counsel wishes to make such a request, the request will be properly considered.

It can be even more foolish to let a witness you represent actually produce documents during a deposition without your prior review. During a deposition in a mortgage fraud case, a bank officer referred to various documents in his personal files that had never been requested earlier by plaintiff and which had not even been reviewed by defense counsel. When asked to produce the documents, the bank officer went to his office to retrieve the documents and without intervention by the bank's counsel gave the documents to plaintiff's counsel. These documents substantially weakened the bank's position. The case then settled for a lot more than it could have earlier when plaintiff did not know of the documents. If defense counsel had known of the documents in advance of the deposition, and after counsel had seen the documents, a different strategy, or even earlier settlement, may have been possible. On the other hand, there may be exceptions. Once during a deposition in another state, a company witness disclosed having certain documents not previously requested. After a short recess, I reviewed the documents and decided to produce them to the other side in order to avoid having to make a return trip out of state.

Although you should not ordinarily allow any witness you are defending to produce or commit to produce documents during a deposition, if a witness you are deposing identifies certain documents not previously seen by you, ask where the documents are located. If the documents are located nearby, recess the deposition and ask the witness to retrieve them. You may or may not be met with an objection. There is no risk in asking. Once during a deposition in Minnesota, a witness described a number of important documents. When he said that they were in his car, we stopped the deposition while he retrieved them. Upon his return, I then made the documents exhibits to the deposition and interrogated the witness based on those documents.

Establishing Authenticity of Documents in Depositions Is Prudent

It is essential, unless admission or authenticity can be or has been established by a response to requests for admission, stipulation or the testimony of another witness, that you establish authenticity of any document you use at a deposition and that you contemplate using at trial.

If a document is damaging, you may want to examine the witness about only the content of the document in the event it becomes an exhibit at trial. If authentication of this type of document is not otherwise established, do not do it only to then have the document be introduced at trial and be admissible only because you laid the foundation. I once had an action for which plaintiff took depositions in Washington, D.C., San Francisco, Chicago, and Dallas, but failed to authenticate any documents identified at the depositions, most of which were needed for plaintiff to prove its case. Two weeks before trial, plaintiff's counsel asked whether I would stipulate to authenticity or admissibility of the documents. I refused. There was too little time to return to the various venues to correct the missing foundational questions, without even factoring in the additional costs, and too little time to submit requests to admit to defendant. The action quickly settled for a nominal amount.

Do Not Offer into Evidence Documents Identified at Depositions

Although you may need to establish authenticity of documents at a deposition, do not offer these documents into evidence on the record at a deposition. I once helped a young lawyer prepare for trial. Reading the transcripts of the depositions she had taken, I noticed that the lawyer offered into evidence all documents by number that were used during the depositions. When I asked why, she said that she did not know. She said that she was at one deposition where that was done and she thought that it was required. Although this never happened to me, I can envision counsel asking a witness at a deposition about damaging documents for which there may be valid objections to their admissibility at trial (especially if the foundational questions were not asked) but being unable to prevent their introduction into evidence at the trial because counsel moved their admission into the record at the deposition.

An Instruction Not to Answer Can Properly Be Used Only Under Limited Circumstances

Rule 30(c)(2) of the Federal Rules of Civil Procedure states:

> A person may instruct a deponent not to answer only when necessary to preserve a privilege, to enforce a limitation ordered by the court, or to present a motion under Rule30(d)(3).

Coaching the Witness Is Prohibited

At times during depositions, defending counsel will intersperse right after the question, "If you know." More often than not, the witness will then say, "I do not know." This has been considered coaching, and upon the issue being referred to the court, counsel has been instructed to cease this practice. Do not run the risk of having this practice called to the court's attention and having the court issue an order directing you to refrain from giving such advice.

Conferences between the deponent and counsel after a question has been asked must be avoided. Such conferences may be construed as an impediment or frustration of the fair examination of the deponent and can subject the deponent or counsel to the payment of costs and attorney's fees. See Rule 30(d)(2), Federal Rules of Civil Procedure. If opposing counsel coaches or engages in conferences with a deponent, make a statement on the record to document what is happening; object, and request that the conduct stop. If it does not, consider stopping the deposition and seeking relief from the court.

Asking Questions of Your Own Witnesses Is Not the Norm

A related issue is whether to ask any questions at a deposition taken of someone you represent. Obviously, if the witness testifies incorrectly, that testimony needs to be corrected as soon as possible. This should be after a recess, lunch break, or the next day of a multi-day deposition. If not done during the questioning by opposing counsel, then you must do so before the deposition is concluded. Otherwise, if you do not make the correction at the deposition and the testimony becomes relevant at trial, the risk of impeachment is great. If the testimony only needs clarification, you must decide how critical the clarification is and how it will appear to the jury if the clarification is not made until trial testimony. If the clarifying testimony is critical, you need to evaluate whether you can provide the evidence in some other way. Likewise, if the witness possesses critical information, the subject of which was not covered in opposing counsel's questions, you must evaluate whether you can present this evidence without this witness, if the witness becomes unavailable. If you can, do not ask the questions. If you cannot, you must ask the questions of this witness.

As Soon as Possible After You Receive a Transcript, You Must Review It to Determine Whether the Testimony Was Accurately Transcribed

Court reporters are not infallible. They do make mistakes. If not accurately transcribed, contact the court reporter directly by letter with a copy to opposing counsel citing the errors. In a lawsuit involving the termination of an employee for theft of company tires, his personal truck was discovered to have tires with the company's logo branded on the inside. The employee claimed that he knew nothing about this. I was probing his position. The following is what I read in the transcript:

> Q. (416) So, are you saying that one day when your car was parked outside, somebody crawled under your truck in broad daylight and put the company mark on 2 tires?
> A. Right.
> Q. (417) Oh, I wish I knew. The son-of-a-bitch wouldn't be alive today.
> Q. (418) Well, what would you do to him?
> A. I don't know what I'd do to him. What would you do if somebody accused you and caused you to lose everything that you've got? What would you do? Put your God damned self in my place, buddy!

What the court reporter listed as my question 417 was really part of the deponent's answer to question 416. Needless to say, I sent a letter to the court reporter, with a copy to opposing counsel, requesting that the transcript be corrected.

Requesting Signature and Reviewing Transcript is Mandatory

As just explained, you need to review all deposition transcripts to be sure they accurately record what was said at the depositions. But you must also insist that all witnesses you represent review their deposition transcripts. You need to have these witnesses confirm that the transcript reflects what they actually said. In addition, the witnesses need to review the transcript to determine whether any changes to what was actually said at the deposition need to be made. A witness may not realize until he or she reads the transcript that what was actually said was incorrect. If you know that the transcript accurately reflects what was said, but that what was said was incorrect, you can call that to the deponent's attention and inquire whether a change needs to be made. You should not tell the deponent to make changes to the transcript.

If a review is not done, or necessary changes are not made, and the witness testifies differently at trial, the witness is subject to being impeached. This could be devastating. The jury may not believe the witness's explanation that the witness or the court reporter made a mistake or the jury may take a dim view of the witness, who, believing that the testimony was incorrect, failed to tell the opposing party.

A specific request is required in order to review a deposition transcript. Rule 30(e) of the Federal Rules of Civil Procedure.

When I first started practicing law, the rules required that the transcript be submitted to the deponents for review and signature. Because court reporters experienced difficulty in having the witnesses return the transcripts, the rule was changed. If you want the signature of the deponent, you must affirmatively ask for it.

Typically, the transcript of the deposition of a person you represent will be sent to you. After you receive the transcript, send it to the witness with a cover letter explaining what should be done. There are time limits on returning transcripts to the court reporter. After being notified by the court reporter that the transcript is available, the deponent has only thirty days to review the transcript and make any changes. Waiting too long could result in no changes being allowed.

Rule 30(e) of the Federal Rules of Civil Procedure requires that if there are changes, the deponent must "sign a statement listing the changes and the reasons for making them." If changes are made, they are usually placed on a separate sheet of paper and the reasons for the changes should be recited, for example, "misunderstood the question," or "made a mistake," or, "based upon further review." If changes are made, the original responses can also be read into the record. The transcript is not physically changed.

Requesting review and signature of the deposition transcript is also a necessity for a party opponent, including key employees or representatives of an opponent. The risk is too great to waive signature. If the deposition transcript contains some very critical evidence on which you can rely at trial, the witness contradicts this testimony at trial, and you then seek to impeach, the witness might say, "That is not what I said; the court reporter made a mistake." If that happens, you will have to call the court reporter to testify at trial and bring the notes or tapes of the deposition. Plus, you will have to wait until you present evidence to do this. In a long trial, this could occur days, or even weeks, later. In the interim, the jury might conclude that you were only badgering the witness, or the jury may have forgotten the whole episode. More important, the court reporter may not be available to testify or may refuse to come to court, especially if the reporter lives beyond the subpoena power of the court.

If the witness has signed the transcript, you will, if you have to impeach, be able to establish that the witness made the statement once at the deposition and then confirmed the statement when the transcript was signed. This highlights the lack of credibility of the witness.

If a witness does change the deposition testimony, it is better to learn that within a short time after the deposition is taken and the deponent reviews and signs the transcript so that you can prepare to attack the change instead of learning of the change for the first time during the witness's trial testimony. As noted above, you can still utilize the earlier contradictory testimony.

You should request that any non-party review and sign the transcript for the same reasons as noted above.

A witness, who declined to review or who had been requested to review and sign the transcript but did not, should not be allowed to argue that the transcript is incorrect.

Video Depositions

Jurors prefer live witnesses to depositions. If depositions must be used, jurors prefer video over non-video and comment favorably on the use of scrolling testimony.

A video deposition has other advantages. For example, in one action, an issue was the measurement of a saw, which was in the courtroom. Plaintiff presented the measurement evidence by way of deposition of an expert. The testimony described the saw and what the witness did to take measurements. This testimony would have been much better by video because the witness could have stood by the saw and shown the jury exactly what he did and what the measurements were. As it was, the deposition testimony confused the jurors as to what the expert did.

Moreover, the jury's responsibility includes evaluating the credibility of witnesses; having the opportunity to observe witnesses on video can have an impact on the jury.

If you are planning to take a video deposition, state the method in the Notice. Rule 30(b)(3) of the Federal Rules of Civil Procedure.

One counsel scheduled a deposition but did not specify that it would be videotaped. Counsel for the deponent objected to videotaping because the notice did not specify that the deposition would be videotaped and the witness was inappropriately dressed. The deposition was nevertheless taken by video. At the final pretrial conference, counsel for deponent renewed his objection. The court did not allow the videotaped deposition to be shown to the jury. If one of your witnesses is going to be deposed using video, make sure that the witness is appropriately dressed and is instructed how to act as a witness.

10

SUGGESTIONS FOR EFFECTIVELY TAKING OR DEFENDING A DEPOSITION

Be Yourself; Do Not Emulate Someone Else

The goal of taking a deposition is to obtain certain information from the witness. Develop a rapport with the witness that allows the two of you to communicate.

Do not adopt the style of another lawyer whom you have observed. If you are normally mild-mannered, do not try to be aggressive at the deposition. Likewise, if you are normally very forceful, do not try to become mild-mannered. The deponent will most likely realize that you are not genuine.

Many years ago, I served as counsel for a national corporation for a litigated matter in Indiana. Because the corporation later was named a defendant in multiple other actions, New York City counsel was selected to be coordinating counsel for all actions. I prepared for and started taking a deposition of a key adverse witness in the Indiana action. After a while, New York counsel began passing me written questions and insisted that I ask these questions. The form of the questions and the style I was asked to use were not mine. I was getting nowhere. Finally, I decided that I was in charge of the Indiana action; I would ask the questions I had prepared, and ask them using my style. When I did, I developed a relationship with the witness and achieved the goals established for the deposition.

Get the Answer You Are Entitled to Receive

Approach each deposition with a goal of obtaining certain information. Prepare questions that will elicit this information. If the witness evades or fails completely to answer a question asked, do not accept the response; instead, continue questioning until you receive the answer you are entitled to receive.

Consider the following examples:

- Q. Tell me the facts or information you know that support the allegation in Paragraph 3 of the complaint that defendants should have known that the statements or representations were untrue.
  A. I believe that Mr. Jones knew. I believe that Mr. Smith knew and I believe that higher people at the company knew these figures as well.

Obviously, I did not receive an answer to my question. So I stated the question again:

> Q. Apparently, you didn't hear my question. I didn't ask you what you believed. My question was, tell me the facts or information you know that support your allegation in Paragraph 3 that defendants should have known that the statements or representations were untrue.
> A. I believe that they should have known that from looking at those documents and everything else that this could happen.

Still not getting an answer, I continued:

> Q. I wish you would listen to my question. I didn't ask you what you believe. You and I can believe it rained yesterday. You and I can believe it rained Sunday. We're not here to talk about beliefs. We're here to gather facts, and I'm here to ask you what facts you know and what your background is, and the question is not what you believe. The precise question is, tell me what facts or information you have that support the allegation in Paragraph 3 that defendants should have known that the statements or representations were untrue.
> A. I have no facts.

The result of this questioning was summary judgment.

- Q. What facts or information do you have to support the allegation that the company knew that the loader was defective?
  A. I would have thought that all the foremen knew.
  Q. Maybe it's a question of semantics. I didn't ask you what you thought. I'm asking you on what facts or information is the allegation based that the company knew that the loader was defective?
  A. All the foremen would have received a copy of a repair report.

Q. You keep saying all the foremen knew or all the foremen would have received a copy of a repair report. You're missing my question. My question is on what facts or information is the allegation based that the company knew that the loader was defective.
A. I cannot say for a fact that the foremen did receive a copy of that repair report, but I would have assumed that they did.
Q. My question again, on what facts or information is the allegation based that the company knew that the loader was defective?
A. I can't tell you any more.

Again, the result was summary judgment.

- Q. So then do you know what the basis of his thoughts was that the plant was going to close?
  A. I can give you my impression, and that is that he had to know.
  Q. I understand your impression, but did Mr. Green ever tell you the basis for his thoughts that the plant was going to close?
  A. The answer to the question is no.

Eliciting a "no" answer led to a successful resolution of this action.

- Q. On what facts or information is the allegation based that Ajax should have known why you were unable to perform your subcontract?
  A. To the best of my knowledge, the architect and the construction supervisor would have or should have known why we were unable to perform our subcontract.
  Q. Is that all you have in the way of facts or information to support the allegation that Ajax should have known why you were unable to perform your subcontract?
  A. I have seen no documents that would indicate anything more than that.
  Q. The question wasn't limited to documents. The question is do you have any other facts or information?
  A. I do not.

The above examples illustrate the value of having questions prepared (see also discussion in Chapter 13). When the questions are prepared, you are able better to determine whether the witness answers the questions asked.

Exhaust the Deponent's Knowledge in Each Area for Which Questions Are Asked

During a deposition, a plaintiff was asked to identify all management personnel to whom plaintiff reported the alleged sexual harassment. When plaintiff identified Mr. Green, counsel asked plaintiff, "What did Mr. Green say in response to your complaint?" After plaintiff answered, counsel went on to another subject and never asked whether plaintiff reported the harassment to any other member of management. At trial, plaintiff identified several other management personnel to whom plaintiff claimed she reported the harassment. Defendant could not successfully impeach by use of the deposition. At trial, plaintiff said that at the deposition, as soon as plaintiff identified Mr. Green, counsel asked plaintiff to state what Mr. Green said in response to her complaint and never gave plaintiff an opportunity to identify any other management personnel to whom plaintiff reported the harassment.

Exhaust the deponent's knowledge on each subject. If conversations are involved, you could ask the deponent to identify all persons with whom conversations were held and then exhaust what was said with the first person identified before going on to the next person; or, you could exhaust the names of all people first and then go back to exhaust what was said by each person.

Consider:

- Q. Did you talk to anybody about your thinking of leaving the company?
  A. Yes.
  Q. And whom did you talk to?
  A. Mr. Brown.
  Q. Did you talk to anybody else?
  A. Mr. Wright.
  Q. And did you talk to anybody else?
  A. No.

Keep asking, "Is there anybody else?" Be sure you get the "no" answer before proceeding to elicit what was said during each person's conversation.

- Q. That's fine. Now, what did Mr. Ford say on the issue of the plant closing?
  A. It was his thinking that the plant would close in September.
  Q. Did he say anything else on that subject?
  A. No. That covers it.

Keep asking, "Anything else?" and getting the "no" answer before proceeding.

- Q. Okay. What else did you talk about with Mr. Jones about the Motors Department closing?
  A. What would happen to the older employees.
  Q. What else did you talk about with Mr. Jones about the Motors Department closing?
  A. Would the Motors employees have a chance to transfer to another department.
  Q. And about what else did you talk to Mr. Jones?
  A. Would the Motors employees be entitled to severance.
  Q. Did you talk to Mr. Jones about anything else?
  A. What or let me say why was the Motors Department closing.
  Q. Is there anything else?
  A. I think that pretty well covers it.
  Q. You say "pretty well covers it." My question was, was there anything else that you and Mr. Jones discussed on the question of the Motors Department closing?
  A. There probably was, but I can't say now that I recall anything.

Preparing the questions in advance will assist in exhausting a witness's knowledge on each area to be covered.

Summarize Several Answers into One Question and Answer

Another technique to use in depositions, when confronted with multiple answers to the same question that may take up several lines or even pages of the transcript, is to summarize the testimony. Such a technique makes any impeachment in this area more hard hitting.

Consider the following examples:

- Q. What did Mr. Lincoln say to you on these occasions?
  A. The most significant thing he said to me was that if I were to leave the company, I might be entitled to retire.
  Q. You said that was the most significant thing Mr. Lincoln said. Can you tell me anything else that Mr. Lincoln said in these conversations about your leaving the company?
  A. I can't really. That was the main thrust of his conversation.
  Q. Again, you said it was the main thrust. My question is, can you tell me anything else that Mr. Lincoln said during these six meetings?
  A. He asked me if I would be interested in a severance package.

Q. Did Mr. Lincoln say anything else in these six meetings?
A. Insofar as my leaving the company, the first subject was if I might be entitled to retire and the second was if I was interested in a severance package.
Q. Again the question is, I'd like for you to tell me everything that Mr. Lincoln said during these six conversations. You've given me two examples. One was whether you might be entitled to retire and the other one was if you might be interested in a severance package and I'd like to have you tell me anything else that Mr. Lincoln said about your leaving the company?
A. To answer your question directly, nothing else was said other than the two subjects that you just mentioned.

Note that by answering, "the most significant thing," the witness did not answer the question. When the question was asked again, the answer was, "main thrust." Because I wanted to find out everything said to the witness, I asked the question again. Finally, at the end, by the last question I attempted to summarize the various answers.

- Q. I don't want any misunderstanding right now, so listen very carefully to my question. And the question is identify for me every person after March 1, 1983, with whom you had any discussion regarding the plant closure? You gave me Mr. Olsen and now you're adding Mr. Carlson. Is there anyone else? I don't care where they are mentioned. I want you to list every single person. Is there anybody else?
  A. Were Mr. Jensen and Mr. Anderson on that list?
  Q. Anybody else?
  A. Counsel.
  Q. Anybody else?
  A. Mr. Jeppsen.
  Q. Anybody else?
  A. Mr. Benson.
  Q. Anybody else?
  A. Mr. Halverson.
  Q. Is there anybody else?
  A. Not that I recall now.
  Q. So I can summarize here, are the only people with whom you had any discussions regarding the plant closure after March 1, 1983, your counsel, Mr. Olsen, Mr. Carlson, Mr. Jensen, Mr. Anderson, Mr. Jeppsen, Mr. Benson and Mr. Halverson?
  A. That's about a three-and-a-half-year period, and to the best of my knowledge, those are the people that I recall at this time.

When Necessary, Clarify and Make A Record

Too much dialogue or comment during a deposition can be a problem. At times, I made comments, when questions were asked, to clarify the record. Arguably, I should have waited until counsel's examination was completed, but I thought it was necessary to clarify the record at that time. This conduct may be challenged, however. One example:

> Q. I next hand you Exhibit 7094. Can you identify the author of any of the handwritten notations on Exhibit 7094?
> A. I cannot.
> Q. You will observe at the top of the page somebody's note, "cc: Larry."
> A. Yes.
> Q. Did you receive a copy of Exhibit 7094 on or shortly after February 21, 2007?
> Mr. Bruess: Excuse me; I need to have a clarification. By your question, do you mean with or without the handwritten notations on it? It could make a difference. Would you please clarify?
> Q. I'll let the witness answer the question, then we'll follow up.
> Mr. Bruess: No, because your question is ambiguous. I want to be sure of your question. The problem is that Exhibit 7094 is not the same document as the letter without the handwritten notations, and the confusion comes in because he may have gotten this letter of February 21, 2007, without all the handwritten scribbles and notations that appear on Exhibit 7094. The two, therefore, are not the same document.
> Plaintiff's Counsel: He may have received it with or without the handwritten notations. If you let me ask questions, I think when we get through with my questions and his answers, we'll understand if he received it and what he received.
> Mr. Bruess: I made my objection.
> Plaintiff's Counsel: Would you read the question back to the witness, please?
> A. After having heard all your arguments, I assumed that I received a copy of this memorandum, and I don't know whether it did or did not have the written words on it.

A problem results when a party produces a document during discovery and opposing counsel has written on it and then uses that document as an exhibit during a deposition. During one deposition, I reacted as follows:

Q. I will show you what's been marked as Plaintiff's Exhibit No. 27 and ask if you can identify this.
A. This appears to be a termination notice.
Mr. Bruess: I will state for the record that Exhibit 27 has all kinds of green marks on there. Can you tell me who put the green marks on there?
Plaintiff's Counsel: I did.

It was better to try to clarify the record at that time, especially if testimony were to follow about the extraneous marks or in case I forgot to make the clarification after opposing counsel completed his questioning. Be certain that you are correct if you do this and that you do not use clarification as a ploy to coach the witness.

Often, during a deposition, counsel or the witness may ask to "go off-the-record." Be very careful in allowing this. Certainly, at times, an off-the-record discussion can shorten a deposition or avoid some objections or arguments. But, at other times, off-the-record discussions can result in problems if counsel later argues that a special agreement was made in an "off-the-record" discussion. Evaluate each instance.

Q. You said that Ms. O'Reily required you to use a lower rate than originally proposed. Do you recall that testimony?
The Witness: Off the record.
Mr. Bruess: No, not with this guy. Stay on the record.
The Witness: I want to go off the record.
Mr. Bruess: I think it's better we stay on the record with him.

You also will have to document the record when strange things happen. During a deposition of his own expert, opposing counsel wanted to leave the deposition room to address other matters. He wanted the deposition to continue in his absence and to conclude. If this happens, be sure that this is reflected in the transcript. In this instance, this witness (plaintiff's damages expert) proceeded in counsel's absence to destroy plaintiff's damages theory. Fortunately, the record reflected the following:

Plaintiff's Counsel: You can show in the deposition I want to be excused.
Defense Counsel: Do you want me to break until you come back?
Plaintiff's Counsel: No, you can continue.
Defense Counsel: Let the record show Mr. Brady has left the room over my suggestion that he not do so and has asked me not to break at this time, even though I'm willing to wait for him to come back.

In another action, questioning counsel sought to leave a deposition during a pending question requiring a long answer. The witness had been asked to detail what facts he knew about fifty interrogatories. After the witness finished his answer with respect to the fourth interrogatory, counsel decided to leave to catch a plane. The following reflects this occasion:

> Opposing Counsel: Why don't you finish answering and if you want to stay, you can.
> Mr. Bruess: No way.
> Opposing Counsel: I don't need to be present. I don't object to this witness finishing his answers, even though I am not present. I am taking off.
> Mr. Bruess: Are you stating this deposition is over?
> Opposing Counsel: I am stating if you would like to miss the plane and listen to him answer the rest of the questions, you can stay here and listen, but I need to get on this plane.
> Mr. Bruess: That is your decision. I am not going on an airplane. I will not be there, and I am instructing this witness if you are leaving that he does not have to answer any more questions. Are you through with your examination of this witness?
> Opposing Counsel: I have asked my last question.
> Mr. Bruess: Fine.
> Opposing Counsel: He is still answering.
> Mr. Bruess: You are instructed that you don't have to answer any questions when counsel is not here. If he is leaving, that is the end of the deposition, as far as I'm concerned.
> Opposing Counsel: I am through asking questions to the witness.
> Mr. Bruess: The deposition is over.

Objections

The issues of whether and how to make an objection if you are defending a deposition are sensitive ones. The problem presents a dilemma between protecting the interests of the client and, at least in federal court, abiding by applicable rules.

What objections must be made? The objection most frequently interposed is, "object to the form of the question." That is short sighted. Many lawyers are not cognizant of the full requirements of Rule 32(d)(3) of the Federal Rules of Civil Procedure, Waiver of Objections, which provides:

(3) To the Taking of the Deposition.

(A) Objection to Competence, Relevance, or Materiality. An objection to a deponent's competence-or to the competence, relevance, or materiality of testimony-is not waived by a failure to make the objection before or during the deposition, unless the ground for it might have been corrected at that time.

(B) Objection to an Error or Irregularity. An objection to an error or irregularity at an oral examination is waived if:

(i) it relates to the manner of taking the deposition, the form of a question or answer, the oath or affirmation, a party's conduct, or other matters that might have been corrected at that time; and

(ii) it is not timely made during the deposition.

The concept of having to make an objection to matters that might be corrected if presented at the time presents some tactical as well as legal issues.

If a party is deposing an opinion witness in another state and fails to establish the witness's qualifications (e.g., competency of the witness), must you object at that time or will you have waived the objection? It is conceivable that if you wait until trial to object, opposing counsel may argue that counsel assumed you were aware of the expert's qualifications since you did not object; and, if you had objected, the deficiency could have been corrected at that time.

If the deposing lawyer asks a witness questions about a document that has not been properly authenticated, do you have to object at the deposition on the theory that if you had objected at that time, the deposing lawyer could have asked the questions necessary to establish authentication and thereby obviate the objection? If you do not object, it is possible that the document can never be authenticated at trial.

You should object on the record in at least the following situations:

1. If a videographer appears at a deposition but the notice of deposition did not specify that it was going to be a video deposition and you did not agree to a video deposition.
2. If a second lawyer starts questioning the deponent.
3. If the deponent communicates with counsel or any other person after a question and before an answer.

If you have any concern that an objection could be obviated by a timely objection, you should object during the deposition. This does make sense. For example, if the deposition is taken 1,000 miles away from the courthouse, and if there is an objection that could be cured by a proper objection, but you fail to object, the court may not allow the objection at trial because of the expense and delay caused by forcing the opposing counsel to return to the venue of the deposition to cure the error.

Content of Objection Is Very Limited

This issue is complicated because of the applicability of various rules. Rule 103(a) of the Federal Rules of Evidence provides that:

> (a) Error may not be predicated upon a ruling which admits or excludes evidence unless a substantial right of the party is affected, and
> (1) Objection - In case the ruling is one admitting evidence, a timely objection or motion to strike appears of record, stating the specific ground of objection, if the specific ground was not apparent from the context. . . .

Rule 32(d) of the Federal Rules of Civil Procedure requires the interposing of certain defined objections together with objections that if presented at that time might cure the deficiencies. Yet, Rule 30(c) of the Federal Rules of Civil Procedure states the following: "(2) An objection (during a deposition) must be stated concisely and in a non argumentative and non suggestive manner."

Local rules are sometimes also applicable. For example, Rule 30.1(d) of the Local Rules for the Southern District of Indiana states, "An attorney shall not, in the presence of a deponent, interpose objections to deposition questions which suggest answers to those questions."

Although, arguably, stating, "Object to the form of the question" might suffice, there is always the argument that the specific ground was not apparent from the objection and was not sufficient to alert the questioning lawyer to the nature of the problem. Counsel always could say that if the objection had been more specific, counsel could have corrected the matter at the time. Since it was not, the objection should be considered waived.

Thus, an objection has to be specific enough to articulate the ground for the objection but not so specific as to alert the witness how to answer; also, the objection cannot be framed in an argumentative manner.

Considering all of the above, I concluded that it was better to provide, in addition to stating, "object to the form of the question," some description of the objection, such as the following: ambiguous; assumes a fact not in evidence (without stating what fact is assumed); is contrary to the evidence; is contrary to prior testimony; misquotes an exhibit; lacks foundation; or is incomplete. Objections to relevancy are truly the sign of inexperienced lawyers.

Examples of objections:

- Q. Does this help you recall the date that you reached an agreement taking over plan termination? Had you reached that oral understanding by December 23, 1996?
  Mr. Bruess: I object. There are two questions built into that.

This example is obvious and demonstrates why an objection needs to be interposed to multiple questions. Here, it is possible that the witness recalled the date and was planning to answer "yes" to the first question. When the second question was added and the answer was, "yes," the witness was then committed to having an oral understanding by December 23, 2006, which may not have been true. This point could become critical at the trial if this witness does not appear to testify and the date is important.

- Q. As a civil engineer, can you read them and understand them and know what they mean?
  Mr. Bruess: Object to the form of the question.

Here, there are three questions. The witness may have concentrated on whether he could "read" them, but without an objection, the witness may have been committed to also understanding and knowing to what "they" refers.

- Q. Did you pass it on to Mr. Smith, Mr. Jennings, anybody else?
  Mr. Bruess: Object to the form.

If the witness passed the information on to only the first person, then without an objection, the witness may have committed to having provided the information to two other people, which may not have been true.

- Q. Was any cover-plating necessary in the Auxiliary Building in the spring or summer of 1996?
  Mr. Bruess: I'll object to the form.

Because the need for the cover-plating was different in the spring than it was in the summer, an objection was proper since the question was compound.

- Q. How long did those meetings last?
  Mr. Bruess: Object to the form.
  Q. Did you have more than one meeting with these counsel?
  A. Yes.

Reference to "those meetings" was ambiguous. Faced with an objection, counsel properly asked new questions based on each separate meeting.

- Q. Were you out at the company when you signed this document 6073?
  A. Yes.
  Q. Who was there?
  A. Both my brother and I.
  Mr. Bruess: Wait a minute. I have got to object to the form of question because there are two different dates on 6073. Which part of it are you referring to? The first part of 6073 is dated March 9th; the last part of 6073 is dated March 26th. I think you have misled the witness and I have to clarify that. What part of 6073 are you asking about when you said, "Were you at the company when you signed it?
  Mr. Hamer. That's a good point.

This example involved two exhibits with different dates that were stapled together. I wanted to have a precise date for when the witness was at the company. This example is included for several reasons. First, I should have objected sooner, before the answer. Second, this is a borderline objection under the rules. Instead of saying, "object to the form," I went beyond. Yet, in the spirit of stating why the question was objectionable, the ambiguity could be corrected at that time. I made the speaking objection. Competent counsel understood the ambiguity and ultimately rephrased the question.

- Q. You knew at the time you wrote this letter that the participants were claiming that they were entitled to all the pension plan assets, isn't that right?
  Mr. Bruess: Excuse me. I'm going to object. I don't think it was a fact that all participants were claiming a right to the money. Because of your assumption of all participants, I object to the form of the question.
  Q. Some participants?

In this action, only some, not all, of the participants were making a claim for plan assets. This objection probably exceeds permissible standards. Probably a better objection would have been lack of foundation. Yet, when I explained the objection, counsel changed the question.

- Q. Did the trustees, the three individual trustees, know that this meeting was taking place?
  Mr. Bruess: I object. You can't ask a question like that unless you can establish that he would have some basis for knowing that that occurred, and you haven't established that he would possibly know what three individual trustees knew.
  Q. You can answer that question.
  A. I have no knowledge as to whether they knew it was taking place or not.

This example demonstrates the interplay of Rule 32(d)(3)(A) of the Federal Rules of Civil Procedure and Rule 602 of the Federal Rules of Evidence. Rule 602 says:

> A witness may not testify to a matter unless evidence is introduced sufficient to support a finding that the witness has personal knowledge of the matter.

Rule 32(d)(3)(A) states:

> An objection to a deponent's competence-or to the competence, relevance, or materiality of testimony-is not waived by a failure to make the objection before or during the deposition, unless the ground for it might have been corrected at that time.

I believed that the witness, who was not a trustee, would not have known about the meeting. I objected to protect the record. I doubt whether saying only "object" or "object to the form of the question" would have been a sufficient objection to have alerted counsel to the need to correct the question. In retrospect, and to comply with the rules, I probably should have stated only lack of foundation. Nevertheless, in this instance, the questioning lawyer refused to change the question. If faced with a meritorious objection, you should recognize it and reframe your question to elicit usable testimony. Do not be so vain as to insist on an answer to a bad question.

11

TRIAL COUNSEL MUST BE FAMILIAR WITH AND USE AVAILABLE TECHNOLOGY

Jurors like and expect technology. When, in one instance, only plaintiff used technology in closing argument, one juror asked defense counsel, "Where was your PowerPoint?" Jurors like to be entertained. Watching a monitor is like watching television. Displaying a document on monitors in the courtroom, in addition to using hard copy, increases juror comprehension in many instances. On the other hand, some jurors complain that unless certain lines or a paragraph of one page of a document are enlarged, it is too difficult to read a document displayed only on the monitors. Older jurors, or those who have had eye problems, complain that the monitors provide blurry images; these people prefer having hard copies. Know your jurors and adjust accordingly.

Some Available Technology to Use in the Courtroom

Although I am knowledgeable only about technology available in the Southern District of Indiana, a description of this system also may explain technology that might be available in courtrooms in other locations. This system is known as a Video Evidence Presentation System ("VEPS"). A detailed description of this system can be found online at www.insd.uscourts.gov. This web site also has a video entitled, Courtroom Technology Training Video. This video is not necessarily limited to the Southern District of Indiana's VEPS System. Following is a brief description of the Southern District of Indiana's System.

VEPS is a modular unit composed of a document camera, videocassette player, and a computer hookup for each party. There are monitors for each counsel table, the jury, the lectern, the judge, the witness chair, and the law clerk. Monitors for the jury are placed at each end of the jury box; alternatively, smaller monitors may be located in the jury box with one monitor for every two jurors.

Document Camera

After the camera is turned on, place the document face up on the base, which is under the camera. The camera has the capability to display white on black or black on white. It also has controls for zooming in or out and scrolling up, down, left, or right. Be careful with zooming and scrolling because they can lead to feelings of motion sickness.

There also is a freeze-frame feature. If the freeze button is pressed, a document placed under the camera will continue to be displayed on the monitors while the document is picked up to be reviewed more closely or to show the document to a witness.

A full 8 1/2- x-11-inch page is not readily legible if displayed on the document camera. If the zoom feature is used, the sides are usually cut off. When this has happened, jurors have complained that they could not read the documents.

Placing documents under the document camera and quickly switching pages can be distracting. In addition, it prevents jurors from sufficiently seeing the documents. Failure to use the freeze frame when changing pages also leads to complaints of feelings of motion sickness.

Display a document long enough for the jury to see it and use the freeze frame when switching pages, and probably also when zooming and scrolling.

The document camera also can be used to display objects, such as guns and defective parts.

When using the document camera, be sure that your nails are clean, and avoid wearing shirts with monogrammed cuffs as well as expensive and large pieces of jewelry.

Videocassette Recorder ("VCR")

To use the VCR, select the proper component of the VEPS, insert the tape, and push Play. As with other VCRs, there are controls to stop, fast forward, reverse and advance frame by frame.

VCR tapes have been used for video depositions, surveillance, accident scenes, demonstrative evidence, accident reconstruction, and damaged property.

Computer

Whatever can be displayed by the document camera or VCR should be able to be displayed by a computer. Stated simply, load the exhibits, arguments, demonstrative exhibits, video depositions, or whatever else to be used on the hard drive of a computer, CD, or DVD and then display this information by use of a laptop computer.

Find out whether the court provides a computer or if counsel must bring their own. In one action, defendant wanted to play a video deposition using a DVD but failed to bring a laptop computer. The court did not provide a computer. Counsel had to get a computer from his office.

If documents are loaded onto a DVD, CD, or hard drive of a computer for display in the court, there are at least three ways to display the documents on the monitors:

1. Placing a bar code on the documents, usually on the copy for counsel or technician, and scanning that bar code into the computer. This is currently the fastest way to retrieve documents.
2. Typing the number of the documents into the computer.
3. Having a list of the documents in a folder on the computer and then clicking on the document desired.

In some actions, an attorney brings a technician or paralegal to the trial to operate the equipment, including the computer that displays the documents. In one action, a technician had an outline of counsel's questions, and as soon as counsel referred to a document, the document was displayed on the monitors. If using the VEPS together with a technician or paralegal operating the document camera or computer, coordination is required. It was embarrassing when one counsel read to the witness a sentence from a document but the technician displayed a different sentence on the monitors.

Monitors

If you plan to display a document or some other object, be sure the document or object has been admitted into evidence. In this regard, ascertain whether the technology will allow a display on the monitors only to counsel, the witness, and the judge, but not to the jurors. This approach is helpful if some documents must be shown to the judge but not to the jurors in case the judge has to rule on any objections.

Except for the monitors at the lectern and witness chair, the monitors are just like television sets. The monitors at the lectern and witness chair are touch-screen monitors. That is, the lawyer doing the questioning or the witness being examined can touch the monitor to draw circles around, underline, or place arrows next to key words or places depicted on the monitor.

There are also controls to change colors for any markings on the monitors. The monitors for the lectern and witness chair have controls to erase any marks, such as arrows, circles, or lines, placed on the screen. Touching one corner of the monitor will remove marks in the order of last in, first out; touching another corner of the monitor will remove all marks. Thus, if a witness places a mark incorrectly on the monitor, the questioning lawyer can remove it quickly to minimize the time the marking is seen by the jury.

Manipulation of a Document

Often, one paragraph, one sentence, or even one word of a document may be important enough to highlight for the jury at the time the document is displayed. Because of the size of an 8 1/2 x 11 inch document and the size of the monitors, it is often difficult to read the entire document. Using a computer and special software to manipulate a document, such as enlarging the language and underscoring or highlighting words, aids the jury's understanding.

If a witness explains or comments on certain words, the words can be highlighted in color. For example, when there was a long list of people from which only certain persons were mentioned, highlighting those mentioned with a colored line or placing a colored arrow next to their names made their names more prominent.

Jurors comment favorably on the use of software that enables the drawing of a box around a paragraph, or several paragraphs or lines of one page and then enlarging the selected material. This makes it easier to read. What works best is to display the first page of the document to identify what the document is and its exhibit number, then display page ten to show the jurors what page is being displayed, then draw a box around the third paragraph, enlarge that paragraph, and then highlight, underline, or place arrows near the key language.

Using VEPS with a computer and software program that permits the use of two documents side by side is outstanding. In an employment discrimination action, plaintiff alleged her discharge from employment violated the Family Medical Leave Act as she was permissibly on company granted family medical leave. Defendant argued that plaintiff's request for leave was fraudulently obtained. On her form requesting the leave, plaintiff claimed she was depressed, had suffered weight loss and had trouble sleeping. Defendant was able to obtain an application plaintiff submitted for employment with another company six days after her family medical leave started. On this new application, plaintiff stated she was not depressed, had no weight loss and had no difficulty sleeping. Counsel displayed both the application for medical leave and the new application, side by side, on the monitors during cross-examination and during closing argument. The comparison was devastating to plaintiff's case.

Although highlighting or underlining may be done in advance with certain software, this is not recommended, especially if there is a possibility of an objection. Besides, it is more effective to do the highlighting or underlining in front of the jury.

Keep in mind that manipulating a document on the monitors will not alter the document. When the document accompanies the jury for deliberations, the arrows, highlighting, or other manipulating done by the touch screen or software will not be on the document. Investigate whether technology is available to print a copy of the document manipulated during the trial.

In the absence of such technology, consider placing another copy of the exhibit under the document camera, placing a mark on the copy of the exhibit where the witness said to do so, marking the copy as an exhibit, and then offering the exhibit into evidence.

Switching Between Components

Often in trials, it is necessary to switch between one of the three components of the VEPS or for the parties to rotate if both parties are using the computer hook ups. This can be done by use of a portable switching device, if available, that can be traded off between the lawyers doing the examination or by requesting court staff to make the switch.

Before the Start of Any Trial or Hearing, Test and Practice with Available Technology

Contact court staff to arrange a time to visit the courtroom to test what technology that may be used at the trial, checking that everything you plan to bring with you to use is compatible with the court's technology and that the technology works. You do not want to appear disorganized before either the judge or the jury. For example, in one action, a party planned to display video depositions. The party came to court before the trial but tested only one videotape. When a different tape was sought to be used at the trial, it was inaudible. The volume on the tape was too low and the court's sound system could not increase the volume sufficiently. The court excused the jury until counsel could decide what to do. The options were to read the deposition transcript aloud or wait to see whether court personnel could increase the volume at a break and call another witness in the interim. Such a situation may upset your strategy.

In another instance, when other counsel came to the court prior to the trial to test the sound level of a video deposition, counsel discovered that the audio was inadequate, so counsel brought their own speakers for the trial. In one action, counsel's planned PowerPoint presentation was not usable because counsel's computer was not compatible with the court's system.

In one action, at five minutes before the start of the second day of the trial, counsel connected his computer to the VEPS only to learn that no display was possible. Counsel had to defer his planned examination until the problem was solved as the judge was not going to delay the trial. Counsel had never been to the courtroom to test his planned technology.

In other instances, there has been a difference in resolution between counsels' computers and the court's VEPS. This can be adjusted, but should not be done while the jury is in the jury box.

Your preparation for the use of the technology should include the following:

> Document Camera: This camera has a magnification feature. Determine how much of the zooming in or out needs to be utilized. Practice this, as well as scrolling and use of the freeze frame.
>
> VCR: Practice how to start, stop, advance frame by frame, and rewind the tape.
>
> Monitors: Practice with the monitors to learn how to place arrows and underline, how to remove the marks, and how to change colors. In one action, counsel was so proficient that she changed colors while marking on a single document.

The person who intends to use the technology during the trial should be the one who tests and practices with the technology. In some instances, counsel sent a secretary or paralegal to test the VEPS. When counsel came for the trial, counsel had no idea how to use the VEPS. This looked unprofessional in front of the jury.

One paralegal inquired about playing a videotape at a trial. I suggested strongly that the person planning to use the tape come to court in advance to be certain that the tape worked and to learn how the equipment worked. The lawyer did not come in advance. During the trial, the tape was inserted into the VCR, so all the lawyer had to do was push the Play button. During the presentation, the lawyer wanted to call the jury's attention to various parts of a jail cell shown on the tape. He just referred to the side or bottom of the monitor. If the lawyer had known how to operate the VEPS, he could have stopped the video and marked the parts of the jail cell he wanted to emphasize by using arrows or drawing circles. Unfortunately, this lawyer did not know these capabilities of VEPS. Another example of lack of preparation occurred when counsel, who wanted to use a PowerPoint presentation, was unable to connect to VEPS.

Jurors were critical of a lawyer who did not know how to operate the document camera. He did not know which side of the document to display, which direction to place the exhibit, or how to zoom. The jurors said the lawyer's ineptness was distracting.

Have a Contingency Plan

In the event that the technology you bring with you to court is not compatible with the court's system, or your technology does not work, or the court's system becomes inoperative, such as because of a power outage, you need a back-up plan.

In one action during which a laptop computer froze, the technician merely switched computers and the examination continued. If the computer does not work, consider using the document camera. If that occurs, a copy of the exhibits needs to be at the lectern so that you can avoid hunting for copies. It is always a good idea to have available in the courtroom a hard copy of each exhibit about which you will be asking questions of each witness. Consider the horrible situation that could result if your computer does not operate and you have no hard copies of documents with you. A motion to continue may be required. If the document camera fails, you will have to consider having a copy of each exhibit for each juror or ask to pass the one available copy to the jury. If a video deposition is on a computer and the computer becomes inoperative, you will need to have sufficient copies of the deposition transcript available so that the transcript can be read.

12

UNDERSTANDING WHEN AND HOW DEPOSITIONS CAN BE USED AT TRIAL IS AN ESSENTIAL INGREDIENT OF TRIAL PREPARATION

There Is No Such Thing as a Discovery Deposition in Federal Court

The Federal Rules of Civil Procedure do not distinguish between a deposition for trial and for discovery. A deposition can be used as permitted by Rule 32. If a deposition is taken, the testimony is preserved and can possibly be used at trial.

At a pretrial conference, defendant objected to the planned use by plaintiff of depositions taken by the defendant on the theory that the defendant had taken the depositions for "discovery purposes and not for trial purposes." Defendant's counsel argued that he asked open-ended questions and failed to ask "impeaching questions" because he believed that the witnesses, who lived outside the subpoena power of the court, would testify in person. Such an objection has no merit and was overruled. Rule 32(a)(4)(B) of the Federal Rules of Civil Procedure provides that the deposition of a witness may be used by any party for any purpose if the witness is more than 100 miles from the place of trial.

In another action, plaintiff deposed the individual defendant. Subsequently, the defendant became sick and could not travel. So, the defense arranged for a video deposition taken by the defense. At the trial, the defense sought to use both depositions. Plaintiff objected, arguing that the first deposition taken by plaintiff was merely a discovery deposition and could not be used for trial. Plaintiff's objection was overruled.

In yet another action, plaintiffs, at a pretrial conference, requested permission to take "trial depositions" of persons previously deposed. Plaintiffs' argument was that the earlier depositions had not been videotaped and now plaintiffs wanted to take video depositions. The request was denied.

Permissible Use of Depositions at Trial

There are four instances when depositions may be used in federal court, as discussed in the following sections.

1. Impeachment

Rule 32(a)(2) of the Federal Rules of Civil Procedure provides that:

> Any party may use a deposition to contradict or impeach the testimony given by the deponent as a witness, or for any other purpose allowed by the Federal Rules of Evidence.

Note, if a witness apparently is impeached, counsel should insist that any clarifying or modifying testimony be read **at that time**, pursuant to Rule 106 of the Federal Rules of Evidence; counsel should not wait until redirect examination to direct the witness to additional testimony in the deposition that corrects the allegedly impeaching testimony.

2. Admissions

A party's deposition can be used as evidence and does not have to be used only for impeachment. Rule 32(a)(3) of the Federal Rules of Civil Procedure provides that:

> An adverse party may use for any purpose the deposition of a party or anyone who, when deposed, was the party's officer, director, managing agent, or designee under Rule 30(b)(6) or 31(a)(4).

One issue that must be resolved is whether, in actions involving a corporation, partnership, and so on, the deponent is "an officer, director, or managing agent" so that this testimony can be utilized as an admission. In an employment discrimination action, an hourly worker would probably not qualify, but the Human Resources Director probably would.

3. Unavailability of Witnesses

Rule 32(a)(4) of the Federal Rules of Civil Procedure provides that:

> The deposition of a witness, whether or not a party, may be used by any party for any purpose if the court finds:
> (A) that the witness is dead; or
> (B) that the witness is more than 100 miles from the place of trial or hearing, or is out of the United States, unless it appears that the absence of the witness was procured by the party offering the deposition; or
> (C) that the witness cannot attend or testify because of age, illness, infirmity, or imprisonment; or
> (D) that the party offering the deposition cannot procure the attendance of the witness by subpoena.

4. Exceptional Circumstances

Rule 32(a)(4)(E) of the Federal Rules of Civil Procedure provides that:

> on motion and notice, that exceptional circumstances make it desirable-in the interest of justice and with due regard to the importance of live testimony in open court-to permit the deposition to be used.

Remember the caveat discussed in Chapter 9 about preserving testimony that may be harmful. If a witness dies, the testimony can be admitted by way of deposition, whereas if there is no deposition, the testimony is not available.

Use of a Deposition If the Witness Will or Can Be Available in the Courtroom Is Not a Good Idea

Assuming that a deposition can be used for testimonial purposes, should the deposition be used if the deponent will be present at the trial or is otherwise subject to a subpoena?

Sometimes, a lawyer believes that a deposition of an opposing party or a representative of an opposing party provides dynamite testimony that will surely be persuasive to the jury. Counsel then plans only to read the transcript or display a video of the deposition at the trial. Although such use is possible, if the witness is available to testify in person, it is a mistake to use the deposition. First, many jurors do not like to listen to or to watch depositions; they find them boring. Second, if the testimony from the deposition is very helpful, it can still be used and in a much better way. Simply call the witness to the stand and frame the questions at the trial based on the deposition testimony. For several reasons, this approach is much more effective than just reading the testimony. In the first place, the damaging testimony comes from a live witness. Also, if the witness denies making the statements, the witness can be impeached. It is always effective to impeach a witness. If the witness is a party or party representative, the impeaching testimony is also evidence as an admission.

Deposition Testimony Offered at Trial Is Still Subject to the Rules of Evidence

Deposition testimony is still subject to the rules of evidence. Depositions usually contain irrelevant questions and answers that cannot be used at trial. Objections can be made at the time that the deposition or portions thereof are sought to be introduced at the trial.

Rule 32(a)(1) of the Federal Rules of Civil Procedure states that:

> Using Depositions.
> (1) In General. At a hearing or trial, all or part of a deposition may be used against a party on these conditions:
> (A) the party was present or represented at the taking of the deposition or had reasonable notice of it;
> (B) it is used to the extent it would be admissible under the Federal Rules of Evidence if the deponent were present and testifying; and
> (C) the use is allowed by Rule 32(a)(2) through (8).

Rule 32(b) of the Federal Rules of Civil Procedure provides that:

> Objections to Admissibility. Subject to Rules 28(b) and 32(d)(3), an objection may be made at a hearing or trial to the admission of any deposition testimony that would be inadmissible if the witness were present and testifying.

During one trial, plaintiff offered the entire deposition of defendant's key witness who was present in the courtroom. I objected, stating that there were numerous objectionable and irrelevant questions; if the deposition was going to be offered, the transcript would have to be reviewed line by line for the court to rule on the objections. The court agreed and told plaintiff's counsel to put the witness on the stand and, if the witness deviated from the deposition testimony, to use the deposition testimony to impeach and as an admission.

Request Rulings Before Trial on Any Objections to Proposed Deposition Testimony

If a deposition is to be used at trial, other than for impeachment, it is very helpful for all parties to know in advance of the trial what testimony is proposed to be presented by way of deposition and what the rulings will be by the court on any objections to the proposed testimony.

Some judges require the parties to designate in advance of a trial which depositions, including as well pages and lines, that will be used for testimonial purposes at trial. This pretrial order may also require the opposing parties to file their objections to the proposed testimony. If this type of order is applicable, hopefully, the court will address any objections in advance of the trial.

If there is no pretrial order, it still is possible to contact the opposing party and suggest, prior to the trial, that the parties designate portions of depositions to be used at trial as well as any objections to the designated portions. If this is done, the designated portions and objections can be submitted to the court prior to trial with a request that the court rule on any objections.

The recommended procedure is for the party planning to use a deposition to designate pages and lines first and then allow the opposing party to counter-designate. The counter-designation may require the originating party to designate further. After all designations have been completed, the parties can list their objections to the proposed testimony.

If there is no court order requiring pre-designation and you do not discuss designations with the other side, then, in the presence of the jury, the questions will be read, or shown by video, objections will have to be made, and the court will have to rule. The trial itself may be when you first learn which portions of a deposition the opposing party seeks to use, or which portions of the depositions you propose to use may be objectionable. If the objections are ruled upon before trial, then only the admissible portions are shared with the jury.

Procedure for Pre-trial Designation of Deposition Testimony

Often, pre-designations result in each party submitting its own list of designations, counter-designations, and objections on separate filings. If the court is to read and rule on objections prior to trial, this requires the court to alternate between the transcript and the different parties' designations, counter-designations, and objections —not an easy task. Likewise, it is a nuisance for a judge in order to rule on objections to have to review each party's separate copy of the same transcript with pages and lines designated by that party in the transcript and then also to have to review objections to the designated testimony listed on separate submissions by the opposing party.

The best approach is for the parties to submit one transcript that contains all designated portions and objections. One party should use a colored magic marker or a computer software program to highlight or bracket its designated testimony, and the opposing party should use a different color to indicate its designations. The objections can be written in the margins in shortened form, such as "irrelevant" or "Rule 106." The judge can read the designated portions and any objections, and write in the margins of the transcript the rulings on the objections. This one transcript, which should be marked as an exhibit, will then provide the record of both the testimony of the witness and rulings on any objections to the testimony. Whether a computer or magic marker is used, be certain that the marking does not obliterate the text.

If one transcript is submitted to the court with objections written in the margins, placing the transcript in a spiral-bound folder is easier to use than a transcript bound on the side.

If there is no requirement or agreement for pretrial designation for portions of deposition transcripts to be read or shown during trial, you must prepare a list of which portions you want to have read or shown. There may be portions of a deposition that you do not want to use but will need to use if the opposing party uses certain portions of the transcript. Prepare a contingent list that states that if the opposing party uses page 10, lines 16–25, then you will want to use page 67, lines 2–10.

If opposing counsel reads or displays only testimony from page 6 of the deposition transcript, which states that the date of the accident was 2005, but does not read from page 95, where the witness said that he made a mistake and the correct date was 2006, you can require that when page 6 is read or shown, that page 95 also be read. Rule 32(a)(6)of the Federal Rules of Civil Procedure provides:

> If a party offers in evidence only part of a deposition, an adverse party may require the offeror to introduce other parts that in fairness should be considered with the part introduced, and any party may itself introduce any other parts.

See also Rule 106, Federal Rules of Evidence.

Edit Deposition Transcripts Prior to Trial

If it has been determined prior to trial which portions of deposition transcripts will be used at trial, confer with opposing counsel to edit the transcripts to remove the testimony not designated and the testimony for which objections were sustained. It is easy to eliminate questions and answers from a deposition transcript to be read. However, it is not so easy to edit deposition testimony presented by video. Although technology allows you to stop a video deposition at various times, when the transcript is fast forwarded and portions of the transcript are being skipped such a procedure is choppy and looks disorganized. Thus, if testimony is going to be presented by video, it is imperative that you try to get definitive rulings in advance of the trial on objections so that, if the video does have to be edited, it can be done prior to trial. There have been trials for which the court ruled on objections one day for a deposition to be used the next day. This meant that the editing had to be done overnight to avoid a choppy presentation.

Often editing of a video deposition results in a gap or jump between segments. Investigate the availability of technology that will allow the use of only portions of a video deposition on a tape, CD or DVD to be displayed without blips or interruptions.

It is helpful, if only part of a deposition is presented, whether by video or reading, to have the judge explain to the jurors that the deposition transcript has been edited to save the time of the jurors and that the court approved the deletions.

If the deposition exhibit numbers are not the same as the trial exhibit numbers (see discussion in Chapter 7), the parties should file a stipulation reflecting the cross-reference of the deposition exhibits with the trial exhibits. The trial exhibit numbers should be written in pencil above the deposition numbers shown in the transcript.

If a deposition is read, the person reading can just read the proper trial exhibit number.

With a video deposition, investigate whether the video can be edited to indicate the trial exhibit number corresponding to the deposition exhibit number. Another option is for the lawyer to stand up and say what the proper trial exhibit number is.

Of course, if parties use the system of one set of numbers for all exhibits starting with the first exhibit at the first deposition, there is no need to worry about conforming deposition exhibit numbers to trial exhibit numbers.

Use of Depositions for Testimony at Trial

If the deposition is presented by video, the entire transcript or edited version is played for the jury. If there was no requirement for pretrial designations and objections, then the video will have to stopped, and possibly fast forwarded if the court needs to hear argument and rule upon objections.

Typically, if a deposition is to be read at trial other than for impeachment, the party seeking to use the deposition places a person in the witness chair. Counsel reads the selected questions, and the person in the witness chair reads the answers to those questions by the deposed witness. In a jury trial, I have never seen a lawyer reading both the questions and the answers.

For court trials, ascertain whether the judge wants the deposition testimony read in open court or only a transcript submitted with the designated testimony and objections that the judge can read before, during, or after the trial.

Inquire if the judge will allow a transcript to be displayed on the monitors when a deposition transcript is being read.

Before a deposition is to be read to a jury, ask the court who should read the questions and when the questions are asked under the following scenarios:

1. If the deposition was taken by one party (plaintiff), but only the other party (defendant) wants to use the transcript.
2. If only plaintiff asks questions at the deposition, but both plaintiff and defendant designate portions of the transcript to be read.
3. If both plaintiff and defendant ask questions at the deposition, and:
   a. Plaintiff designates only questions plaintiff asked, and defendant designates only questions defendant asked.
   b. Plaintiff designates questions asked by defendant, or defendant designates questions asked by plaintiff.
4. Can the reading be done out of order, such as from page 6, to page 34, to page 20, to page 72, and so on, or must reading be done in numerical page order? (Likewise for a video deposition, inquire if the video can be edited to present testimony out of order? Can testimony about, for example, Exhibit 10 found on page 165 be added after testimony about Exhibit 10 found on page 20? Can the testimony skip from page 65, to page 5, to page 54, to page 90?)
5. If objections are to be read to the jury, which counsel reads the objections?

Comments from jurors have indicated that using a male to read the answers of a male witness and a female to read the answers of a female witness is better. If possible, do not use the same person to read the testimony of several witnesses.

By all means, practice with the person who is going to read the transcript of a deposed person. Be certain that the witness can pronounce all the words correctly. Having a witness stumble with words, or having the witness stop to ask counsel about what page or line is next, is not impressive to a jury.

Not only practice, but preparation should take place. Some lawyers prepare a copy of the transcript by using a magic marker to highlight the question and answer to be read on each page and then either tag each page or give only the designated pages to the witness. This method expedites the use of the deposition better than saying, "Turn to page 10, line 5."

The person reading the answers should read with appropriate inflection, indignation, or whatever is appropriate to emphasize to the jury the evidence that is being presented.

Whenever a deposition is being used, it is important to follow along with the transcript as the testimony is being read or shown. It is important that only the designated parts of the transcript are read or shown, that no designated, non-objected parts are left out, and that no part is read or shown for which an objection was sustained. It is also a good idea to provide a copy of the transcript for the judge to assist in the judge's understanding of the testimony and, also, in the event that a ruling is needed on testimony being presented.

A technique sometimes used with video depositions is scrolling testimony, which helps juror comprehension. As the witness is displayed on the monitor, the bottom of the monitor displays five or more lines of the witness's actual testimony as it was being spoken. The testimony is continuously scrolling so that only five to six lines are present at any one time. Some people learn by hearing; others by seeing. Using the two senses together increases the possibility of reaching more jurors. Scrolling testimony is extremely helpful when the witness speaks with an accent.

There is also software that utilizes three split screens showing the deponent, scrolling testimony, and a document being shown to the witness.

You will need to know whether the judge will allow the use of scrolling testimony in the event that there is an objection from the other side. Do not plan to use scrolling testimony only to learn later that it will not be allowed.

If a deposition is used, either as a video or read, neither the transcripts nor the video are provided to the jury. They are, however, retained by the court. Confirm that this is the procedure for your case.

However, ascertain the following: when depositions are to be used as testimony at trial if the court reporter will be recording the testimony; whether the jury, during deliberations, can request that the testimony be re-read or the video re-shown; and how the deposition testimony is to be preserved for appeal.

Whenever evidence is presented at trial by way of deposition testimony, either in a bench trial or jury trial, the transcripts should be assigned exhibit numbers. These transcripts should also be marked to document which pages and lines were read in open court or submitted to the court for its consideration.

If objections to proposed deposition testimony are sustained by ruling at a conference prior to trial, ascertain how these rulings will be preserved for any appeal. If there is a filed document reflecting the ruling, inquire whether this document will protect your record or if you need to renew your request for this testimony to be read on the record during the trial, either by an offer of proof or otherwise. If there is no record of the ruling and you do not make an offer of proof at trial, there will be no way to raise this issue on appeal.

If objections are overruled prior to trial, insure that the rulings are preserved for appeal. Is there a filed document reflecting the ruling that will preserve the objections, or must you object as the deposition is being read or shown to the jury?

If a video deposition is used, and the objections were ruled upon prior to trial, ascertain whether the objections will be edited out of the video or shown to the jury, requiring the court to rule at that time.

Summaries of depositions should be avoided. Some courts prefer, or perhaps even mandate, the use of deposition summaries to be read to the jury or tendered to the court. If required to use summaries, good luck. They are, in many instances, very difficult and time consuming (and thus expensive) to prepare. They result in protracted arguments with opposing counsel. If you have an option to use summaries, think twice before agreeing to use them. They are not as effective as questions and answers read or shown to the jury.

13

PROPOSED EXAMINATION OF WITNESSES SHOULD BE PREPARED WELL IN ADVANCE OF DEPOSITION OR TRIAL

After determining what needs to be accomplished to win the litigation, it is the testimony of the witnesses and exhibits introduced, by way of questions asked and answered, that will achieve these objectives. Each direct and cross-examination must be approached with a goal of what needs to be established with this witness or, at least, what needs to be done to discredit the witness.

Consider Preparing Exact Questions for Each Witness Instead of Relying Only on Notes or a Sketchy Outline

Lawyers have varying levels of skill; all lawyers are not created equal. I have witnessed one lawyer who conducted a magnificent cross-examination without an outline or note of any kind. Even though this was a successful example of talent, this method is not recommended. Litigation is too important to rely merely on one's memory.

Some lawyers prefer to use merely an outline or a few notes. This method can vary from using a topical outline to a more elaborate listing of facts to be established. I have seen lawyers do a very effective and thorough examination using only one page or several pages of notes. This method is rare and also is not recommended.

By preparing questions in advance of deposition or trial, you can be more assured that you will elicit the appropriate testimony from each witness, as well as to introduce into evidence the required documents, in the order that you want to present this testimony and these exhibits.

A proper form of question is necessary to avoid objections and to create a proper record. Framing questions as you go often results in objectionable, ambiguous, and incomplete questions.

Litigation can be stressful. It is easy to get sidetracked, especially if objections are made by opposing counsel during depositions or at trial, or by intervention of the judge at trial. There are lawyers who intentionally try to distract questioning lawyers by making objections or using other obstructionist tactics.

One story illustrates this point. In my early years as a lawyer in private practice, I was asked by a senior partner, who was at that time Chairman of the Labor Law Section of the American Bar Association, to assist in defending an Equal Pay Act case. There were four categories of jobs, with more than 100 persons to be deposed. I was assigned to prepare the outline/questions for these depositions. When the senior partner took one deposition in each of the four job categories, there were no objections. When I took the remainder of the depositions, using the very same questions, innumerable objections arose. I concluded that the only purpose of these objections was to try to distract me, as a young lawyer, from what I was trying to do.

In any event, it is impossible to avoid objections or distractions, especially at a deposition; also, distractions can cause you to lose your train of thought. My preference, and hence my recommendation, especially for newer lawyers, is to prepare in advance exact questions to be asked at depositions, or at trial, for both direct and cross-examination. If you have the questions prepared and are met with an objection, you can easily return to the same question, if desired, or proceed to the next prepared question without having to try to remember what question you just asked.

Moreover, if a witness testifies to something unexpected, thereby causing you to deviate from your planned examination to pursue this matter, you might lose your train of thought or simply forget to ask questions that you meant to ask. Having your questions prepared enables you to get back on track to continue with the questions you believe are necessary based on your preparation.

There are other advantages of having questions prepared in advance, as follows:

- Sometimes, a witness does not understand the question or wants the question repeated. Having the question prepared ensures that the restated question is the same. If you, as the questioning lawyer, have only a topic or idea written down, you might not restate the question exactly the same way and, therefore, might not elicit what you had originally hoped to elicit; or, you might not even remember the question that you just asked.

This situation does happen. In one case, counsel asked a question; there was an objection; there was a brief argument; the objection was overruled; the witness asked for the question to be restated; counsel could not do so; and the judge had to restate the question using the real time displayed on his monitor. If the questions had been prepared, counsel could have simply restated the same question instead of appearing to be flustered and unprepared.

- Having the questions prepared enables you to evaluate better whether the response actually answers the question. When, for example, the question is, "What facts do you know?" but the witness keeps responding with matters other than facts, you must continue to ask the same question until you get an answer to that question. It is very dramatic when a witness consistently evades a question with a nonresponsive answer and you keep repeating the very same question to elicit the answer to which you are entitled. It is even more effective, during impeachment at trial, if you had to ask the same question two or three times at a deposition before getting the appropriate answer and then, at trial, the witness changes the answer that was given at deposition.
- Having questions prepared allows the examination to flow more smoothly and makes you look organized; also, it demonstrates to the jury, court, and witness that you know exactly where you are going with your questions and that you are in control of the witness. This is especially important in cross-examination when you do not want the witness to have time to think between the last answer and the time it would take for you to formulate your next question if it has not been prepared.
- Having prepared questions will help ensure that you will be able to include the proper number of any exhibit referred to in your question. Referring to exhibits by number in questions creates a better record. If exhibit numbers are not referred to in your questions, it can be impossible for a reviewing court on appeal to connect the testimony to an exhibit; likewise, it will be virtually impossible to connect deposition testimony about exhibits to trial testimony. If an exhibit is important and you want both the court and jury to review the exhibit at the same time that the witness is testifying about the exhibit, if the court and jurors have their own copies, you need to refer to exhibit numbers in your questions. You do not want jurors fumbling around looking for documents instead of concentrating on the testimony. Refer-

ring to exhibit numbers in your questions allows jurors to include the exhibit numbers in the jurors' notes that can be used during deliberations.

Frequently, lawyers merely say: "Let me show you this document;" or, "Please review this letter." In one action, counsel said, "On the second page of your letter, you state that you wish to have a meeting as soon as possible." Twenty minutes later, the question was, "In the next paragraph, you refer to the loss of sales in the amount of $250,000." Jurors could not connect this testimony to any exhibit. Likewise, judges reviewing transcripts, especially on appeal or in drafting opinions or findings, have difficulty in connecting testimony to exhibits when the questions do not include reference to specific exhibits.

In another action, several memoranda were sent to plaintiff regarding plaintiff's performance. Counsel kept referring to "that memorandum." It would have been better to have asked, "Does that memorandum, Exhibit 13, refer to sales?"

In using medical records, one counsel frequently told the witness, "Turn to the next page." A better request would have been, "Turn to Exhibit 51, page 10." Another request was, "Turn to the next entry." The better request would have been, "Turn to the entry dated March 20, 2007, found on page 11 of Exhibit 51."

Questioning a witness about an exhibit and not referring to an exhibit number — or referring to the wrong exhibit — gives the appearance of disorganization and runs the risk that the jury may conclude that you and the party you are representing have no idea of what you are doing. Ultimately, you will lose the jury's concentration and possibly the case.

Preparing questions in advance with the exhibit number included will ensure that you have the correct number instead of trying to remember the number during your questioning.

In one action in which counsel was not prepared for trial, his approach was to review exhibits in several notebooks, page by page, decide while reviewing the exhibits about which exhibits he would ask questions, and then formulate questions. At times, lengthy delays occurred as counsel reviewed documents in the notebooks. The jurors commented on this lack of preparation; they resented having their time wasted. They believed that counsel should have made decisions about which documents to question witnesses before coming to court. The jurors were even more resentful when counsel asked some of his questions while facing the wall, as he was reviewing exhibits in notebooks on a table, instead of facing the witnesses.

Not having questions prepared with the exhibit number leads to delays. At one trial, counsel wanted to ask a witness about Deposition Exhibit 17, but counsel did not know the trial exhibit number. Counsel stopped to ask a paralegal to find the trial exhibit number. After an eternal and silent two-minute delay, the trial exhibit number was found.

Lawyers who have their questions prepared in advance seem to be more effective in eliciting what they desire, are better prepared, and are more favorably received by jurors, even when their style is relatively plodding and not flashy, TV like. Jurors have commented that they appreciated lawyers who were organized with their presentations; these trials proceed more smoothly. Jurors prefer presentations with some type of order as opposed to skipping around. A clear organization seems to provide a trustworthy guide to the evidence. Jurors do not like disorganization and delays.

In a criminal case in which the direct examination of witnesses was very effective, I confirmed that counsel had her questions prepared before trial. She knew exactly what she had to prove and how to get there. In another case in which the jurors commented how impressed they were with counsel's examination of witnesses, especially the cross-examination of the defense's key witness, I confirmed that the questions were prepared before trial. In another instance, the lawyers did not have their questions prepared. Instead, they formulated questions during their examination of witnesses. This resulted in delays in asking questions, a number of requests to "strike that," some withdrawn questions, compound questions, negative questions, and objections. After the trial, the jurors commented on how disorganized these lawyers were with their examinations.

Having questions prepared in advance helps focus on what needs to be established and to do so efficiently. The preparation of one counsel who presented fifteen witnesses on the first day of the trial and twenty on the second day of the trial included a folder for each witness with proposed questions typed, the exhibit numbers included; and a list of exhibits to be introduced through that witness on the left side of the folder.

Organizing Questions by Subject Matter Is Recommended

My practice was to prepare questions by subject matter and to place each subject matter on a separate sheet of paper, or several sheets of paper stapled together, with a title or heading in the upper-right corner of the first page of each subject matter.

For depositions (see Appendix A for the format), I used the following: one sheet for name, address, and prior addresses; one sheet for educational history; one sheet for employment history; and other, separate, sheets for the events of February 6, the events of February 7, the events of February 12, etc. I also used other, separate, sheets for other topics. Then, I laid these sheets on top of each other with only the title of the subject matters in the upper-right corners visible, in the order in which I planned to use them. If an answer from the witness led to one of the other subject matters, I located the pages devoted to that subject matter and covered it at that time. If, as a result of some answers, I concluded that some prepared questions should not be asked, I simply removed the pages with those questions from the outline and did not ask those questions. During questioning of a witness, if the witness mentioned something that was not in my outline but needed to be pursued, that topic was covered at that time without the benefit of prepared questions.

For direct examination of witnesses and cross-examination of witnesses at trial for whom no deposition or statement existed, I used the same format as I used for depositions. I first determined what information needed to be elicited from each witness. I placed each subject matter on a separate sheet or sheets of paper stapled together with the title in the upper-right corner of the first page of each subject matter visible. These subjects included every conceivable matter I wanted to cover at trial, as well as matters about which I did not plan to ask questions but would do so if the subjects were raised by the other side. I organized these subjects in the order in which I planned to use them and placed them in a folder for each witness.

As preparation for trial or the trial itself proceeded, I might eliminate or rearrange certain subjects. If any subjects were eliminated, those subjects were placed in the back of the witness folder in case I needed to use them after all. There was the possibility during the trial of having to add new questions based on trial testimony. If these were non-adverse witnesses, I hoped that there would be time to review the questions with the witnesses before having to ask the questions.

The system that I used for examination at trial of adverse witnesses for whom I had a deposition transcript was different. My guiding principle for this type of examination was to ask only those questions for which I knew the answers and for which I could impeach — with a deposition transcript, I hoped. The format for this system is found in Appendix B and is described in the following paragraphs.

I copied the entire transcript. Then, I cut the pages into distinct subject matters, e.g., name, address, education, employment history, the events of February 17, testimony about a certain document, and testimony about purchasing a certain stock. Each subject matter included all testimony on that subject; every page from the transcript was collected into one subject matter. Nothing was omitted; thus, if I found testimony about the January 10 meeting on pages 20, 97, and 313, all that testimony would be collected together.

Next, I taped each subject matter on a separate sheet(s) of paper with the title in the upper-right corner of the first page of each subject matter visible.

If there were certain subject matters from the deposition transcript that I did not plan to use at trial, I placed those subject matters at the back of the witness's trial folder, keeping them readily available in case I subsequently decided that I needed to question the witness about those subject matters.

Next, I arranged the subject matters into the order I planned to use them at trial. Keep in mind that my goal in cross-examination of any adverse witness was to elicit certain information and not necessarily to cross-examine on precisely the same topics covered on direct examination. If certain direct examination does not merit cross-examination, do not do it.

Some trial lawyers will take notes on direct examination and then cross-examine based on what was said or, at least, most of what was said on direct and try to formulate questions during the cross-examination based on the direct examination. This can be risky if the direct examination did not cover all the points on a certain subject that need to be presented.

Frequently, counsel will start a cross-examination with a question based on the last answer given on direct examination. This can be done, but it can also lead to trouble, especially if you receive an answer that you did not expect.

The direct examination may dictate that the order of cross-examination be different from what you had planned. You may want to start with the last answer given on direct examination instead of asking the questions based on the proposed order of your pretrial preparation. If this happens, merely shuffle your subject matter sheets; and, of course, you may want to add some questions based on direct testimony for which you do not have a prior statement available for possible impeachment. If so, do this questioning cautiously.

When I had the subject matters organized, I then prepared the actual questions I planned to ask. The best technique is to frame the questions based on the actual questions and answers found in the deposition transcript. This technique ensures that, if the witness deviates from the deposition testimony, the questions at the trial will be the same language used in the deposition.

On one hand, asking a question and receiving an answer not identical to the deposition testimony can be problematic. On the other hand, asking a question based on the exact words from the deposition transcript can be very effective. I have observed witnesses trying to explain impeachment at trial by suggesting that the question at deposition was not the same question at trial.

Using the system described above and shown in Appendix B for the examination of adverse witnesses ensures that the trial question will match the deposition record. When lawyers merely have notes from a deposition, sometimes the notes are interpretations of the deposition testimony and not the exact testimony. Then, asking a question based on an interpretation of the deposition testimony, especially if someone else did the interpretation, may not result in impeachment because the trial question may not match the deposition record.

Using the system shown in Appendix B makes impeachment go faster; it is more dramatic; and it is more effective. By asking questions at trial, based on the deposition testimony collected as described, you can quickly direct the witness to the page and line of the transcript as soon as the witness deviates from the deposition testimony. This shows everyone — jury, judge, and witness — that you are in control. I have seen too many instances in which, when a witness testifies differently at trial than at deposition, counsel fumbles to find the transcript and then looks further to find the line and page, and then reads to himself the deposition testimony before questioning the witness about it. This takes too much time and gives the witness an opportunity to create a reason for the differences in testimony.

Examination of Witnesses Should Be by Questions and Not by Statements

There is general agreement that direct examination of witnesses should be done by nonleading questions. Using leading questions on direct examination may result in the interposing of objections or even intervention by a judge who, without waiting for an objection, may state that the question is improper, saying that the testimony should come from the witness. On the other hand, leading questions are permissible and should be used during cross-examination or direct examination of a hostile witness or adverse party. [Federal Rules of Evidence, 611(c)]. There is some controversy as to what is a leading question. I have always thought that a leading question is one in which the question itself suggests the answer. For example, the question, "To what was the tow strap attached?" would not be a leading question; on the other hand, "Was the tow strap attached to the luggage rack?" is a question that suggests the answer, a classic example of a leading question.

Somehow, a philosophy has developed that the only appropriate form of a leading question is a statement such as:

"The tow strap was attached to the luggage rack?" or,

"The patent has six claims?" or,

"You have issued a report?" or,

"The report was prepared on October 6?"

I suppose that counsel argue that the inflection in counsel's voice at the end of the statement makes the statement a question. This is not questioning of a witness; it is testimony by the lawyer, which should be susceptible to a motion to strike. When I was defending depositions, I would advise deponents, when the questioning lawyers made statements, that there was no question for the witness to answer; the lawyer was testifying. Some witnesses, when a lawyer makes a statement, even ask, "Is that a question?" In response to a question that was only a statement, one witness during a trial responded, "Are you asking me or are you telling me?"

At trial, an opposing counsel may object to the "question" stating that the "question" is testimony by the questioning counsel. The court could sustain this objection, or, not even waiting for an objection, interrupt and instruct counsel to refrain from the use of such "questions," or, even ask, "Is that the testimony of the witness or your testimony?" In one action, counsel asked the following "question": "I assume that the rate of return was 4%." The witness responded by saying, "Why would you assume that?" Counsel then demanded, "Answer my question." The court said, "There was no question; counsel was testifying." This supports the view that making statements is, in effect, testimony by counsel, which is improper.

To circumvent this possibility, lawyers have adopted a style of making a statement followed by the words "correct," "right," or "agreed." For example:

"You called her Mayor, correct?"

"Different batting order today than you had in New York, right?"

"You are an expert, agreed?"

"There is a warehouse, true?"

The fact that counsel adds the word "correct" or a similar word at the end of the statement does not really change the fact that the lawyer is testifying.

If this were the ideal cross-examination, then every "question" on cross-examination should be a statement followed by "correct," or, "right," or, a similar word. I have observed numerous cross-examinations featuring a steady stream of statements followed by "correct" or "right." After a while, it becomes distracting and obvious that the lawyer is testifying.

Discussions with jurors reveal that some — not a majority, but some, are turned off by the use of statements alone or statements followed by "correct" or "right." These jurors have stated (accurately, in my opinion) that the lawyer, and not the witness, is testifying. Keep in mind that many jurors do not like lawyers to begin with and believe that the technique of making statements is manipulating the witness and not giving the witness an opportunity to speak. These jurors state that they want to hear the witnesses testify, not the lawyers. One juror, commenting on a lawyer whose cross-examination style was to make statements, thought that counsel was a "corporate shark." I want to emphasize that these comments do not come from a majority of jurors. But, there are enough comments that competent counsel should consider them.

These jurors do see a difference between:

1. "Was the tow strap attached to the luggage rack?"
   and
2. "The tow strap was attached to the luggage rack?" or, "The tow strap was attached to the luggage rack, correct?"

The answer of, "Yes" to each of these "questions" should establish that the tow strap was attached to the luggage rack. There is a small difference in form between 1 and 2, but a big difference in the perception of some jurors.

The Use of Statements to Prove Negative Facts Creates an Ambiguous Record and Can Be Devastating to the Action

In one case, plaintiff's first two witnesses described the scene of the accident. Defense counsel tried to establish that the witnesses did not see the accident. The first "question" on cross-examination for both witnesses was, "You didn't see the accident?" Each witness said, "No." Defense counsel believed that she established that the witnesses did not see the accident. Grammatically, if the witnesses did not see the accident, the answers should have been, "Yes" (I did not see the accident). When the witnesses answered, "No," this meant, grammatically, due to the double negative, "Yes" (I did see the accident).

The jurors may have understood that the witnesses did not see the accident, because many of us use negatives in our normal conversations. Yet, some jurors have looked perplexed at the answers to such negative "questions" as:

- "You never hit plaintiff?"
- "You never kicked plaintiff?"
- "You never saw the report?"

- "You didn't use a taser?"
- "You are not aware?"

Other examples of negative "questions" are:

- "You did not look at the machine?"
- "That's not one you checked?"
- "You weren't referring to the rules?"
- "That was not true?"
- "You did not see the weapon?"
- "You don't deny this?"
- "Employees cannot be terminated for disability?"
- "You cannot tell how many times he slept there?"
- "You don't know the amount of lead present when the tenant took possession?"

Although everyone at the trial may have believed or known what these witnesses meant by their answers to these negative "questions," the records were ambiguous, especially for an appeal. Consider an appeal of a denial of a motion to suppress with the following testimony from the hearing:

"Q. You did not consent to the search?
A. No."

Imagine the opposite question and answer:

"Q. Did you consent to the search?
A. No."

These are not the same two questions.

Because of the ambiguity resulting from negative questions, some judges have even interrupted, in certain instances, to clarify the record by requesting counsel to rephrase the "question."

Use of negative "questions" can be very detrimental to your case. In an employment discrimination action, plaintiff died shortly after the action was filed. His Administratrix was substituted as plaintiff. At her deposition, the Administratrix was "asked," "You have no facts regarding your husband's termination." Her response was, "No." At the trial, the Administratrix testified as to facts of her former husband's termination. Defense counsel tried to impeach the Administratrix by use of her deposition. The attempt failed because her trial testimony grammatically was consistent with her deposition testimony. Thus, although everyone at the deposition might have thought that the Administratrix knew of no facts because her deposition testimony is typical of how we talk casually, that assumption turned out to be incorrect.

Similarly, in another employment action, a witness, who was a salaried employee, testified that she had asked several times in the past to return to hourly status. Defense counsel tried to impeach at the trial based on the following deposition testimony:

"Q. You never asked to go back to hourly status?
A. No."

This attempt failed as the judge said the question and answer were too ambiguous.

"Questions" containing **double** negatives create further ambiguities:

- "It is not your testimony that you had no input as to the HUD standards?"
- "You are not aware that he didn't do that?"

Some lawyers try to solve the ambiguity resulting from negative statements by adding a positive statement such as "correct," or "true." For example,

- "It was not your job to post those boards, true?"
- "The government never filed that motion, right?"
- "You never saw the report, correct?"
- "You never left, true?"

Adding words such as "correct" or "right" does **not** resolve the ambiguity; it only emphasizes the problem. In one action, defense counsel tried to establish that plaintiff did not expect to get paid overtime. The record reflects:

"Q. You didn't expect to get paid for overtime, correct?
A. No."

More philosophically, is that one "question" really two questions? Is the first question, "You did not expect to get paid for overtime?" Is the second question, "Is it correct to state you did not expect to get paid for overtime?" Whenever you have two questions or statements, there is always the issue of which question or statement the witness answered. In this case, the witness did not expect to get paid for overtime. But when the witness answered, "No," what did the answer really mean? Did it mean that the witness, who probably was tense and nervous, was concentrating on the first part of the "question", "You did not expect to get paid for overtime?" and responded, "No" because she did not expect to get paid for overtime (and because that is the way we talk)? Or, did the "No" response mean that the witness meant, "No, it was not correct to say that she didn't expect to get paid for overtime"? A, "Yes" answer, however, would have meant, "Yes. I did not expect to get paid for overtime." and, "Yes, it is correct to state that I did not expect to get paid for overtime." A better approach to have solved this ambiguity would have been to ask, "Did you expect to get paid for overtime?"

In another action, Mr. Bravo was not on the promotion list. Counsel wanted to confirm that Mr. Bravo was not on the promotion list. The "question" was, "Mr. Bravo's name is not on the promotion list, correct?" The answer was, "No." Did the witness mean that Mr. Bravo was not on the list or that it was not correct to state that Mr. Bravo was not on the list?

In yet still another example, one lawyer tried to establish that the witness had never worked as an hourly employee. Counsel simply could have asked, "Did you ever work as an hourly employee?" Instead, the following occurred:

"Q. You never worked in the hourly work force, true?
A. No."

Which question did the witness answer and what does the answer mean? This question and answer are clearly ambiguous. In fact, they were so ambiguous that the judge intervened and requested counsel to re-state the "question." If you use such ambiguous questions on critical matters, you might not be fortunate to have a judge help you out.

Other examples of adding a positive question to a negative statement:

- "You didn't think there was a problem, did you?"
- "You were not handcuffed, were you?"
- "You had not been advised of your Miranda rights, had you?"
- "It doesn't say that, does it?"
- "No one ever told you, did they?"

There are lawyers who obviously confuse witnesses by deliberately combining positive and negative statements together. In a criminal trial, counsel asked, "The cocaine was powder, was it not?" How in the world can this dialogue make sense? The question starts with a positive (the cocaine was powder) and ends with a negative [was it (the cocaine) not powder?]. Which question did the witness answer?

Other examples of a positive statement followed by a negative question:

- "The relationship deteriorated, didn't it?"
- "You were there, weren't you?"
- "The Agreement was in effect, was it not?"
- "He explained this, did he not?"
- "You were concerned, were you not?"
- "You are still in the Plan, are you not?"
- "You remember, do you not?"
- "This is acceptable, is it not?"
- "You have done that, have you not?"
- "You defined it, didn't you?"

Rather than "ask," "The catheter can be pulled back further, can it not?" just ask, "Can the catheter be pulled back further?"

The "do you not"/"was it not" habit creates havoc when combined with negative statements:

"You didn't do it, did you not?"
"You don't know, do you not?"

Avoid the Use of, "Is it Correct?" or, "Isn't it Correct?"

Some lawyers start questions with, "Is it correct that. . . ?" or, "Is it true that. . . ?" For example, "Is it correct to say that Sylvester's firm resolved this?" This sounds more like a question, although, arguably it is still testimony by the lawyer. A steady use of questions starting this way gets boring quickly and establishes that the lawyer is testifying. If this were an appropriate style of cross-examination, then every "question" should be prefaced by, "Is it correct that. . . ?" or, "Is it true that. . . ?"

A worse situation occurs when lawyers start each question with, "Isn't it true that. . . ?" or, "Isn't it a fact that. . . ?" or, "Isn't it correct that. . . ?" Using the negative as part of the "question" actually can result in proving the opposite of what you are intending to establish.

Consider the following:

1. "Is it true that the tow strap was attached to the luggage rack?"
2. "Isn't it true that the tow strap was attached to the luggage rack?"

These are two different questions. If you want to establish that the tow strap was attached to the luggage rack, simply ask, "Was the tow strap attached to the luggage rack?" Adding "Is it not true?" creates a horrible record, most certainly creates an ambiguity, and may prove the reverse of what you are trying to establish. Why would you want to ask, "Is it not true (in other words, false) that the tow strap was attached to the luggage rack?"

A key issue in one action was whether a wife severely scratched her husband's back. The question to the husband was, "Isn't it true (is it not true) your wife scratched you?" Just ask, "Did your wife scratch you?"

Following are other examples of confusing questions using, "Isn't it true" or, "Isn't it correct":

- "Isn't it true that you reported to Thelma?"
- "Isn't it a fact that the patent is an important patent?"
- "Isn't it your opinion that the patent was invalid?"

Additional confusion results when, "Isn't it true" or, "Isn't it correct" are used when trying to establish negative facts:

- "Isn't it true that none of the funds were used for the loans?"
- "Isn't it correct that you were not in that position?"

- "The jokes did not offend you, isn't that true?"
- "They do not measure this, isn't that correct?"
- "The company did not allow calls to be screened, isn't that correct?"
- "Plaintiff hasn't told you all of the things he cannot do, isn't that true?"
- "You didn't call sooner, isn't that correct?"
- "You do not consider yourself an expert, isn't that correct?"
- "Isn't it correct that you do not know?"
- "He didn't have vision of the car, isn't that correct?"
- "It wasn't given to the foreman, isn't that correct?"

Actually, some lawyers during the same cross-examination will alternate between, "Is it correct" and, "Isn't it correct" or, "Is it true" and, "Isn't it true." This creates even more confusion.

Extreme Examples of Combining Positive and Negative Statements and Questions

- "You would agree, would you not, it does not count, does it?" (a positive followed by a negative, followed by a negative, followed by a positive.)
- "Isn't it true that you did not want them to leave, did you?" (a negative followed by a negative, followed by a positive.)
- "Isn't it true that the government did not promise you it would not prosecute you?" (triple negatives).
- "But you don't say, do you not, that it could not have meant that the legislation could not have been passed in this legislative year?"(quadruple negatives). Once counsel heard this question, he and everyone else in the courtroom smiled and had a laugh together.

Some Fundamentals of Asking Questions

Only One Person Should Talk at a Time

It is extremely difficult, and impossible in most instances, for the court reporter to record all that is said if two people talk simultaneously. To have a good record, be absolutely certain that only one person talks at a time.

Confusion results when a witness and counsel or two lawyers talk simultaneously. If you are interrupted, back off and let the witness or other lawyer look rude. You then may want to ask the judge for help by making some self-serving statement about being interrupted.

Unless justified possibly to prevent a mistrial (see the next paragraph), allow a witness to finish an answer before you ask the next question. If the answer being given is nonresponsive, you can move to have the answer stricken. If you purposely interrupt the witness, ask another question, or start to ask a question before the witness answers the pending question, you may be met by an objection by opposing counsel, followed by a reprimand from the judge. The judge might intervene without waiting for an objection, as the judge should, because such conduct is inappropriate. In one action in which counsel kept interrupting the witness, the judge first cautioned counsel and then sternly rebuked counsel for interrupting, and then finally said, "This is the third time." You do not want to have this happen to you in front of a jury. In this action, jurors, who rendered a verdict against this counsel's client, later stated that counsel was badgering the witnesses; the jurors believed that counsel did not properly respect the witnesses. Generally, jurors identify more with witnesses than with counsel.

If the answer being given by the witness is highly prejudicial, you should take the risk by interrupting before much prejudicial material is said. For example, if the witness starts to testify about some matters that the court has previously stated were inadmissible, you need to stop this testimony as soon as possible rather than risk a mistrial. Doing so may incur the wrath of the court, but sometimes this has to be done.

When asking a question, a witness will sometimes start answering your question before you finish asking the question. If that happens, stop asking your question. When the witness finishes, you may want to ask the court to strike the answer, but you should restate the question that you intended to ask. Failure to restate your question after the witness responds to only part of the question can create an ambiguity in the record. Although it may be obvious at the deposition or trial as to what was meant, the record may still be ambiguous. Before you restate your question in full, you should ask the court to request the witness to let you finish your question before answering.

Questions on Direct Examination Should Be Framed to Elicit Fairly Short Answers, not Long, Narrative Responses

Often, a series of questions like the following is very effective:

> Q. I want to review with you the events of August 30. What time did you leave for work?
> Q. What happened next?
> Q. What happened next?
> Q. What happened next?

Cross-examination Should be Done with Short, Crisp Questions, Seeking Only a Yes or No Answer

If the answer is wrong, use the deposition to impeach, if necessary.

Be Certain that the Witness Answers the Question Rather Than Avoids the Question by Arguing or by Answering Another Question, or by Trying to Provide Some Explanation

If the witness does not answer the question asked, continue asking the same question. It is very dramatic on cross-examination to ask the same question, if necessary, three or four times before you get the appropriate answer. Advantages of having the questions prepared are that you can ask the exact same question again without having to request the court reporter to read the question or you do not have to try to remember what the question was that you just asked.

Be Careful with Predicates Such as, "Do You Know," "Do You Recall," or, "Do You Remember"

In one situation, defendant tried to establish that plaintiff was never removed from the job list. The question and answer were as follows:

"Q. Are you aware if plaintiff was removed from the job list?
A. No."

All this established was that the witness was not aware if plaintiff was removed from the job list. The answer did not establish that plaintiff was removed from the job list, as counsel believed had been established. This question and answer were ambiguous. Follow up questioning was required.

Likewise, there is a difference between the following two questions:

"Do you know if the company considered Mr. Lincoln for the job?"

and

"Did the company consider Mr. Lincoln for the job?"

If the first question is answered, "No," all it means is that the witness does not know whether Mr. Lincoln was considered not *that* Mr. Lincoln was or was not considered for the job. If the first question is answered, "Yes," all it means is that the witness *knows* whether the company considered Mr. Lincoln for the job, not *that* the company considered or did not consider Mr. Lincoln for the job. Additional questioning is required. The second question is the better question.

One plaintiff's action was based on the presence of a contaminant in his well. On cross-examination, defense counsel tried to establish that plaintiff had his well tested and no chromium was found. The following occurred:

> "Q. Did you have your well tested for the presence of chromium?
> A. Yes.
> Q. Do you know if the test disclosed the presence of chromium?
> A. Not at this time."

Because defense counsel said, "No further questions," defense counsel believed that he established that the test showed that no chromium was present. However, based on the question asked, all defense counsel established was that the witness did not know at that time whether the test disclosed the presence of chromium.

There is a difference between:

> "Did you turn the machine on?"
> and
> "Do you recall if you turned the machine on?"

If the answer to the second question is, "Yes," this does not mean that the witness turned the machine on but only that the witness recalls if he turned the machine on or off. Follow up questioning is required. Likewise, the question, "Do you recall if the door was open?" is not sufficient. This question does not prove one way or the other if the door was open. Just ask the question, "Was the door open?"

A question using, "Do you remember?" can also create an ambiguity. "Do you remember if plaintiff told you he planned to quit?" with a, "No" answer is ambiguous. The answer establishes only that the witness does not remember. The better question is, "Did plaintiff tell you he was going to quit?" This sets up a possibility of a direct conflict. Failing to remember does not create the conflict.

An answer of, "Yes" to the question, "Were you able to determine if she understood?" requires additional questioning. Likewise, an answer of, "No" to the question, "Do you have any memory of the foreman seeking your approval to lay off the plaintiff?" establishes only that the witness had no memory of the foreman seeking the approval, not that the foreman did not seek the approval of the witness. If the foreman never sought the approval of the witness, the better question would be, "Did the foreman seek your approval to lay off the plaintiff?" not, "Do you have any memory?"

Receiving an answer of, "Yes" to the question, "Did you have the opportunity to see if the dye packs were taken?" did not establish that dye packs were taken. The answer required follow-up questions. Here, after the witness said, "Yes," counsel then asked, "Were dye packs taken?" This was very efficient questioning.

Avoid Irrelevant and Silly Questions

Be certain that the questions asked seek relevant material. Having a judge sustain objections to your questions, especially if there are many such instances, could affect your credibility with the jury. In an ADA accommodation case, the fact that plaintiff was injured on the job had been established. After ten minutes of plaintiff's counsel asking questions of a witness about how the accident happened, the court intervened and said that no reason existed for this series of questions; thus, the jury knew that counsel was wasting the jury's time.

Likewise, in an action seeking employment benefits, plaintiff, who was in his fifties was asked to describe the farming he did thirty years earlier. The judge intervened and instructed counsel to move along.

Why do lawyers, usually on cross-examination, believe that they must begin by asking, "Have we met before?" Or, more typically, "We haven't met before?" Who cares? Are the lawyers trying to show that they can examine without a deposition? If so, how does the jury know this?

Likewise, why bother to ask a witness whether the witness is married or has children or grandchildren? If these matters could be issues, by all means obtain this information, but do not bother otherwise because these questions are a waste of time. In a class action trial, plaintiffs' counsel asked one class representative to state names, ages, and occupations of all thirteen grandchildren. The judge stopped counsel and, in chambers, said that if counsel did not stop the "hearts and flowers" routine, the judge would declare a mistrial and get people into court who wanted to try a case.

In another action, on rebuttal, counsel asked a witness about where he was raised, his education, and his work history. Counsel then asked if the witness was married and for how long. When counsel asked about children, the court interrupted without an objection and said to move on. It also is a waste of time to elicit information about military service and education, unless these matters have some bearing on the case.

When defendant's net worth had no possible relevance to the action, some jurors resented plaintiff placing into evidence the defendant's income tax returns. The jurors, ruling for the defendant, stated that they knew the only reason for introducing the tax returns was to try to prejudice the defendant.

Avoid Using Repetitive and Unnecessary Predicates to Questions

All too frequently, lawyers preface their questions with, "Is it your testimony that. . . ?" If that is the standard, then every question should be so prefaced; otherwise, it would be logical to assume that the testimony is not the witness's testimony. Each witness is expected to give that witness's testimony, not the testimony of someone else, so why bother to ask, "Is it your testimony that. . . ?" Just ask the question without those predicate words.

Do not use, "Can we agree that . . . ?" or "Will you agree with me that . . . ?" Who cares whether the witness and questioning counsel agree on anything? Counsel and the witness can *agree* that plaintiff was absent from work on nine days, but that is not the issue. The issue is, *was* plaintiff absent from work on nine days, not the number of days upon which counsel and the witness agree. Objections to such questions have been sustained.

Eliminate from your questions the phrase, "as we sit here today." These are meaningless words and add nothing to the testimony.

Do not ask, "Is it fair to say?" The issue may be whether defendant produced twenty defective parts. That is what needs to be proved. To elicit from the witness that, "it is fair to say defendant produced twenty defective parts" does not prove that defendant produced twenty defective parts. As in other areas, if the other questions do not start with, "Is it fair to say?" does that mean that the answers are not fair? Also, what is the definition of fair? Objections to the use of, "Is it fair. . .?" have been sustained.

A steady use of starting questions with, "Tell the ladies and gentlemen of the jury. . . ." is too stilted.

In one case, a lawyer continually began direct questions with, "Is it the case that. . . ?" On cross-examination, the "questions" overwhelmingly were, "It is the case, is it not, that. . . ?" These questions raise issues about making statements and using negative statements, and six days of these predicates became annoying. Just ask the question. Here, apparently only thoughts were written down and in order to make "questions," counsel reverted to the monotonous predicate words.

Avoid, "Look the jurors in the eyes and tell them. . . .," especially a repetitive use of this preface.

These predicates are usually a reflex while the brain is forming the heart of the next sentence or question. Preparing questions in advance should eliminate the use of these predicates.

Ask Specific, Not Ambiguous, Questions

In a heroin case, ten defendants were indicted, but only two went to trial. There was testimony about the defendants not on trial. Questions and answers were replete with references to "him" and "he." Include proper names in your questions; do not use pronouns. These are too ambiguous. If you really want to prove that a defendant on trial was involved in the charged offense, leave no doubt by naming the defendant. Referring to a particular defendant by name places emphasis on the guilt of that defendant.

In one action, there was a Randy Jones and a Steve Jones. Randy was deceased and only Steve was a defendant. Although both brothers were a part of a conspiracy, there were questions referring only to Mr. Jones, without specifying which one.

In an action involving two companies, there were too many questions referring to "the company," such as, "When did the company learn that the regulation was issued?" When referenced, the company name should be used.

When several phone numbers were involved, the question, "Did you call the same number?" was a problem.

When police forced plaintiff to the ground, the takedown involved several sequential procedures, some of which a witness observed and some of which he did not observe. The cross-examiner kept asking or stating, "You didn't see it?" What is "it," and why the negative question/statement?

In an action seeking damages for an arrest stemming from a domestic dispute in September 2005, defendant introduced evidence of other domestic disputes in December 2004 and March 2005. Counsel switched questioning among all three incidents. The questions were ambiguous: "Who was present at that incident?" and, "Who precipitated that incident?" Counsel should have specified in each question the incident for which the question was being asked.

When many of the same type of exhibits are involved, refer to each item by exhibit number. In an action involving ten guns, there were numerous questions referring to "that gun." Rather than say, "Where did you find that gun?" ask, "Where did you find the 38 caliber revolver, which is Exhibit 2?"

In another action, counsel sought to establish what records an expert had reviewed. The question was asked, "Did you review all of the records?" Why not lay out all of what the expert reviewed rather than create an ambiguity as to what the expert did review?

Include a Specific Time Reference in Questions if the Lawsuit Involves a Series of Events Over an Extended Time Period.

"Did you sleep there that night?" is too ambiguous. What night and place are meant by the question? It is better to ask, "Did you sleep at 18 West Street on the night of July 21, 2007?" Even if a new topic is introduced by saying, "Now, let's turn to the events of March 25, 2008," be sure to add in subsequent questions a reference to March 25 rather than saying, "At that time" or, "Then" or, "At this time."

Preferably include in your question or confirm with the witness the full date of an event:

Best: August 28, 2007
Better: August 28
Good: The 28th

Do not accept less. The full date of an event may matter. For example, you may, at a deposition, start a series of questions with the date stated, but you become careless with subsequent testimony and eliminate any reference to a date. Later you may want to use at trial, either by reading or video, a portion of the testimony that is not complete with the date. Confusion can result. Which is better form:

"What happened at that meeting?"

or

"What happened at the meeting of September 8, 2007?" (Optional: "between you and Sally Jones.")

Clarify Ambiguous Answers

When testimony concerned the amount of sales, the witness answered, "twenty-six ninety and seventy-five twenty." Was this $26.90 or $2,690.00, and was it $75.20 or $7,520.00? Counsel clarified by stating, "two thousand, six hundred and ninety dollars" and "seven thousand five hundred and twenty dollars," thus removing the ambiguity. It is your job to make a good record.

One witness said that the lead inventor received 3–4 percent of the royalties and that the witness, a co-inventor, received 27 percent of what the lead inventor received. The next question was, "How much was received in 2000?" The answer was "$11,000,000." It was unclear whether the lead inventor received $11,000,000 or the co-inventor received $11,000,000. Be specific; don't leave an ambiguity like this on the table.

Avoid the Windup; Just Ask the Question

Too often, there is a tendency to start a question by commenting on the evidence, such as what another witness said, what was said on direct examination by the witness, what a certain exhibit says, or what was said in opening statement. This is improper because the lawyer's recitation may not be accurate or it could be considered as testimony. Even without objection, some courts have intervened and instructed counsel in front of the jury to stop this practice.

Judge S. Hugh Dillin of the Southern District of Indiana used to say during questioning by lawyers, "Forget the windup; just pitch the question." What he meant was, just ask the question and don't load the question with such things as, "Yesterday you said" or, "On direct you said" or, "Witness Jones said" or, "Exhibit 10 says." Sometimes the windup gets long and often it may not be accurate. Using a windup may result in a rebuke from the court, such as, "Skip the windup" or, "Just ask the question," even without an objection. It is not good to have a judge tell you that your question is improper, especially when there is no objection.

In one action, counsel prefaced his question with the comment, "On direct examination, counsel asked you a question using emotion in his voice." The judge quickly interjected in front of the jury that counsel's job is to ask questions and not make editorial comments about other counsel or witnesses.

In another action, counsel, as a possible preface to a question, stated, "You went on leave on May 6, July 10, September 15, and October 12," at which time the court interrupted counsel and said, "Stop the review of prior testimony; just ask the question."

Likewise, do not try to summarize a witness's prior testimony. For example, when counsel said, "You just told me . . . ," the court interrupted and said, "Just ask the question."

Examples of improper windup that were met with an instruction by the court to avoid the windup and just ask the question are the following:

- "On direct examination, you testified that. . . ."
- "In your prior testimony, you said. . . ."
- "I think it has been established. . . ."
- "I do not understand why this is only an estimate. . . ."
- "Now, let's see if we can get a straight answer. . . ."
- "Now, will you answer my question. . . ." (implying that answer just given did not answer the question).
- "There is some confusion in the record between what you said on direct examination and what you just said."
- "A prior witness has testified. . . ."

It is improper to ask whether a witness agrees or disagrees with the testimony of another witness.

Do Not Ask a Question Unless You Know the Answer

As a Navy trial lawyer, I was assigned to prosecute a defendant charged with the theft of clothes. The clothes in question were in the custody of a Navy investigator, wrapped in brown paper and sealed with tape. The investigator wrote his name on the tape and paper so that the writing would be disturbed if the package were opened. When I first interviewed the investigator, he asked whether I wanted him to open the package. Being concerned with the chain of custody, I said, "No." At the end of the first day of trial, counsel agreed that the court reporter could retain custody of the package overnight. On return to the courtroom the next day, I had the investigator open the package and identify the clothing. Even though I had all the stolen clothing identified, there was still another package at the court reporter's table. All persons in the courtroom looked at me. As I picked up the package to take it to the witness, the court reporter said, "Wait — that is my laundry."

In a criminal action, the undercover agent identified the purchases of drugs but did not identify either of the two defendants as buying drugs. On cross-examination, counsel for defendant Jones asked, "Did you see Mr. Jones at any of these buys?" The answer was, "No." Counsel for defendant Smith asked, "Did you see Mr. Smith at any of these buys?" The witness said, "Yes." There was no reason for either defense counsel to ask these questions because neither defendant was identified during the direct testimony. Counsel for defendant Jones was successful, but counsel for defendant Smith certainly did not help defendant Smith.

As with so many rules, there are exceptions to this rule, the most interesting of which shall be called the "Eisenhower Exception." In a false arrest and excessive force action, plaintiff, on cross examination, explained how his ROTC training allowed him initially to resist efforts by the police officers to hand cuff him behind his back. His testimony continued, with minimal questioning by defense counsel, to explain his most important ROTC assignment. Plaintiff said he had been certified by the ROTC staff as an expert marksman. When asked how good he was, plaintiff answered, "Right eye or left eye?" Plaintiff then testified he was asked to and did accept a special assignment. He was taken by plane and limousine to a farm in Pennsylvania; he was told to go into the back yard. There, plaintiff saw a man painting a picture. The man was President Eisenhower who asked plaintiff if he would be willing to go on a special mission to assassinate Fidel Castro. When plaintiff volunteered to do so, he said there was a second meeting with President Eisenhower. Defense counsel, without having any idea what plaintiff would say, then asked plaintiff to describe what happened at this second meeting. Plaintiff proceeded to relate another bizarre story. Not surprisingly, this case resulted in a defense verdict.

Know When to Stop Asking Questions

A witness testified at trial that she complained to management many times. On cross-examination, she was impeached with her deposition testimony, in which she stated that she complained only one time. Instead of stopping there, counsel asked whether there were other complaints, thereby giving the witness an opportunity to bolster her testimony rather than just leave the record with inconsistent testimony.

If there is nothing that can be accomplished with a witness on cross-examination, based on the direct testimony, consider not asking any questions or limiting the cross-examination. To go beyond, especially in a criminal case in which, in most instances, there is no material with which to impeach or contradict, can be dangerous. A government witness said he read the Consent to Search form to the defendant. Defendant then testified but was not asked if the Consent to Search form was read to him. On cross-examination of the defendant, government counsel asked whether the form was read to the defendant; the defendant said, "No." Thus, there was a conflict in the testimony and a credibility problem that never should have happened. If you have already established a fact, do not ask another witness to confirm the fact if you do not have a written statement or deposition testimony establishing that same fact. Certainly, never ask this type of question if you do not know what the answer of the witness will be.

After counsel develops impressive employment history on a witness, it makes no sense for opposing counsel to review the same information. It makes the witness more credible to the jury.

14

WITNESS AND EXHIBIT LISTS SHOULD BE PREPARED CAREFULLY, SHOULD DISCLOSE SPECIFIC WITNESSES AND EXHIBITS WHENEVER POSSIBLE, AND SHOULD NOT INCLUDE GENERIC CATEGORIES

Exhibits and Witnesses Are Required to Be Disclosed

Witnesses that have not been disclosed, and exhibits that have not been disclosed, in civil cases as directed will not, with certain limited exceptions, be allowed to be used at trial. If you require certain witnesses or exhibits at trial, list them specifically on your witness and exhibit lists.

The Federal Rules of Civil Procedure direct disclosure of exhibits and non-expert witnesses on two occasions: (1) Initial disclosures (Rule 26(a)(1) — at or within 14 days after the Rule 26 conference; and (2) trial exhibits and witnesses (Rule 26(a)(3)) — at least 30 days before trial. Rule 26(a)(3) also allows each federal district court to order disclosure at other times. For example, the Southern District of Indiana uses a case management plan that proposes the filing of preliminary witness and exhibit lists five months after the action is filed, final witness and exhibit lists fourteen months after the action is filed, and a list of exhibits "that will be used at trial" and a list of witnesses "who are expected to be called to testify at trial" two weeks before trial.

The process adopted by the Southern District of Indiana recognizes that at the initial stages of an action, five months after the litigation is filed, when the preliminary exhibit lists and witness lists are required to be filed, the parties probably will not know what exhibits and witnesses will actually be used at trial, so the preliminary lists may be over-or under-inclusive; but, as discovery and trial preparation progress, counsel should be in a better position to know what exhibits and witnesses will be used at trial.

The final witness and exhibit lists should include only those specifically listed witnesses and exhibits from the preliminary lists that are still expected to be used at trial, plus those specifically identified witnesses and exhibits *actually* discovered since the preliminary lists were filed.

The trial exhibit and witness lists should be a further winnowing of the prior lists, with the possible exception of additional witnesses and exhibits only *recently* discovered despite diligent discovery and investigation. Whereas earlier lists were probably overly extensive, the trial lists should include only those exhibits and witnesses actually needed for trial. Except for extraordinary circumstances, there should not be any witness or exhibit on the trial lists not disclosed on the final witness and exhibit lists. The obvious reason for this is the requirement to identify specific witnesses and exhibits in order to allow for proper preparation for trial; in other words, to avoid the old system of "trial by ambush."

When parties have included witnesses or exhibits for the first time on their trial lists and were unable to establish that despite proper investigation and discovery, these exhibits or witnesses were only recently discovered, some judges have ruled that the newly listed exhibits and witnesses appearing on the trial exhibit and witness lists will not be allowed to be used at trial.

It is poor practice to withhold disclosure of witnesses and exhibits until the last opportunity and then argue that the witnesses and exhibits were only recently discovered. Thus, if, after you file your final or trial lists you do *actually* discover new documents or witnesses, file supplemental lists and notify opposing counsel as soon as possible. The longer you wait to disclose these allegedly newly discovered witnesses and exhibits, the less chance you will have of using them. For the same reason, if you are in a district that requires only initial disclosures and trial exhibit and witness lists, and you *actually* discover other witnesses or exhibits after the trial lists were filed, disclose these new witnesses or exhibits and advise opposing counsel as soon as you become aware of them.

Remember, Rule 26(e) of the Federal Rules of Civil Procedure requires supplementation of witness and exhibit lists under certain circumstances.

Witnesses and exhibits should neither be placed nor kept on the various lists as a means of deceiving the other parties to the litigation and forcing them to do more preparation than is necessary. Remember, this could happen to you in the same case or future actions. If your trial lists include exhibits and witnesses that you have no intention of using and, in fact, you do not use the bulk of them, you may lose credibility with the judge in that action or future actions.

If you are aware of witnesses and documents at the time initial disclosures are required to be served that you may use to support your claim or defense, you must list them. In an ADA case involving the issue of accommodation, plaintiff testified at trial he should have been transferred to certain jobs. Defendant then sought to introduce the written job descriptions that were not on any of defendant's exhibit lists to establish that plaintiff could not do those jobs. Plaintiff objected and argued that the job descriptions were never disclosed in discovery. Defendant argued that plaintiff never requested them. The court sustained the objection, stating that the job descriptions were not on any of the defendant's exhibit lists. More important, they should have been listed in defendant's initial disclosures, but were not.

It Is Quite Possible That an Opponent Can Use an Exhibit or Witness Listed on Your Exhibit or Witness Lists

In a federal false arrest case, plaintiff listed as an exhibit, "a certified copy of the file/record in State of Indiana v. Louise B______." At the final pretrial conference, plaintiff's counsel said that he had been unable to find the record. During the trial, defense counsel went to the state court, found the record, and sought to introduce it, because the record contradicted some of plaintiff's evidence. Plaintiff objected. Defendant's response was that because the exhibit was on plaintiff's trial list, plaintiff's objection was without merit. The court agreed. After all, the purpose of an exhibit list is to apprise opposing parties of what to expect at a trial. How can a party be surprised by the use of an exhibit on that party's own list? It is inconsistent for a party to include an exhibit on its exhibit list and then object to the admissibility of that same exhibit.

Similarly, at a preliminary injunction hearing, defendant offered Exhibit 102 into evidence. Plaintiff objected, stating that although the exhibit was discussed during a witness's deposition, the document was not produced until after the deposition was concluded; however, Exhibit 102 was specifically listed on plaintiff's exhibit list. The objection was overruled.

The same issue holds true for witnesses. If you list a person on your witness list, you might be unsuccessful in objecting to an opposing party's calling that witness based on the argument that you should not be surprised by a witness who is listed on your own list. One defendant included on its witness list Samuel Adams, a person not within the subpoena power of the court. The witness was present in Indianapolis during the presentation of defendant's case but was not called as a witness. Plaintiff then announced that it wanted to call Mr. Adams in rebuttal. Defendant objected, stating that Mr. Adams was not on plaintiff's witness list. The court overruled the objection, stating that there could be no prejudice to defendant by having a person already on defendant's list testify in plaintiff's case in rebuttal.

Some courts may sustain an objection to the use by one party of an exhibit or witness not specifically listed on that party's lists, even though it is on an opponent's lists; other courts may allow it. Thus, if you do not want an exhibit admitted into evidence, do not include the document on your exhibit list; likewise, if you do not want a witness to testify, do not put that person on your witness list. It even could be malpractice to list an exhibit or witness on your lists without ever having seen the exhibit or knowing what the witness will say and later having the exhibit or witness used by the other side to the prejudice of your client.

The Use of Broad Generic Categories of Witnesses and Exhibits Should Not Allow the Use of Unspecified Witnesses and Exhibits and Could Result in the Opposite Effect of What Was Intended

The purpose of exhibit and witness lists is to enable opposing parties to prepare for trial by being informed of specific witnesses and exhibits and to eliminate surprise. Using broad categories does not accomplish these purposes; nevertheless, many lawyers hesitate to be too specific with their lists for at least two reasons:

1. They do not want to disclose specific persons or exhibits, thereby alerting opposing parties to potential evidence.
2. Counsel want to have a fallback position in the event that they fail to identify specifically any witness or document that counsel later believes may be needed at trial.

Examples of these broad categories include:

Witnesses

1. "Any person identified in any discovery response, including interrogatory answers, responses to requests for production, responses to requests for admissions, depositions, statements or correspondence."
2. "Any witness identified in any document produced in discovery."
3. "Persons identified in or pursuant to pleadings, motions, objections, memoranda, briefs, or other court papers in this case."

What if Louis Lincoln is mentioned in one document among thousands of documents produced? If Louis Lincoln is called by your opponent, can you prevent the testimony of this witness when you have listed this person in your witness list by this broad reference?

Documents

1. "All documents produced in discovery."
2. "Any and all documents or exhibits which are identified, mentioned or referenced in any discovery response, including interrogatory answers, responses to requests for production, responses to request to admissions, depositions, statements, or correspondence."

It is foolhardy to believe that the general category of "all documents produced in discovery" will enable you to seek to introduce into evidence a document not specifically identified but only included in a mass of documents made available for inspection by the opposing party. I once had an action in which the party I represented was required to make available for inspection a warehouse full of documents. It certainly would have been unfair and defeated the purposes of the Federal Rules of Civil Procedure if any party could have used at trial one document from the hundreds of thousands of documents in the warehouse that were never specifically identified on any list, on the theory that the document was identified in the category of "all documents produced in discovery."

Such broad categories are useless and should not allow a party to utilize these categories to seek to introduce an unspecified exhibit or call an unidentified witness at trial. These categories provide no notice to an opposing party. In one action, plaintiff's trial exhibit list included 280 specifically identified exhibits that were not included on plaintiff's prior exhibit lists. When defendant objected, plaintiff had the audacity to argue that the prior lists included "documents produced in discovery" and the additional 280 documents now identified all fit within this category. Plaintiff was not successful in this endeavor. Plaintiff's counsel clearly appeared to be trying to prevent defendant from proper preparation for trial.

If these broad categories are not sufficient to call unidentified witnesses or use unidentified exhibits, why use them in the first place? If you think that these broad categories will enable you to utilize some exhibit or witness not specifically identified, then your opponent, relying on your same category, should have the same opportunity. Of course, you can argue that no party should be able to use any exhibit or witness not on that party's lists or that the witness's testimony or admissibility of the exhibit are still subject to the rules of evidence and this witness is not competent to testify or the exhibit is not otherwise admissible. Keep in mind, however, that you are sure to be met by an argument that a party should not be allowed to object to a witness or exhibit on that party's own lists.

The use of broad categories can, in fact, result in prejudice to the client you represent. In one action, defendant's witness list included a general category of "plaintiff's co-workers." Plaintiff, for the first time, on its trial witness list, listed Abigail Smith. Abigail Smith was never listed on plaintiff's preliminary or final exhibit lists. Defendant objected. The court overruled the objection, stating that plaintiff could call anyone on defendant's trial witness list and defendant, by including "plaintiff's co-workers," listed Abigail Smith by reference.

Although I have no personal instances to report, I can envision problems with the following broad categories:

- A defendant's trial witness list that includes "any and all witnesses identified on plaintiff's preliminary trial and final witness list." Plaintiff seeks to call as a witness a person who is listed on plaintiff's final and trial witness lists but whom defendant believes is incompetent to testify. Defendant objects. Plaintiff responds by arguing that defendant should not be allowed to object to any witness listed on defendant's trial witness list. Defendant might respond by stating that such a broad listing by defendant should not encompass witnesses who are incompetent. If defendant's position is correct, then just what does defendant's broad category of witnesses mean in the first place? Imagine the hypocrisy if this defendant, relying on the incorporation by reference technique, subsequently might try to call a witness or use an exhibit not specifically listed by defendant but on one of plaintiff's lists?
- "Any expert named by any party." If an opposing party seeks to call as a witness a person whom the opposing party states is an expert, but you contend is not competent to testify as an expert, have you waived your right to object by having this person on your witness list by reference? If not, then do you think your broad category only applies to witnesses that you want to call?
- "Any expert retained by any party." What happens if you have employed an expert for consulting purposes only, but an opposing party learns of the existence and identity of this expert and then wants to call that person to testify? Can you object because your witness list included "any expert retained by any party?"

- A defendant's witness list includes, "Any person deposed in this matter." Plaintiff does not list Mary Jones on any witness list but calls Mary Jones as a witness at trial. If defendant objects, plaintiff is sure to argue that Mary Jones was deposed, and because defendant's witness list included "any person deposed in this matter," Mary Jones was on defendant's witness list by reference.
- A defendant's witness list includes, "Individuals identified by any party in its initial disclosures." Plaintiff lists Alan Smith in its initial disclosures. Plaintiff does not list Alan Smith on any witness list. Defendant does not list Alan Smith by name on any witness list. At trial, plaintiff calls Alan Smith. Defendant objects. Plaintiff says that Alan Smith is on defendant's witness list by the general category of, "Individuals identified by any party in its initial disclosures."
- A defendant's list includes, "All documents identified on any party's initial disclosures." Plaintiff includes a document on its initial disclosures that is harmful to defendant's case, but neither plaintiff nor defendant specifically lists it on any exhibit list; yet, plaintiff seeks to use it at trial on the theory that the document is on defendant's exhibit list by reference. Can defendant object successfully?
- "Any exhibit listed on any exhibit list filed by any party in this action." If an opposing party seeks to introduce an exhibit on its list that you believe is not admissible, will you lose the right to object to its admission by the fact that the exhibit is on your exhibit list by reference?
- "All exhibits identified or used at any deposition taken in this case." Plaintiff seeks to use at trial an exhibit used by plaintiff at a deposition and properly authenticated but that is highly prejudicial and irrelevant or a document never even authenticated. If plaintiff seeks to introduce the exhibit over defendant's objection, defendant is sure to be met with a response questioning how defendant can object to a document on defendant's trial exhibit list.
- "All pleadings in this action." If representing a defendant, would you like plaintiff to seek to introduce the complaint on the theory that it is on your exhibit list? If there are certain portions of a pleading that you want to introduce into evidence, simply list them specifically and, better, by page, paragraph, and line.

- "Any and all answers to interrogatories and requests for production of documents." Do you want your opponent to place into evidence all of your client's answers to interrogatories or responses to requests for production of documents, especially if they contain objections, or evasive responses, or prejudicial but otherwise inadmissible statements, on the theory that these items were included on your exhibit list? If there are admissions by an opposing party in interrogatory answers or responses to requests for production of documents, by all means list them, but specifically list those you want to introduce into evidence. Do not be careless enough to list all responses to all forms of discovery.
- "All affidavits taken in this action." Typically, affidavits are not admissible at trial. Do you want to have your opponent at trial seek to introduce into evidence a prejudicial affidavit that was submitted as part of the summary judgment filings on the theory that "all affidavits" are on your exhibit list?
- "All expert reports, résumés, curriculum vitas, and/or notes." Why would you provide an opportunity for your opponent to place into evidence a prejudicial report from your opponent's expert on the theory that the report is on your exhibit list?
- "All documents contained in expert witness files for any expert." The files of your opponent's expert could contain damaging documents. Do you want to give your opponent an opportunity to introduce these documents on the theory that you have listed the documents on your exhibit list?
- "All supporting literature for expert opinions or documents relied upon by any expert witness, including diagrams, charts, drawings, and/or computer-generated documents relied upon or generated by any expert in forming his opinion." Why give your opponent a chance to introduce exhibits from the opponent's expert on the theory that they are on your exhibit list?
- "Any and all depositions taken in this action." Depositions can be used only under certain conditions. Does use of this category allow any deposition to be used for any purpose? What if a deposition provides prejudicial information, the deponent is not listed on the opponent's witness list, and your opponent seeks to use the transcript? Can you object since your own exhibit list includes "all depositions?"

- "All documents produced by non-parties." A non-party could have produced prejudicial documents, some of which might not be admissible. Do you want to give your opponent a basis to introduce these documents by including them on your exhibit list?
- "Demonstrative exhibits of all expert witnesses." Why would you want to provide your opponent an opportunity to introduce into evidence a demonstrative exhibit prepared by your opponent's expert, especially one you believe is not accurate or is prejudicial?
- "Any physician, psychologist, psychiatrist, therapist or other healthcare provider who has knowledge of plaintiff's medical and/or psychological condition." In many lawsuits involving medical treatment, a defendant will contest the testimony of the plaintiff's medical providers, often on the grounds of incompetence. Why run the risk of losing that objection by including these people on your witness list if you are a defendant? If you want to call one or more of these witnesses, list them specifically.
- "Any and all documents which may be necessary to support the testimony of any witness." It is unlikely that this category would enable you to introduce into evidence a document not previously listed. If you could rely on this broad category to introduce documents not previously listed, then why bother to list any documents at all? If you rely on this category to introduce exhibits, is there a chance your opponent could also rely on it?

If these broad categories are only included on preliminary lists, the argument that these broad categories should not allow a party at trial to call a specific witness or introduce a specific exhibit that fits within a broad category carries more weight. But, the argument has less weight if the broad categories are included on final or trial lists.

Other categories of exhibits and witnesses that are ridiculous to include on any exhibit or witness list are represented by the following examples:

- "Any and all exhibits subsequently identified."
- "Any evidence, documents or exhibits that may come to the attention of Plaintiff subsequently."
- "All documents yet to be produced in discovery."
- "Any other documents that may be discovered pursuant to continuing discovery."

- "Any and all exhibits that may be discovered between the date of this exhibit list and the trial of this matter."
- "Any witnesses that may be identified pursuant to continuing discovery and investigation."
- "Any person yet to be deposed." Does this cover anyone in the world?
- "Any expert witnesses who may be obtained prior to trial."
- "All witnesses subsequently identified."

Who possibly could contend that these categories would enable any party at trial, to call a witness or use an exhibit not previously identified on the theory that the exhibit or witness was identified in subsequent discovery?

There is another reason for not using broad categories. In one action, plaintiff failed to file any exhibit or witness list. Instead of dismissing the action, the court ruled that plaintiff could call as witnesses and use as exhibits only those contained in defendant's exhibit and witness lists. Thus, if defendant had been bold or careless enough to include on defendant's lists "any document disclosed in discovery," or "any person identified in discovery," or other broad categories such as "plaintiff's co-workers" or "plaintiff's medical providers," plaintiff might have been able to prove its case anyway.

In conclusion, witness and exhibit lists should not include broad categories. The lists should contain only specifically identified exhibits and witnesses, and those exhibits and witnesses should be only those you will or may want to use. You should not list any exhibits or witnesses to which or about whom you will need to object.

15

A FINAL PRETRIAL CONFERENCE SHOULD HAVE AN AGENDA FOLLOWED BY AN ENTRY DOCUMENTING RULINGS MADE AND TRIAL PROCEDURES ESTABLISHED AT THE CONFERENCE

Some courts have local rules requiring that parties to a lawsuit prepare an agenda for a final pretrial conference in accordance with a specific format. Other courts simply may require that the parties jointly prepare an agenda for a pretrial conference. Other courts may not have any requirements at all. If the court does not have any published rules or procedures, contact court personnel to determine what typically happens at a final pretrial conference.

If there is no requirement for an agenda, contact opposing counsel to prepare a joint agenda. If the other party or parties will not cooperate, you still should prepare an agenda, serve it on the other party or parties, and file with the court sufficiently in advance of the conference so that the court can review it. At a minimum, bring with you an agenda that lists items you believe need to be addressed at the final pretrial conference.

Be prepared for the following matters:

- Review of witness lists to determine who will testify, the subjects of their testimony, and any objections to this testimony.
- Review of exhibits and discussion of authenticity, admissibility, and objections. Bring to the conference a copy of at least the proposed exhibits to which there are or may be objections.
- Motions in limine.
- Status of settlement.
- Requirements and procedures for voir dire, opening statements, and closing arguments, including the length of time allotted for each.

- Proposed deposition testimony, including the procedures for designating which portions of the transcripts will be used, how objections will be submitted and ruled upon by the judge, and the need to edit depositions, including video depositions.
- Calling of certain witnesses to testify out of order, such as physicians or persons with other commitments.
- Scope of cross-examination, if plaintiff calls a defense witness in plaintiff's case, or for witnesses testifying in defendant's case.

In all likelihood, the judge will make rulings at a final pretrial conference that will govern the conduct of the trial on some or all of the items listed above. These decisions should be documented by an appropriate entry. Ask whether the court will be preparing an entry. If not, ask whether you, or all parties jointly, can prepare and submit an entry for the court's consideration. You must determine, in the case of adverse rulings made at the conference, whether this entry will be a sufficient protection of the record, or whether you will need to make a record at trial by making objections either in the presence or outside the presence of the jury, or whether you will need to make an offer of proof, presumably outside the presence of the jury.

16

ALL COUNSEL, PARTIES (INCLUDING FAMILY AND FRIENDS), PARTY REPRESENTATIVES AND WITNESSES SHOULD BE APPROPRIATELY, NOT FASHIONABLY, DRESSED, FOR ALL COURT PROCEEDINGS

Federal court hearings and trials are still conducted as formal proceedings, as opposed to the casual atmosphere currently in vogue in many businesses and even law firms. All counsel (including paralegals and assistants), parties (including family and friends), party representatives, and witnesses should be appropriately, not expensively or fashionably, dressed for all court proceedings. A male should wear a coat and tie; and the coat and tie should be kept on at all times when in the courthouse and courtroom. Females should wear a dress or preferably, a suit, which would include a jacket either with a skirt or pants. A skirt or pants with only a blouse or sweater is inappropriate, as are short skirts or dresses and low-cut dresses or tops.

Jurors do notice the dress of people in court; these extraneous matters may influence their decisions. The testimony of an expert witness who came to court with no jacket, wrinkled shirt, and three days' growth of beard was not well received. In an action in which plaintiff lost his thumb in a table saw accident, jurors commented that by wearing shirts without buttons for three days of the trial, plaintiff demonstrated that he had adjusted to the loss of his thumb. Because he wore a shirt with buttons on the one day that he testified, jurors concluded that the plaintiff coped with his disability by wearing buttonless shirts, but wore a shirt with buttons only when testifying to emphasize the disability.

In one personal injury action, plaintiff claimed that she had hurt her back and was partially disabled as a result of falling on ice. On different days of the trial, plaintiff wore a sweatshirt from Florida and a jacket from

Alaska. Plaintiff could have acquired these items before she was injured, but that is not what the jury concluded. Jurors commented on the dichotomy between being disabled and traveling to Florida and Alaska.

In another instance that involved defendants being tried for distribution of heroin, two women, identified with the defendants, came into the courtroom during the trial wearing fur coats, expensive clothes, and flashy jewelry. Jurors commented on the appearance of these visitors and thought these clothing items and jewelry were purchased with drug money.

Jurors in another action commented that a female attorney was dressed inappropriately for trial. They said that her jacket and skirt did not match and that her hair was disheveled. They thought she needed to go to a hair stylist.

By all means, do not select a clothing style that will not look good on you. For instance, an older female lawyer should not wear clothes more appropriate for younger women. A witness who probably did not own a suit came to court wearing a suit that was too big, plus the sleeves reached below his hands. It was thought that the suit was purchased or borrowed for trial. The witness would have looked better without the jacket.

Be conservative and neat, not fashionable and chic. You do not want to appear too successful in front of the jury because some jurors may think that if plaintiff can afford such an expensively dressed lawyer, plaintiff will not need a big recovery. On the other hand, some jurors may conclude that if defendant can pay such an expensively dressed lawyer, the defendant can afford to pay a big verdict.

Do not underdress, either. Look presentable. Years ago, when lawyers from my firm went to outlying rural counties to try cases, we used to wear worn-looking and somewhat wrinkled suits. I recommend that you not do this.

There is the question of whether a law enforcement officer should wear a uniform or a suit. There probably is no answer applicable to all situations. For example, in an action in which a deputy United States Marshal wore a suit to the trial, there was testimony about an entry into an apartment. The deputy was questioned about what he was wearing on the night of the entry. He described what he was wearing, including a vest with letters stating "U.S. Marshal." It would have been better to have worn the actual vest in the courtroom, or at least to have brought the vest with him.

Clothing items to avoid:

- Wrinkled clothes.
- Untied tie.
- Tie that says, "Our Father Who Art in Heaven, Hallowed Be Thy Name," with matching socks, and a wrist band with the initials W.W.J.D.

- Blue jeans.
- Cowboy boots, unless you are in Oklahoma or Texas.
- Designer clothes or shoes.
- Expensive jewelry or watches, such as a Rolex watch.
- Excessive jewelry; bracelets, or big rings for males; large jewelry for females. Be wary of the male witness who wants to wear large diamond rings on each hand, plus a gold bracelet, plus an expensive-looking watch, plus a gold tie clasp, plus gaudy cufflinks. Pierced lips, tongues, and eyebrows should be avoided; these could be viewed as offensive by some jurors. Males should avoid pierced ears altogether, especially double and triple piercings with dangling earrings.
- Unshined shoes. You may have a juror or a judge who is as eccentric as I am, and who thinks that unshined shoes are a sign of disorganization. You will never offend anyone with shined shoes, but you might lose someone if your shoes are unshined.

17

SUGGESTIONS FOR EFFECTIVE COURTROOM PRESENTATIONS

Matters to Determine Before the Start of a Proceeding

1. Sufficiently in advance of a trial or hearing determine if the following equipment and supplies are available in the courtroom:
   a. Video Evidence Presentation System. If so, what are its components (e.g. document camera, VCR, computer hook up, monitors)? If there is no VEPS System available, are any of the usual components of the system available individually?
   b. If there are monitors, where will they be located (e.g. in the jury box, or elsewhere, on the bench, at counsel tables, at the witness chair); do any monitors have touch screen capability?
   c. Overhead projector and screen, if desired.
   d. Easel, if desired.
   e. Marker board or large pad of paper and markers, if desired.
2. If technology is not available and you want to use some equipment, or if all you want to use is not available, ask court staff whether you can bring your own technology. In one action, the parties brought, at their own expense, computers and monitors for the counsel tables, judge, witness, and jurors. In another action, in addition to the monitors available in the courtroom, one party brought a projector and a movie screen, approximately 4 feet by 5 feet. When both monitors and the movie screen were utilized, jurors reported that they liked both.

3. Learn how all equipment works.
4. Is there a sound system? If so, how should counsel and witnesses use it?
5. Is there a requirement for which party sits at which table? If not, how is it determined at which table each party sits?
6. When, how, and where are side-bar conferences held? Is the sound system turned off?
7. Where should witnesses report? If witnesses are to report directly to the courthouse, find out and tell them the room number to which they should report. If the witnesses are not sequestered, you may want them to report to the courtroom. If the witnesses are sequestered, or if you do not want opposing counsel to know who your next witnesses will be, tell the witnesses the room number or location to which they should report. Also, advise your clients and witnesses to bring appropriate identification to be able to clear court house security.
8. What time will the courtroom be opened the first day of the trial and what time every day thereafter? Can the courtroom be opened earlier by special request?
9. Will the courtroom be locked during the lunch break?
10. Will the courtroom be locked at night? If so, at what time? Can the courtroom be kept open later by special request?
11. Is there a room available to store files, meet privately with witnesses, or eat lunch?
12. Trial schedule:
    a. Start time each day?
    b. Morning break(s), time and length?
    c. Lunch break, time and length?
    d. Afternoon break(s), time and length?
    e. Stopping time each day?
13. Does the judge have a rule or preference for where you can be or must be during voir dire, opening statement, questioning of witnesses, closing arguments, and arguments to the court? If there is no lectern or if you are not required to stay at the lectern, ascertain how far you can move and how close you can get to the jury box or bench. Generally, it is better to stay at the lectern, if there is one, except for times, if necessary, to approach a witness.
14. Do you need permission from the judge before approaching a witness? If you do approach a witness, resume your regular questioning position as soon as possible thereafter.

Promptness Is a Necessity

When scheduled for a court appearance, be sure to report to the courtroom at least thirty minutes early. (This suggestion also applies to every day of a multi-day trial or hearing.) Sometimes the court may want to confer with counsel before each day's proceeding begins. If you are late or come at the last minute, the trial or hearing may be delayed. Arriving early allows you the opportunity to get organized. Whenever you try a case, you need to organize your materials (witness folders, exhibits, demonstrative exhibits) in the courtroom for that day's proceeding. Arriving at the very last minute prevents this from being properly accomplished, may cause you to look disorganized in front of the judge or jury, and may cause you to be flustered.

Reporting early also allows you to familiarize yourself, your client, and your witnesses with the courtroom and facilities. You can show these people where they will sit, allow them to practice walking from where they will be sitting to the witness chair, learn how the witness chair spins or tilts, practice using the microphone, learn where to look when listening to a question and where to look when answering a question, and learn how to use the touch screen, if available. Actually, it is better to bring your client and witnesses to the courtroom at least one day prior to the start of any proceeding for this purpose. In this way, they will be familiar with the courtroom. Unfamiliarity can be traumatic in an already tense situation. Your client and witnesses should be as relaxed as possible.

Being late for court hearings or trial can be embarrassing. Consider these situations:

- At the final pretrial conference held one week before the scheduled trial date, which plaintiff attended, the judge said that the trial would start at 9 o'clock. The trial did start at 9:00 o'clock, in plaintiff's absence, although plaintiff's counsel was present.
- In another action that started on schedule, defendant walked into the courtroom during voir dire.
- Calling for a recess, the court stated that there would be a ten-minute break. Although plaintiffs' counsel and one plaintiff returned to court, two of the plaintiffs did not. After fifteen minutes, the court said to bring the jury in. The two missing plaintiffs had to tiptoe into the courtroom while the trial was in progress. This was disruptive and created a bad impression.
- In a bench trial, the court stated that there would be a five-minute break. After ten minutes, the judge took the bench. Just as plaintiff's counsel was starting his rebuttal argument, defendant's counsel returned to the courtroom.

Do Not Overstaff Your Trial Team

Frequently, two lawyers appear for one party. Except for unusually large actions, such as patent infringement or contract actions involving hundreds of thousands of dollars, having more than two lawyers raises questions about why. This may influence the jurors when they assess the action. If a party comes to court with four lawyers, the jurors may think that money is no object for that party and take that into consideration in determining whether to award damages or the amount of damages.

Staffing a six-day trial with five lawyers, two of whom did questioning, two of whom just sat, and one local counsel who also just sat, plus a paralegal, seemed excessive and sent the wrong message. Three lawyers for a three-day trial was inappropriate, especially when the third lawyer merely sat at counsel table and had no other role in the action.

In lieu of a second lawyer, one lawyer may consider using a paralegal. Ascertain prior to the start of the trial whether the court will allow secretaries or paralegals to sit at counsel table. If allowed, use common sense. In one action in which plaintiff was seeking $6,000, plaintiff's counsel had two paralegals sitting at counsel table. Jurors, who ruled against plaintiff, questioned why three people were needed for such a small case. For smaller cases, two counsel plus two paralegals at counsel table is also too much, as might be two lawyers, plus one paralegal.

If these extra lawyers, paralegals, or secretaries need to be present during the trial, they can always sit in the gallery. They should be careful not to communicate with trial counsel when the jury is present.

No Matter How Many Counsel Participate in the Trial, These Counsel, and Especially Lead Counsel, Need to Be in the Courtroom at all Times When the Court Is in Session

Sometimes, lawyers leave the courtroom to work on other aspects of the case, such as preparing a future witness. Do not do this. Prepare witnesses or do this other work at night, at noon, or on weekends, not during the trial. Some jurors wonder why counsel is absent. Also, it may inhibit counsel's ability to object or respond to objections if counsel later presents a witness, because that counsel will not know what happened in the courtroom during his absence. Lead counsel, especially, must be totally involved and familiar with what happens in the courtroom.

In one action with multiple lawyers and multiple witnesses, the lawyers were in and out of the courtroom like revolving doors. Apparently the lawyers shared the witnesses, so lawyer Anderson presented witness

Michael and left when witness Michael was completed. Lawyer Benjamin then presented witness Nelson and left when witness Nelson was completed. Lawyer Anderson returned for witnesses Grand and Hagge. No one lawyer was present for all of the proceedings. The jury wondered why this happened and especially wondered why all lawyers were not in the courtroom on a Friday afternoon when the jurors had to be there.

It is best to keep the trial team as small as possible and keep all of the team in the courtroom throughout the trial. The smaller the team, the more likely the whole team will know the trial strategy, as well as being aware of exactly what is happening in the courtroom.

For Jury Trials, All Named Parties Should Be Present at All Times the Court Is in Session

If you represent a corporation, governmental agency, or partnership, you must have a representative of that party present during the entire trial. Consider how it looks to a jury if the other side has a representative and you do not, or your representative is in and out of the courtroom. This sends a message that your party does not take the case seriously.

In a Fair Labor Standards Act action involving thirteen plaintiffs, four named plaintiffs appeared for the first day of trial, but only three stayed for the whole day. On the second day, five different plaintiffs appeared at different times and left when their testimonies concluded. No plaintiff appeared for the last day of trial. Plaintiffs certainly failed to show any interest in their action. It was no surprise that this action ended with a defense verdict.

If there is an action with several corporate officers or employees of a governmental agency as defendants, these defendants, even if not at counsel table because of the large number, should be present at all sessions of a jury trial. If the trial is extended, and these people are needed to oversee the agency's or the company's operations, their absence could be accepted but should be explained to the jury. In the case of a bench trial, ask whether the court wants or requires all of the individual defendants, especially if they are officers or key personnel who are needed to operate the company or governmental agency, to be present at all sessions of the trial.

Be Selective as to Who Sits at Counsel Table

Individual parties (unless there are too many to be accommodated) and party representatives should sit at counsel table and not in the gallery. However, think twice about having another family member who is not a party, and especially think about including a "significant other" at counsel table. In one trial, plaintiff's live-in boyfriend sat at counsel table with plaintiff. This is not a good decision because some jurors may take offense to such involvement by the boyfriend or to people who are unmarried but living together. Although the relationship will certainly be evident during the trial, it is better not to be so obvious.

You, Your Clients and Witnesses Should, at all Times, Act in a Polite, Professional Manner, Especially After an Adverse Ruling by the Court

- No person in the courtroom should ever exhibit by facial expression, bodily movement or other conduct, any opinion (e.g., surprise, happiness, laughter, disbelief, or displeasure) concerning any testimony, attorney argument, or any particular ruling by the court. Such conduct has resulted in a rebuke from the court. Counsel should admonish their clients and witnesses to avoid such behavior. Visitors who cannot abide by this requirement probably will be asked to leave the courtroom. In one action, the court, in a side-bar conference, told counsel to advise plaintiff that if plaintiff did not stop indicating disagreement with the testimony of a witness by facial expressions, plaintiff would be reprimanded in front of the jury. Even without a rebuke from the court, jurors notice these actions and believe they are inappropriate. Jurors will draw their own conclusions. Some jurors have even been offended by inappropriate conduct by visitors and have commented that the jurors knew these visitors were aligned with one of the parties.
- Do not attack, belittle or disparage anyone, whether a witness, opposing counsel, or a party. Treat everyone with respect, including court staff, jurors, opposing parties, court reporter, and witnesses. Do not treat anyone with contempt in front of the jury. Jurors comment that they do not appreciate counsel engaging in personal attacks on opposing counsel and refer to such attacks as "mud slinging." In one action, a witness answered a question by stating, "I do not have any recollection of that." Counsel then stated, "You don't have a recollection of many things." Without even an objection, the court said, "Stop the editorial comment; just ask the question."

- Do not converse with co-counsel, parties, or witnesses when opposing counsel is asking questions of a witness or presenting argument. This is distracting to others, including the witness, jury, and judge.
- Do not argue or discuss the case or objections directly with opposing counsel. Address all remarks to the court.
- During any opening statement or argument of opposing counsel, remain seated at counsel table and be respectful. Never divert the attention of the court or the jury. Counsel should so instruct their clients and witnesses.
- Do not shout or scream. The best approach is to remain calm and, by so doing, try to make the witness become agitated or excited. Being polite when confronted with a shouting witness often causes the witness to become even more out of control and, thus, less likely to be believed. You never want a jury to think you are impolite to any witness.
- Do not toss or throw papers on the table.
- Do not exhibit familiarity with witnesses, jurors, or opposing counsel. Generally, do not use first names. During opening statement or argument to the jury, no juror should be addressed individually by name.

It Is Inappropriate to Refer to the Size of Any Party

Typically, instructions from the court will advise a jury that all parties stand equally before the court regardless of size. It is inappropriate for counsel to refer to the "little guy" against a "giant corporation." When one plaintiff's counsel did this without objection by defendant, jurors later told plaintiff's counsel not to play the big guy/little guy approach.

Often when large corporations are involved in litigation involving an individual or a much smaller party, counsel for the large corporation elects to raise the size issue first in voir dire. Consider whether this is good strategy. In a fraud case in which a large company was seeking to recover damages from a smaller company, plaintiff's counsel said that plaintiff had thousands of employees and billions of dollars in revenue and asked whether that presented a problem for any juror. One prospective juror said, "Yes, if plaintiff had that much money, the money should be given to the poor."

Expressing Personal Beliefs and Opinions at Any Time During a Trial Is Inappropriate

Rule 3.4 of the Indiana Rules of Professional Conduct, entitled, "Fairness to Opposing Party and Counsel," states that a lawyer shall not "state a personal opinion as to the justness of a cause, the credibility of a witness, the culpability of a civil litigant, or the guilt or innocence of an accused. . . ."

I have been surprised at how many lawyers violate this admonition by making such comments as:

- "I have never met such an outstanding person as Robert Jones in all my years of practice."
- "I have never experienced such a dishonest witness."
- "I have never had a stronger case in 20 years."
- "This is the most frivolous suit I have seen in 25 years."
- "These are the finest men I have ever met. I believe and respect them."
- In one action, counsel was bold enough to argue that he knew it was improper for counsel to express his personal beliefs, but he just had to do so because of the righteousness of his client's position.

If opposing counsel objects, and the court instructs the jury to disregard the comments and admonishes the counsel making the inappropriate comments, the impact on the jury may be great. What is even worse is when the court, without waiting for an objection from opposing counsel, interrupts and instructs the jury to disregard the statement and sternly rebukes counsel.

Use Lay Terminology, Not Technical Jargon

At times, lawyers get so immersed in their actions that they either forget to make the explanation simple or become so enamored with themselves that they try to show off by using highly technical terms. Know your audience. Use words that will explain in lay terms what happened. Do not try to impress the jury with technical terms. Make it simple. For instance, say arteries were "blocked," not "occluded."

The use of technical terms can result in losing or confusing jurors. In a telephone case, defendant contracted with plaintiff to purchase unlimited outgoing local calls. Defendant then added switches to allow these local calls to become long distance calls. Defendant then obtained customers for long-distance calls. Defendant paid plaintiff only for the local calls and kept the charges defendant received for the long distance calls. In this action for fraud, both parties kept referring to the practice of "terminating calls," a term of art in the phone industry. This was confusing because the calls were not "terminated," they were "switched."

In another action, a copyright lawyer presented a very technical opening statement to the jury explaining all the details about how computers and computer software functioned. He also exceeded the prescribed time limit. In response, defendant's counsel said, "Did you understand what counsel just said? I didn't. Let me tell you what this case is about: They stole our stuff." This definitely got the jury's attention, and counsel proceeded in lay terms to explain what the evidence would be. The action was settled shortly thereafter.

Do not use initials or abbreviations unless they are well-established ones, such as IRA, GM, GE, AT&T, with which jurors are familiar. It is not a good idea to use initials or abbreviations that are specific to the action when complete identification would be better. Rather than refer to "implantable cardiac defibrillators" as "ICDs," refer to them as "defibrillators," at least until the jury has an opportunity to learn for what ICD stands.

If your action does involve a number of technical terms, acronyms, or business-specific jargon that will be used throughout the documents and testimony, preparation of a glossary of terms, marked as an exhibit, could be very helpful to the jury. It is a good idea to work with opposing counsel to create this as a joint list. You will need to ascertain from the judge whether the exhibit will be merely a demonstrative exhibit that does not accompany the jury during its deliberations or if it will go with the jury. Even with a glossary of terms, it is appropriate to have a witness, probably the first witness, explain the terms. Even though this may seem dull, it is less dull than trying to explain each term as it is mentioned in later testimony. It is recommended that you use an otherwise nontestifying witness for this purpose.

Counsel and Witnesses Should Use Good Grammar

In one opening statement, plaintiff's counsel kept saying that defendant is "gonna do this" or "gonna do that." Other counsel have said, "Sally was off work more than her," or he "arrove at the house." A response of "yea" or "yeah" should be avoided.

Address Professional Persons Appropriately

When referring to a medical doctor or person with a Ph.D., address that person as "Doctor." Of course, one strategy might be to refuse to address a nonphysician, whom you believe is incompetent, as "Doctor" in order to make your point that this person is incompetent and should not be addressed as "Doctor." However, the jury may be offended by your refusal to use the proper title that the witness legitimately earned.

When addressing a member of the clergy be sure to use Father, Sister, or Reverend. With respect to police officers or military personnel, refer to them by their title, such as detective, sergeant, major, officer, but not patrolman.

Do Not Refer to a Party You Represent as a "Client"

In any action, there are parties, such as plaintiff, defendant, and third-party defendant. These parties have names such as Joan Brown, General Motors Corporation, and Harrison Foundation. Too often during trials, lawyers, and especially young lawyers, refer to the parties they represent as "my client." Such references to "my client" are inadvisable. It is better to personalize the party you represent by referring to the party as Joan Brown or General Motors. References to "my client" suggest that this is a professional or business relationship and that you are providing this representation for money only.

All Cell Phones, Beepers, and Pagers Should Be Turned Off or at Least Silenced

Not only is it rude to have a cell phone ring during a court proceeding, it could be damaging to your case if a phone rings during an important piece of testimony and the jurors look to the ringing phone and tune out the testimony. Some judges take a dim view of phones ringing during a court proceeding and verbally reprimand the rude person. In one action, a visitor's phone rang and he tried to speak by covering his head in his jacket. The judge instructed the Marshal to escort this person out of the courtroom. This could be harmful if this person is associated with your client and the jury knows this.

Talk Distinctly, Loudly, and Slowly

Those famous words of Teddy Roosevelt, "speak softly, but carry a big stick," do not work in the courtroom. Some jurors complain when lawyers or witnesses talk too softly. Jurors opine that a lawyer who speaks softly with a monotone voice and no emphasis puts the jury to sleep.

If the court has an amplification system, use it. If you need to leave the amplification system to approach a witness or put something on the

VEPS, elevate the volume of your voice. You must be certain that the court reporter, judge, and jury hear what you have to say. If the court reporter asks you or a witness to speak up, the jurors probably cannot hear either. Jurors have even interrupted witnesses to say that the witnesses cannot be heard.

In one of my first trials, I wanted to demonstrate to the judge that I was prepared. So, during my questioning and without notes, I walked around the courtroom. The senior lawyer with me stopped that by telling me how difficult it was for others in the courtroom to hear when my voice was projecting to the side or rear of the courtroom, and how the judge had to strain to hear my questions. I learned my lesson early. In this regard, whether using a microphone or not, keep your voice up, do not drop your voice, and do not mumble.

Do not talk too fast. You want to be sure that the court reporter can record what you are saying. If you or a witness is asked to "slow down" by the court reporter, the jury probably has a problem keeping up with you (or the witness). Speaking too fast can result in a poor record if the court reporter cannot record all of the testimony and arguments. Talking too fast can result in losing your audience. Jurors also complain when the lawyers or witnesses talk too fast, and, on occasion, have asked the fast talker to slow down.

A wicked combination is speaking softly, or mumbling, coupled with fast talking. In addition to the risk of losing the jury, there is a great chance that the record will be inaccurate.

Be Dramatic

According to Shakespeare, "The whole world is a stage." A good lawyer should follow this advice. Do not drone on. Use some expression in your voice; be dramatic. This applies to opening statements and questioning, but is particularly applicable to closing arguments. Use some emotion, show some outrage, evoke some sympathy, change your tone of voice, but do not shout. Use different inflections and emphases. Keep the jury's attention. Be confident. Those lawyers who may be legally correct and precise but deliver with a monotone style are very ineffective. Some jurors, however, believe that the change in voice inflection can be overly dramatic or manufactured.

Jurors have commented that they like lawyers who can laugh at themselves, who are human, who can be relaxed, and who can portray themselves as ordinary people as the jurors are. One particular comment stands out. The lawyer was explaining the burden of proof in a civil action.

He rhetorically asked the jurors whether they were familiar with the scales of justice. He said that all plaintiff had to do was tip the scales slightly to one side. He then spread his arms out to his sides so that he looked like the letter "T." He then bent one arm slightly up and the other slightly down; he said that that was all plaintiff had to do, and plaintiff had done that. The jurors were highly complimentary of this demonstration.

In another action, the evidence was that plaintiff threw away some papers sent to him relating to the action. Defendant argued that had plaintiff read those papers, the whole matter could have been avoided. To make the point about tossing out the papers, defense counsel, in closing argument, took a piece of paper, noisily crumpled it up in front of the jury, and tossed it away.

Although it is advisable to be dramatic and show some passion, too much drama can upset a jury. In one employment discrimination action, the defendant had failed to comply with certain procedures in the company's personnel manual, most of which were insignificant or irrelevant; nevertheless, plaintiff's counsel emphasized these in his closing argument. In an effort to defuse these allegations, defense counsel reviewed each one, after which he jumped from behind the lectern and toward the jury, shaking his finger and saying, "Got ya." The first time this happened, the jurors jumped back in their seats. Later, they said they were offended by this conduct. In this action, plaintiff's counsel did not even mention a specific damages figure, but the jury awarded $3 million.

Jurors were quite critical of one argument that was basically all shouting and screaming from beginning to end.

Have Rulers, Calculators, and Calendars Readily Available in Case They Are Needed

Be prepared for measurements and calculations. In a drug case, government counsel asked how big the pile of cocaine was. To estimate the measurement, the witness used his hands. Counsel said, "8 inches by 12 inches?" It would have been better to have had a ruler available so that there would be no mistake or dispute as to what the witness's testimony and demonstration was.

If you want a witness to do complicated computations, it is a good idea to have a calculator available for use.

If dates will be important, bring a calendar of the pertinent years or months.

Do Not Bring Soft Drinks, Coffee, or Food into the Courtroom

In the last ten or fifteen years, bottled water has been the "in" thing to use; however, there are many people who grew up drinking tap water from a glass. Also, there are people who are frugal and think that bottled water is ostentatious and a waste of money. Why take a chance on offending a member of the jury? If the court provides tap water in pitchers with cups, use this water and these cups, or pour your bottled water into cups when the jury is not present. By all means, don't drink from a bottle of water during argument or questioning of a witness; use a cup.

Counsel, Parties, and Witnesses Must Pay Attention at All Times

Counsel, parties, and witnesses should pay attention to proceedings and sit erect at all times; not slouch or rock in the chairs; no one should sleep or give an appearance of sleeping by resting his head on the back of the chair. Jurors notice these things. Jurors were very critical of a lawyer who used his Blackberry during opposing counsel's argument.

Miscellaneous Suggestions

- Stand when speaking for the record, including making objections, questioning the witness and addressing the court. Jurors will notice if you do not and the other side does, and jurors will notice especially if the judge asks you to stand and you subsequently do not do so.
- When finished with your examination, do not say, "Pass the witness" unless this is a requirement of a particular court. I do not know why some lawyers say this unless it is an old state court practice. "Pass the witness" sounds too stilted. Just say, "No more questions" or, "I have no further questions."
- Do not ask the court reporter directly to mark testimony or read a previous question. All requests for rereading of questions or answers should be addressed to the court.
- Do not enter the judge's chambers or jury room except on invitation of court staff.
- If you need glasses, wear them. Do not put them on when you read a document and then take them off when you look at the witness. This is distracting. Get bifocals so that you do not have to do this.
- If you have a pen in your hand, do not flip the cap on and off.

- Do not rub your pen or pencil between your hands as you are speaking.
- In one case, jurors told counsel, after the trial, that she should not have kept twisting her hair while questioning a witness; it was distracting.
- Be certain that there is a proper line of sight for the jury, court, witness, and counsel and that you can be heard when using easels, oversize exhibits, models, and VEPS.

18

SELECTION OF A JURY REQUIRES APPROPRIATE INVESTIGATION AS WELL AS EFFECTIVE VOIR DIRE

Information to Ascertain Before Voir Dire

1. From which counties or areas are the prospective jurors summoned?
2. How many prospective jurors will be summoned?
3. Will juror questionnaires be available to counsel and, if so, when can they be obtained; from where can they be obtained; and must they be returned to court staff and, if so, when?
4. Do the questionnaires present any conflict issues? In one action, prior to the start of the trial, defense counsel disclosed to the court and to opposing counsel that one of the prospective jurors was a neighbor. This was a proper action to take rather than have this fact come as a surprise during the trial.
5. Will the prospective jurors be reporting to the courtroom or some other location? You will want to know whether the jurors report to the courtroom in the event that prospective jurors are there when you arrive.
6. Will prospective jurors be seated for voir dire by order of draw, alphabetical order, or some other way?
7. Will a seating chart be provided to you in advance of the voir dire?
8. Will all prospective jurors be examined at the same time or will they be examined in different groups?

9. What if prospective juror number 2 does not appear on the day of trial? Do all other prospective jurors move up one seat, or is the seat filled from the back of the list of prospective jurors, or in another way, or is the seat left empty?
10. If a prospective juror being questioned is excused, do all remaining people move up one seat or does the seat remain vacant?
11. Who does the voir dire — the lawyers, the judge, or a combination?
12. If the lawyers are permitted to do voir dire, how much time is allotted to the lawyers? (Do not even think about splitting voir dire time with co-counsel.)
13. From where must the questioning take place — counsel table, lectern, or wherever counsel desires?
14. Can questions be submitted to the court, either if the judge does all the questioning or there is a sensitive matter that counsel would prefer to be asked by the judge? If so, when do the questions need to be submitted to the judge and must they be provided to the other side?
15. Can a prospective juror request that a matter be discussed privately with only the judge and counsel present? If so, how and where are these discussions held?
16. How many jurors will be selected for a civil case; do all of the jurors selected participate in deliberations, or will those beyond six be alternates and excused? If any are excused, when are they excused?
17. How many alternates will there be for a criminal case? When are they excused?
18. How many peremptory challenges will be allowed?
19. If a large number of prospective jurors appear and few are excused for cause, will more peremptory challenges be allowed?
20. After all challenges have been exercised, which people ultimately will comprise the jury? For example, if seats are filled in due to no shows or excuses for cause, what is the priority for selection of the jurors?
21. How, when, and from where in the courtroom are challenges for cause handled?
22. How are peremptory challenges exercised? Some courts do this by allowing the parties alternately to strike jurors; other courts require the challenges to be done simultaneously and in writing.
23. How will peremptory challenges be handled if jurors are examined in different groups?
24. Will back strikes be allowed?
25. How will those people selected as jurors be seated?

Arguing the Case in Voir Dire Is Improper

Voir dire is not the time to argue the case, make a speech, or to present your opening statement. Trying to extract commitments to give a plaintiff a million dollars or to refuse to give plaintiff a penny are not proper.

Voir Dire Questions Should Be Framed to Learn About the Jurors in Order to Ascertain Who Should Be Challenged from the Venire as Opposed to Who You Would Like to Have on the Jury

In one action, counsel's approach was to ask at least one question of each person on the venire. These questions were not designed for any purpose other than to try to develop a rapport with the prospective jurors. These questions included:

Where did you go to college?
Have you ever been married?
What do you do in your job?

These questions were not only a waste of time but were also inappropriate. It is ill advised to ask some prospective jurors where they went to college, thereby perhaps causing someone who wanted to go to college, but was not able to, feel inadequate. Likewise, asking a single woman whether she had ever been married could be regarded as offensive. Do not do it. Instead, try to find out whether any prospective juror should be eliminated.

Avoid questions that will make jurors uncomfortable. In one employment discrimination action, jurors were noticeably uncomfortable when asked how they would correct the problem of race discrimination in the United States.

Refer to Prospective Jurors by Name, and Be Sure to Pronounce Names Correctly After Pronunciation Has Been Established

A very effective technique to use in voir dire, when directing a question to a prospective juror, is to address the person by name. As the prospective jurors are seated, prepare a seating chart if it is not otherwise provided by court staff. Refer to the seating chart when asking questions. Better yet, memorize the names. There is no excuse to conduct voir dire without a seating chart in hand and then look silly by pointing to prospective jurors and stating, "the person in the top row, third from the left."

If You Are Confident that Damaging Evidence Will Be Admitted During the Trial, Consider Raising Those Issues in Voir Dire

When a plaintiff had a live-in boyfriend, who was going to be a witness, plaintiff's counsel elected to address the issue in voir dire. Counsel stated that plaintiff and her partner had lived together for 14 years, in all respects just like in a marriage, except they were not married. Counsel asked whether this fact alone would cause the jury to find against the plaintiff. If this relationship is going to be an issue in the action, it is better to raise it early in the trial; however, plaintiff's counsel could have been a little less direct. For example, counsel could have asked a prospective juror some general questions, such as, "Do you know any people who live together without being married?" "Does this cause you any concern?" Then, counsel could have addressed the plaintiff's particular situation at that time or perhaps even waited until plaintiff testified.

In a criminal case in which the evidence included audio tapes containing vulgar language, defense counsel defused the harshness of the language coming into evidence at trial by repeating it during voir dire and asking whether the language would be a detriment to the jurors in considering the charges against the defendant. After the trial, one juror said that she considered the language offensive and was upset when she first heard it; however, after having heard counsel use this language several times in voir dire, she was used to it when the evidence was introduced during the trial, and the vulgar language played no role in her decision.

If one of your witnesses has prior convictions that may be used for impeachment, consider asking the jurors whether they could believe testimony from any person who has a previous conviction.

Additional Thoughts

In one action, after the judge talked about the inconvenience to the prospective jurors, plaintiff's counsel said that he wanted only jurors who desired to be jurors and then asked all prospective jurors whether they wanted to be in court. Asking any prospective juror whether he or she wants to be a juror puts that person in an awkward position. After all, no one should *want* to be on a jury. Anyone who wants to be there should be a suspect juror. A juror may believe he or she has a duty to be there and will fulfill that duty, but it is doubtful that any person wants to be on a jury. How do prospective jurors express that fact? To say, truthfully, that they do not want to be in the courtroom will suggest they do not want to fulfill that duty. Probably no one will say, "No." To say, "Yes" suggests that the people are too eager. Asking this question places any prospective juror in an awkward position. That is, prospective jurors who will not want to be in court will most likely resent having been asked that question. The use of the word "inconvenient" is much better.

Study the information about jurors and, where possible, use this information to make your case more understandable. When the defense of one case was going to be that the perpetrators of the fraud were individuals who were independent contractors who could not bind the defendant company, defense counsel reviewed the juror questionnaires and learned that one prospective juror was a contract employee. Defense counsel engaged in a dialogue with this prospective juror concerning the fact that as an individual contractor the juror could not bind the company hiring her to contracts even if she were provided office space at the company's headquarters. Drawing on parallel experiences can help in voir dire to get jurors thinking your way.

19

THERE IS MUCH MORE TO AN OPENING STATEMENT OR ARGUMENT THAN THE CONTENT OF THE PRESENTATION

Ascertain How Much Time the Court Has Allotted for Opening Statement or Argument

For opening statements and final arguments at trials, the determination of how much time will be allowed should be raised at the final pretrial conference, if not established before. For an argument on a motion or other hearing, ask court staff sufficiently in advance of the argument or hearing so that the staff can ask the judge about any time limits, if not already established.

If submitting a motion requesting oral argument, tender a proposed order granting the motion and include empty spaces for the court to include the date, time of day, and amount of time for the argument.

If a party is permitted to open and close an argument, inquire how the time may be divided if division of time is desired. For example, if thirty minutes are allowed, can plaintiff or the moving party initially take ten minutes and reserve twenty minutes for rebuttal?

If the Court Has Allotted a Specific Number of Minutes for Opening Statement or Argument, Inquire if the Court Will Provide Intermittent Time Indicators if Desired

An indication of elapsed time may be helpful in the following situations:

- For an argument by a plaintiff or a moving party, when reservation of some time to respond to the opposing party's argument is desired.
- When a certain number of minutes of your allotted time is left so that you can properly conclude.
- When sharing an opening statement or argument with co-counsel or a co-party.

If the court will not provide notice of elapsed time, then create your own unobtrusive system of timekeeping, such as placing a watch on the lectern or having somebody at counsel table provide notice at appropriate intervals. In one case, defense counsel brought a timer that beeped when it was set and when the time expired. This was tacky. In another action, during which co-counsel periodically orally advised arguing counsel of the time remaining, most people in the courtroom looked around to see who was interrupting the argument.

When There Is an Allotted Time, Abide by the Limitations; Do Not Risk Having the Judge Terminate Your Statement or Argument

It is not only embarrassing if the judge terminates your statement or argument but it could also be devastating if you have not properly concluded or even failed to make your strongest points.

Even though the court allows a set time for opening statements or arguments, you have no obligation to take the allotted time. A short presentation may be all that is required. In one criminal case, defense counsel argued for only eight minutes and convinced the jury to render a verdict for the defendant. This was the only criminal jury case in which I was involved that resulted in a total acquittal.

Jurors have stated that they resent long closing arguments. In one action in which ninety minutes were allowed for final argument, defense counsel was doing well and seemed to have concluded. Counsel then turned to the judge and asked how many minutes remained. The judge said seventeen minutes. Counsel proceeded to argue additional matters for seventeen more minutes. The jury did not appreciate this. The jurors later said that the lawyer just wanted to talk for seventeen more minutes and not really tell the jury anything important. Important matters should have been presented during the first seventy-three minutes.

Do not continually promise that you will conclude in a few minutes and then keep speaking. Likewise, do not say that although the court has allowed thirty minutes for argument, you will not take that long and then proceed to take all the allotted time anyway.

The Most Effective Opening Statements and Arguments Are Those Using Few or No Notes

Opening statements during which both counsel elected not to use notes, nor stand at the lectern, preferring instead to stand in front of the jury box, were the most effective opening statements in any trial I have observed.

The most ineffective opening statements and arguments are those that are read. At most, only notes should be used. I have listened to some well-organized and grammatically correct arguments that were read word for word. Examples of poor argument style are the following:

- A lawyer who not only had her argument written out but also kept her place on each sheet of paper with her finger, read a few words, and looked at the jury to speak the words, returned to the paper where her finger was to find her place, and then repeated the process. When she finished one sheet of paper, she stopped, removed the top sheet, and placed it on the lower shelf of the lectern.
- A lawyer who had his argument entered on a laptop computer, placed the computer on the lectern, and then read the argument.
- A lawyer who copied the principal summary judgment brief and reply brief, and did nothing more than read arguments contained in briefs.
- A lawyer who typed her opening statement and placed it in a notebook. She put the notebook on the lectern and referred to the typed statement periodically during the argument. She appeared to be familiar with what was contained in the typed statement and used the typed pages only as a prompt for the next portion of her argument. She looked like an orchestra director who directs for a while and then turns about two or three pages to catch up to where the orchestra is at that moment.

Some of the reasons why reading an opening statement or argument is ineffective are the following:

- Reading generally results in speaking too fast.
- Reading generally results in a more monotone presentation with less inflection or emotion.
- Reading appears too legalistic; it appears that you are not sincere, as though you are being paid to do a job and do not really believe in what you are saying.
- Reading results in less eye contact with the jury.

One of the risks of reading an opening statement or argument is that when counsel loses the place in the written material, a delay occurs while counsel attempts to find the proper place in the written material.

One juror opined that reading a closing argument indicated that counsel had no passion or sincere interest in the case; the lawyer should have prepared his closing argument before the start of the trial.

Be Certain that the Facts, Theory of the Action, and Legal Arguments Are Accurate

It could be embarrassing and lead to a loss of credibility with the jury if:

- You misstate the facts and this is pointed out to the jury by the opposing party in a responsive argument.
- You misstate the facts, there is an objection by the opposing party, the court sustains the objection, and the court reprimands you in front of the jury.
- You misstate the facts and the court, without waiting for an objection, interrupts, directs the jury to disregard your comments, and tells the jury what the evidence was.
- You misstate the law and the other side objects, the court sustains the objection, and the court correctly instructs the jury on the applicable law.
- You misstate the law and the court, without waiting for an objection, interrupts your argument to state that you have misstated the law and then instructs the jury as to the proper legal standard.

Examples of these principles follow.

- In a breach of contract action, one issue involved the financial statements of an insurance company. Plaintiff's position was that the financial statements were guarantees. Defendant's position was that they were projections (estimates only). In opening statement, plaintiff's counsel said that the financial statements were guarantees. Defendant objected. The court sustained the objection and specifically told the jury that the financial statements were projections only and chastised counsel.

- In opening statement, plaintiff's counsel said that due to flaws in the jury system, there was no way plaintiff could be made whole. Without objection by the defendant, the court interrupted and instructed the jury that if the jury followed the instructions and sufficient evidence was introduced, plaintiff could be made whole.
- One counsel referred to pounds of marijuana. The court interrupted, without waiting for an objection, to state that the proper measure under the statutes and instructions was kilograms, not pounds.
- Plaintiff sued for a violation of his constitutional right under the Fourth Amendment to be free from excessive force from a governmental officer. At the outset of the argument, plaintiff's counsel argued that plaintiff had a constitutional right to free speech (arguably, it was plaintiff's mouthy comments that led to the confrontations). Defendant objected. The court sustained the objection, stating that the only constitutional claim in the case was the Fourth Amendment; no free speech was involved.
- In an excessive force case, plaintiff argued that the defendants improperly arrested plaintiff. Defendants objected, stating that the court instructed the jury that defendants had a legal right to arrest plaintiff; therefore, plaintiff was trying to argue that the defendants improperly arrested plaintiff. The court sustained the objection and told the jury that the court had previously instructed the jury that defendants had a legal right to arrest plaintiff.
- Counsel argued that there was certain evidence on damages when there was not. Following objection, the court told the jury that there was no such evidence as stated by counsel.

If arguing facts, do not rely on only part of the evidence. One counsel, arguing that the only reason given to plaintiff for his termination was excessive absenteeism, read from a part of a document. Defendant subsequently displayed the entire document on the monitors to show other reasons that were provided to plaintiff as reasons for his termination.

Know which exhibits are in evidence before making a closing argument. Referring to an exhibit not introduced into evidence most likely will be met by an objection from opposing counsel and, possibly, a rebuke from the court. There is no reason for this to happen.

Division of Argument Is Not Recommended

Often in jury trials, a team of lawyers divide either an opening statement or closing argument. It is not recommended that this be done. When two lawyers share an opening statement or a closing argument, it appears disorganized and suggests that the lawyers just want to talk. If it is necessary for client demands or for other purposes to share an argument, the better way to accomplish this is in closing argument for a plaintiff, during which one lawyer can do the first part and a second lawyer can respond to defendant's argument.

Another acceptable use of two or more lawyers arguing is when a court schedules oral argument on multiple motions and lawyers divide the argument based on the motions to be addressed. The downside to this procedure is when the court asks a question of lawyer Johnson, and lawyer Johnson states that lawyer Samuel, who will be arguing other motions, is the one to respond to that question. It is frustrating for the court to ask a question and be told that the question will have to be answered by another lawyer. After all, the court has to prepare for all arguments, so counsel should also be prepared.

A third acceptable use of multiple lawyers arguing is when there are multiple parties and the court allots a certain number of minutes per side. If essential for each multiple party to present argument, division of the time is acceptable. Clear any proposed division first with the judge or court staff.

Use of a non-active lawyer to present opening statement and final argument is another option. In one high-stakes patent infringement trial, plaintiff utilized one lawyer whose only responsibility during the trial was to make the opening statement and closing argument. He examined no witnesses and made no other comments during the trial. He was present at all proceedings, taking notes and reflecting. His presentations were very well done.

Do Not Make Condescending Remarks to the Jury or to the Court

Do not spend time thanking jurors, either during voir dire, opening statement, or closing argument. Some jurors believe that this is too condescending. After all, the jurors have no choice but to be in court and accept this. If anyone should thank the jurors, that person should be the judge.

In one action, counsel thanked the court and jury on behalf of:

> All the employees of Ajax Corporation, a Fortune 500 company.
>
> All the lawyers and staff of a 400-lawyer firm from Chicago.
>
> All the lawyers and staff of local counsel's firm of 40 lawyers from Indianapolis.

For some reason, counsel forgot to thank all the people in their office building in Chicago, in Illinois, in Indianapolis, in Indiana and all humankind!

Do not say it is a great honor to represent a party.

Use common sense and respect when addressing a judge. Do not say to a judge, "to make it simple for you," and then explain that in the accounting field there are "debits" and "credits," and if a person had a mortgage of $500 and paid $300, there was still a debit of $200.

Avoid Making Inappropriate Comments and Relating Personal Experiences

In one closing argument, a lawyer not only presented an inappropriate argument but fabricated his argument. Borrowing a story from Western political lore, he said that formerly he assisted in a political campaign. The candidate for whom he was working addressed a group assembled in a cattle barn at an Indian reservation. The candidate said that if he were elected, he would increase unemployment benefits. The group shouted, "Hoday." Next, the candidate said that if elected, he would increase Social Security benefits. The group shouted, "Hoday." As the candidate was leaving the cattle barn, an attendee advised the candidate not to step into the cows' "hoday." As part of his closing argument, the lawyer said that the defense case was "just a bunch of hoday." Such references may be considered inappropriate by some or all members of the jury. (Also, inaccurately telling the jury about participating in a political campaign may cause some or all jurors to disbelieve everything counsel said.)

Some jurors have reported that it is inappropriate for counsel to incorporate instances from their personal lives into arguments. These jurors have commented negatively on stories of marriage proposals, a son serving in the Marines, and other activities of children.

Do Not Refer to Pretrial Rulings or Non-Rulings by the Court

One defense counsel argued that there was no evidence that would allow the jury to determine that plaintiff was disabled. In response, plaintiff's counsel said that he could tell the jury there is no way the judge would have allowed the matter to get this far if that were true. The argument was met by an objection, the objection was sustained, and the jury was told to disregard the statement by plaintiff's counsel.

Look at Your Audience When Speaking

Keep eye contact, but do not stare. In one action, counsel stood at the lectern, which was in front of the bench, but turned ninety degrees to look out the window while continuing to argue. Counsel later said that he was thinking during the argument. Not looking at the judge, witness, or jury but instead looking elsewhere may create an impression that you are looking for confirmation from co-counsel, the client, or party representative.

Try to Be Certain that Your Objection Will Be Sustained Before Making the Objection

It is dangerous to make objections during opening statements and closing arguments. If you are correct, the objection is sustained, and the court admonishes counsel and instructs the jury to disregard the objected material, this will be a benefit; but if you are wrong, you will be considered as interrupting and rude. Two examples illustrate this point. In closing argument, counsel objected to opposing counsel's misstating the evidence. The court overruled the objection, saying that the jury had heard the evidence. In the second case, defense counsel objected to a portion of plaintiff's opening statement, claiming it was inadmissible hearsay. The court refused to strike the comment, stating that this was opening statement and this evidence may or may not be admissible during the trial.

Additional Thoughts about Opening Statements

An opening statement should be a statement of what counsel expects the evidence to be. You do not want an objection followed by an adverse ruling, or even to have the court interrupt to say that the statement is argument, personal opinion, or the responsibility of the court to instruct as to the law.

Although the purpose of an opening statement is to preview what the evidence will be, continued references by counsel to, "what the evidence will show" seem too formal and may be a "turn off" for the jury. After all, the whole purpose of an opening statement is to state what the evidence will be. The jury probably will have been so instructed by the judge.

Give an overview. Don't tell every little detail. Devise a theme and go with it. Consider a defendant in a wrongful discharge case, for example, stating only that plaintiff never complained about the treatment plaintiff received on each prior suspension instead of detailing all of the events leading to each suspension. The jury will never remember all these details. Tell them what will occur like a puzzle and let the jurors help solve the puzzle.

Do not make promises for which you cannot deliver. In a trademark action, plaintiff's counsel told the jury that defendant's former president selected, as a company name, the same name as the plaintiff company in order to capitalize on the widespread recognition of plaintiff's name. In response, defendant's counsel stated that this was not correct and that this former president of defendant company "will be here to testify and he will tell you exactly how he picked the name." The former president who was beyond the subpoena power of the court failed to appear at the trial. Plaintiff's counsel began his closing argument by reading from the opening statement of defendant's counsel, emphasizing the promise by defense counsel that the former president would testify. Plaintiff's counsel then argued that plaintiff's position on selection of the name was not rebutted and defendant's other evidence was a futile attempt to compensate for the missing evidence that had been promised. This case resulted in a large jury verdict for plaintiff.

If there is a possibility certain testimony or exhibits may not be admissible, do not take a chance of mentioning these matters in an opening statement. If you do mention this evidence and it is not admitted, you will be certain to hear about it during your opponent's closing argument.

If you are confident that damaging evidence will be admitted during the trial, tell the jury, unless it was earlier disclosed in voir dire. Bring out bad facts, especially if you represent a plaintiff, rather than wait until defendant raises these matters. In an emotional distress case, for example, plaintiff's counsel should alert the jury to any psychological problems plaintiff experienced prior to the events forming the basis for the current lawsuit. If a witness or a party has a prior conviction that could be used to impeach, jurors should be made aware. Also, mention such facts as a party having had seven prior marriages, or a party's involvement in a previous lawsuit.

Think twice about mentioning damages in opening statement. In fact, consider whether as plaintiff, a damages number should ever be mentioned. If the action involves a contract, describing the terms of the contract is not a problem. It is fine to state that plaintiff agreed to buy a certain number of items at a certain price, but that defendant breached the contract. Or, it is fine to state that plaintiff was employed at a salary of $2,000 a month but was fired from that position.

Do not mention a total number for damages. Save this information for the closing argument. First of all, realize that the damages number suggested in opening statement may not be supported by the evidence. In one action, during opening statement, counsel said that plaintiff's damages were $50,000. The evidence supported $30,000 at most. In closing argument, counsel argued that damages were $20,000. Counsel lost credibility with the jury. Second, the evidence that is or is not introduced in evidence may support an even larger verdict than what might have been suggested in opening statement. Third, asking for a definite amount of damages in opening statement emphasizes money too much rather than focusing on the merits of the action.

During voir dire in a Fair Debt Collection Practices Act action involving a $350 check, one prospective juror expressed disbelief about having all the prospective jurors summoned for a trial over $350. Then, during opening statement, plaintiff's counsel spent most of the time explaining how much money plaintiff was seeking, including the supposed twelve hours of wages plaintiff lost and mileage from traveling to court and seeing lawyers, and then tripled this amount. Counsel stated that all these damages authorized the jury to award more than $6,000 in damages. Stressing money so much more than the facts in opening statement suggested that the lawyer and client were greedy, which offended the jurors. This was a defense verdict.

If there is a possibility of punitive damages, it is not a good idea to mention these in opening statement. Discussion of the facts that would provide a basis for such an award should be sufficient. Wait until admissible evidence is presented to justify the award before mentioning punitive damages. Credibility will be lost if punitive damages are requested but no evidence to support them is introduced.

As a defendant, there is little value in mentioning damages other than to say that you will ask the jury to render a verdict in defendant's favor. Even if it is a case in which liability is conceded, the most that should be said is that the evidence will show that plaintiff is not entitled to the damages requested. Do not say that plaintiff is requesting $100,000, but the evidence will support only $40,000 in damages.

There are exceptions, of course. In opening statement in an FLSA case, defendant stated that plaintiffs were not entitled to any overtime compensation because they were exempt employees. If, however, the jury determined that plaintiffs were not exempt, the defendant would introduce evidence to document the proper amount of overtime hours at issue in the action.

Visual aids have a place in opening statements. Although the purpose of an opening statement is to apprise the jury of what the evidence will be, some lawyers show the actual evidence to the jurors, such as an e-mail or critical language from a contract. In a covenant-not-to-compete action, showing the jury the document containing the restrictions would alert the jury to the main issue. If there is a dispute as to whether plaintiff is a named insured under an insurance policy, counsel may elect to show to the jury the policy definition of a named insured. This can be done by mounting an enlargement of the page from the contract or insurance policy on a poster board, perhaps even with the critical language in bold type or highlighted. If VEPS is available, the page can be displayed on the monitors and, with the appropriate software, the critical language enlarged or highlighted.

In an FMLA retaliation claim action, counsel's opening statement mentioned the start and stop dates of each FMLA leave. As counsel mentioned each date, she marked it on a big calendar that was on an easel to show that the plaintiff was away from work more than she was there. When dates are important, some counsel construct a timeline on an easel while making an opening statement.

Some counsel use PowerPoint to show highlights or a summary of their opening statement. Arguably, what ever could be stated should be allowed to be displayed on VEPS. However, it is a good idea to confirm this with the court in advance of the trial.

An opening statement may be used to alert the jury to deposition testimony that counsel knows will be read or shown to the jury during the trial. The transcript could be read to the jury or possibly even displayed on the monitors; or, parts of a video deposition that would be displayed at the trial could be shown, including the use of scrolling testimony and highlighting of important testimony. In an action involving the sale of a company, plaintiff played a video of a shareholder meeting at which the CEO of the defendant company promoted the sale. In another action, plaintiff's counsel displayed parts of a video deposition of defendant's CEO in which the CEO outlined the terms of a contract to be offered to plaintiff.

Pictures can also be effective, such as of the following:

- A car that had burned while an unconscious plaintiff was locked inside.
- A plaintiff's appearance right after sustaining the injuries that are the subject of the action.
- The hole in the surface of a parking lot into which plaintiff fell.
- A $1.5 million house purchased for cash by a defendant charged with not paying taxes.

Exhibits and visual aids can also be used to educate the jury. In a securities action in which counsel believed that few jurors had ever seen a securities offering circular, counsel placed a sample of an offering circular on the monitors, rapidly displayed all the pages, and then read a portion of one key page. In an action involving satellite TV, the plaintiff prepared a diagram depicting digital signals from the point of origination to the customer's house and displayed this on a poster board. It could just have easily been displayed on the VEPS. In an action involving the alleged illegal switching of telephone calls, defense counsel used a poster board to explain more easily how the telephone system worked. This method was better than trying to explain by words alone. Again, VEPS could have been used.

In a patent case in which there usually are more detailed preliminary instructions, counsel was very effective by referring in opening statement to these instructions, displaying them on the monitors and alerting the jury about the evidence as it would relate to those instructions.

Disclose to opposing counsel exhibits intended to be used in opening statement in case there may be an objection to their use.

If you intend to use, during opening statement, an exhibit to which admissibility has not been stipulated, raise the matter in advance with the court and opposing counsel. Likewise, check with court staff to ascertain a particular judge's rule for the use of demonstrative exhibits or visual aids; that is, inquire whether the court requires disclosure to the other parties, or if they can be used at your peril without advanced disclosure. Nevertheless, provide to other counsel a copy of any demonstrative exhibits you plan to use. If you do not, there is always a risk that the court will not allow these exhibits, which could be devastating if you try to show the exhibits to the jury only to find that the court will not allow their use.

Additional Thoughts about Closing Arguments

If a plaintiff intends to suggest a damages number to the jury, the only way a defendant can respond is if that number is mentioned in the opening segment of plaintiff's closing argument. Do what you can to require that any damages number plaintiff chooses to suggest be disclosed in the opening segment of the closing argument.

The use of visual aids is also very helpful in closing argument. Some lawyers, either because of having arranged for daily copy of transcript or otherwise having ordered certain testimony, display key testimony either by either use of a poster board or VEPS. Counsel will also enlarge, underline, or highlight certain sentences, phrases, or words. Likewise, if depositions were used during the trial, counsel have been known to display the text of depositions read, or even play excerpts of video depositions shown, during the trial. Likewise, if there are two different versions of testimony, either from the same witness or different witnesses, either from deposition testimony used at trial or trial testimony, consider placing them on the monitors side by side. Having the actual testimony gives it more credibility to the jury. This will not work for big segments of testimony; use this approach only for critical short testimony.

Frequently, lawyers display portions of key exhibits, either enlarged in size on a poster board or through the use of VEPS, possibly enlarging, underlining, or highlighting. This is more effective, even if the jurors have individual copies of the exhibits, than just referring to the exhibits. When defendant argued that she never received a certain package, plaintiff's display of the delivery receipt with her signature on it emphasized the unreliability of defendant's testimony. If you intend to use the VEPS to display exhibits or testimony, be prepared to show the exhibits or testimony instead of fumbling at the appropriate time and being disorganized. Jurors comment on the lack of preparation. Because some jurors take notes, be sure to refer to an exhibit number of the document being displayed.

If the court reads the instructions prior to closing argument, some lawyers display key instructions on the monitors to emphasize certain words, even underlining or highlighting them. Displaying the instructions on the monitors and going through certain critical instructions can help the jury conclude that you have established, or that the opposing party failed to establish, what the court's instructions stated had to be proved. Some counsel will display the verdict form to the jury and then write in or check mark what the lawyer thinks the jury should do. If you review the verdict form with the jury, this may assist the jury.

Counsel can use VEPS either with the document camera or a PowerPoint presentation to summarize their argument. Again, what could be stated should be allowed to be displayed on VEPS. One defense counsel argued that there were five reasons why plaintiff should not recover; these five reasons were then displayed on the monitors. Counsel argued with respect to each reason, leaving the five reasons displayed on the monitors during the argument. Another PowerPoint presentation consisted of major portions of the argument followed by quotations from trial testimony and exhibits. As these items were shown on the monitors, counsel read them to the jury. In one criminal action, government counsel placed the bulk of his presentation on a computer, using almost complete sentences. As counsel started each new point, he pressed a button on the remote control for that point to be shown on the monitors as he argued that point. The jury was very impressed with this. Keep in mind, though, this style could result in rapid changes of displayed material and become confusing. With this style, you must be careful not to speed up. Also, counsel still needs to emote and not just speak in a monotone voice.

While some lawyers who use a computer to display their arguments use a handheld remote that allows counsel to switch screens as the argument progresses, other counsel prefer to use another attorney, paralegal or technician who has an outline of the argument to switch between screens. As counsel turns to a certain argument or document, this other person displays it on the monitors. This does take practice and coordination to make sure that the correct item is displayed at the correct time.

If VEPS is used, the jury may focus more on the monitors than on counsel. This could be good or bad.

If your opponent displays something on the VEPS or easel, remove it before you argue. In one criminal action, the government put a gun under the document camera. Defense counsel failed to remove the gun during defense's argument, so the jury viewed the gun during all the closing arguments. In one action involving an allegation that concentrations of lead at the premises were too high, plaintiff, in closing argument, put a chart under the document camera showing the high levels of lead. When defense argued, defense left the chart under the document camera. This was a mistake. If faced with such a situation, remove the document from the monitors as soon as possible if the document is unfavorable, but avoid acting overly concerned about the item being displayed.

Think Twice Before Using Technology for Bench Trials and Arguments to the Court

Frequently, lawyers ask whether the VEPS is available for oral argument to the court, in a bench trial or other court proceedings, such as a Markman hearing. Although the VEPS system certainly can be used for such matters, you should first find out whether the judge really wants technology. Some judges may insist on it or prefer it, but if the particular judge does not insist or prefer its use, think twice before using technology. Some lawyers are enamored by technology and by PowerPoint in particular. These lawyers will prepare their entire arguments, summary of their arguments, or excerpts from testimony or documents and then display these using the court's VEPS. Trial lawyers know their facts and documents well. Often, they believe that one or more documents are very critical and perhaps determinative of the action. The problem is that as familiar as counsel is with the documents, the court is just as unfamiliar. If lawyers plan to display documents only on the VEPS, they may not be effectively presenting the argument to the judge.

A judge has many cases. To expect a judge to remember why a certain document is critical by a one-time display on VEPS is unrealistic. Of course, a judge will be taking notes, but with a one-time showing of a document on VEPS, the judge will have to record the exhibit number, description of the document, summary of the document, or critical part of the document, and then write why it is or is not important. It is better to provide the judge with a copy of all exhibits to be used during the proceeding before the proceeding starts. This way, the judge can highlight or write notes directly on the documents as they are being utilized in the proceeding. This is much easier than having to find later the appropriate document and compare the judge's notes to the documents.

If you intend to use documents, be prepared. One counsel intended to provide the court with actual documents instead of only placing them on the document camera. Just before the argument, counsel was sorting documents that would be used and then gave a stack of documents to the judge. These documents had no numbers on them and were not in the order in which they were going to be used. Confusion arose when counsel referred to a document. Counsel could not find it, and it took the judge a while to find it as well. This situation resulted in a loss of presentation time, plus it demonstrated disorganization and a lack of professionalism. Here are the recommended choices: Hand the documents to the judge at the time you refer to them; or provide them all to the judge at the start of the proceeding; place exhibit numbers on the documents; or arrange the documents in the order in which you will use them.

If you have a typed summary or PowerPoint presentation for an argument, provide it to the judge in advance rather than use the VEPS to display it during the argument so that the judge can mark on portions of the written material that the judge believes are important and can make any appropriate notes during the argument. Above all, do not wait until after the argument to give it to the judge. One lawyer who was an advocate of PowerPoint presentations used to provide a copy to the judge only at the conclusion of the argument. When I suggested that he provide a copy at the beginning of the argument, he said that he never thought of doing that but he was going to start using that procedure. Of course, you also will need to provide a copy to opposing counsel prior to the start of the argument.

Using VEPS in addition to hard copies may, however, be of value for certain purposes. Even if you have provided a copy of the exhibits or your written presentation to the court prior to the start of the trial or argument, you may still want to utilize VEPS if you want to underline, place arrows, highlight, or draw on a particular page. In one action, counsel deposed each of the four plaintiffs. For each major point of the argument, defense counsel used VEPS to display the title of each section of the argument, followed by excerpts from the video deposition of each plaintiff discussing that section of the argument. This was more effective than merely reading those portions of the deposition.

Miscellaneous Comments

During argument, some lawyers frequently address the court as, "Your Honor." Although this is polite and acceptable, a steady use of this is strikingly noticeable and annoying.

Do not comment on what you may perceive to be a reaction by the judge to your argument by saying such things as, "I see you smiling" or, "You look troubled."

Lack of preparation for oral argument can impact your message. Consider the following situation: Defendant filed a motion in limine seeking to limit testimony of plaintiff's expert. The court scheduled a hearing. At the hearing, counsel was asked by the court about what the expert said at the deposition on a certain matter. Counsel could not respond because he did not bring the transcript to the hearing.

20

SUGGESTIONS FOR THE CARE AND PRESENTATION OF WITNESSES

There have been many treatises written and seminars devoted to the issue of preparing witnesses for deposition and for trial, as well as how witnesses should conduct themselves in the courtroom. One chapter in this book cannot possibly discuss all of these caveats and suggestions. Instead, the suggestions in this chapter are limited to the issues that I believe are the most practical based on what I have observed and comments received from jurors.

The Most Important Advice to a Witness Is to Tell the Truth

All witnesses should follow the adage of Samuel Clemens, "When you tell the truth, you don't have to remember anything." Second, witnesses should not try to evade damaging testimony on ultra-technical grounds. In one action, a witness who worked for Atlas Engineering testified against Butler Architects. On cross-examination, the witness denied seeking and being rejected for employment at Butler. Counsel for Butler then produced the witness's résumé from Butler's files. The witness's explanation was that he did not apply for the job at Butler. He said he gave the résumé to a third-party, who then delivered the résumé to Butler Architects. This witness lost credibility.

Likewise, at a deposition a witness testified he **never** requested to return to the hourly work force. At trial, the witness testified he did request to return to the hourly work force. After being impeached with his deposition testimony, the witness "explained" his answer at deposition by stating he thought the deposition question meant written requests only and since he made oral requests only and not written requests, there was no inconsistency.

To Avoid Impeachment, Witnesses Must Be Instructed to Review and Study All Prior Statements, Including Depositions, Written Statements, and Any Trial Testimony

A witness whose testimony is inconsistent with a prior statement is not as credible as a witness who is consistent. A witness who at deposition said that she complained of sexual harassment to one supervisor, but then at trial testified that she complained to six supervisors was not believable.

Questions of credibility are also raised at trial when witnesses have no recollection of prior statements or of documents about which the witnesses were previously questioned. In a false arrest case, a defendant was asked at his deposition to draw a line, and did draw a line, on a picture to signify the location and length of a scratch that was the alleged cause of the arrest. At trial, defendant said he did not remember placing the mark on the picture, even when shown the deposition transcript. There was no excuse for a witness not to remember what was done or said at the witness's deposition. The deposition transcript must be studied, studied, and studied again.

In this regard, some lawyers advise witnesses to do no review of documents or of facts or to do any other preparation until after a deposition; then, if asked about certain matters at a deposition, the witnesses are to say they do not remember. They then are advised to prepare for trial. If asked at trial why they can remember at the trial but could not remember at the deposition, they are to say that they did the research and review after the deposition. This is risky and can lead to a loss of credibility. On the other hand, if a witness is properly prepared for deposition and trial, there should be no impeachment at trial, and the answers provided at deposition may assist in the granting or defeating of a motion for summary judgment, or lead the opposing party to consider settlement.

In one excessive force case, the police officers were not prepared for their depositions and so were not able to testify about the details of the arrest. Just before trial, the officers went to the scene of the arrest, and took meticulous measurements and numerous pictures. At trial, the officers gave detailed testimony of the incident incorporating the measurements and pictures into their testimony during the trial. The discrepancy in testimony between their depositions and trial made the officers vulnerable to impeachment and a loss of credibility. Moreover, had the deposition testimony been as thorough as the trial testimony, it is possible that a favorable settlement, or even the granting of a motion for summary judgment, might have resulted, thereby avoiding a trial.

Meet With Your Witnesses Before Trial to Advise Them What You Will Be Asking Them and for You to Learn How They Will Answer the Questions You Propose to Ask

This is especially applicable for your first witness. In a drug case, the government's first witness was an undercover officer who was asked on direct, but could not answer, the following questions:

> "How much heroin did you buy?"
> "How much did you pay for the heroin?"
> "To whom did you give the heroin after you bought it?"

If counsel had properly prepared the witness, this never would have happened.

Consider the impact on the jury of the following answers by plaintiff to questions asked by plaintiff's own counsel in a wrongful termination case:

> "Q. How much did the former employer contribute for dental insurance?
> A. I don't know.
> Q. How much did the former employer contribute to a retirement plan?
> A. I don't know.
> Q. How much did you earn in your new job?
> A. I don't know.
> Q. What was your cost for medical expenses in the new job?
> A. I don't know."

In a real estate action, a key witness was asked to describe the physical conditions of the property. The witness could not answer the questions. If counsel was going to ask these questions, counsel should have made certain that the witness knew what questions would be asked so that the witness would have been prepared to answer them.

In an action involving an alleged deceptive offering circular, plaintiff's counsel presented three investor witnesses, ostensibly to establish that these investors purchased the bonds based on the circulars. All three investors stated that they had never seen the circular. This weakened plaintiff's theory.

One special problem that deserves appropriate care is preparing witnesses to identify defendants or other parties during a trial. In two separate criminal cases involving African-American defendants, the Assistant United States Attorneys and their witnesses were embarrassed when the witnesses were asked to identify the defendants. On both occasions, the witnesses pointed to a member of the court's staff. Witnesses must be properly prepared to identify witnesses; they must not be advised or allowed to assume that the party or witness to be identified is of a particular race. Improper identification under these circumstances could be devastating.

Advise Witnesses to Admit Meeting with You or a Colleague, Even If Just for an Interview, Prior to Testifying at a Deposition or at Trial

It is appropriate to interview witnesses, other than opposing parties. Many jurors are aware of this practice. Yet, some witnesses believe it is improper; however, by denying a conversation with counsel, there is potentially a loss of credibility.

Explain How to Use Exhibit Notebooks

Explain to your witnesses how the notebooks are arranged, if notebooks are used, especially if multiple books are used, so that the witnesses can quickly find an appropriate exhibit when asked to review it.

Advise Witnesses or Parties That They May Be Called to Testify by the Opposing Party

Any party that you represent, that party's representative at counsel table, any employee or agent of that party, or any witness for that party present in the courtroom may be called to testify as a witness by the opposing party. Unless you so advise your client, client representatives, employees and witnesses, they may be unprepared and appear nervous if called to testify by the opposing party. To be prepared for such a scenario, review with your client, its representatives, employees, or witnesses their proposed testimony and knowledge of the case before the trial starts rather than expect to do so sometime during the trial.

If you decide to call the opposing party or one of its representatives as your first witness, the testimony should be extremely effective. It is not impressive if you plan to establish certain points with such a witness and fail to do so.

Advise Witnesses on Proper Positioning in the Witness Chair

- Sit erect; do not lean back in the chair.
- Do not sit sideways.
- Do not spin around on the chair.
- Do not put your arm around the back of the chair.
- Do not lean forward to rest your chin on your hands.

- Do not bring your own bottle of water or other bottled drink to the witness stand; a cup of water is fine.
- Look at the questioning lawyer when the question is asked and then turn to look at the jury or judge, in a bench trial, when answering questions.
- Do not look down at the floor or into your lap when answering a question. When a witness did this, jurors said they would never believe someone who looked down at the floor and refused to make eye contact with the jurors.

Advise Witnesses to Be Careful What They Do or Say Outside the Courtroom

Some witnesses do or say things in the hallways or restrooms that are seen or overheard by jurors, an opposing party, or opposing counsel. A plaintiff testified at trial that she had no way to call for help at the time of her injury because she had no cell phone. Yet, plaintiff was seen walking around the hallway of the courthouse with a cell phone during the trial. Of course, plaintiff could have obtained a cell phone after her injury, but this conduct suggested inconsistency with her trial testimony.

This admonition applies to counsel as well. When prospective jurors were asked during voir dire if they had read or heard anything about the action to be tried, one woman said that she had heard plaintiff's lawyers, who sat at a restaurant table next to her table at dinner the prior evening, discussing the action.

When a Party Is a Corporation or Governmental Agency Avoid Allowing Witnesses to Refer to "My," "Mine," and "I," or Even "We"

Not using the above pronouns will keep corporations and governmental agencies separate from individuals. It is confusing for these ambiguities to be in the record, plus the jury may be left with an unanswered question as to who is to pay or who is entitled to damages. In an action involving a suspension of an employee, the Human Resources Manager, who testified that he did not make the decision to suspend the plaintiff, later stated, "*We* suspended plaintiff." (emphasis added). Plaintiff's counsel then asked why the witness earlier said that he did not participate in the decision to suspend. The witness then said that by "we," he meant, "the company." Without the clarification, there was the potential for a suggestion of inconsistent testimony.

Do Not Let Witnesses Direct Counsel What to Do

Jurors resent witnesses who try to control the litigation by directing counsel, for example, to take such action as to re-position documents on the VEPS or find certain exhibits.

Use of Notes By a Witness Should Be Limited

See also Chapter 9.

Unless the testimony of a witness is very detailed as, for example, references to many dates and quantities, witnesses should not take notes or other documents with them to the witness stand. Use of notes suggests that the witness does not really remember what happened or maybe even that counsel prepared the notes for the witness. If a witness refers to notes during testimony, every lawyer has a right to inspect those notes during the examination. If you review the notes, you might learn something. Looking at the notes does not mean that you have to use them or introduce them into evidence. Just calling the jury's attention to the notes may cause the jury to believe that the opposing party's lawyer prepared the notes, or that the testimony is structured and scripted in advance. Wait until you finish questioning the witness before you ask for the notes in case the witness refers to the notes on more than just the one occasion.

Have Witnesses Spell Their Names

As a courtesy to the court reporter and court staff, ask witnesses to spell their names for the record. Doing so ensures accuracy in the record in the event of an appeal. Remember, it is possible to spell names in different ways. Carlson could also be Karlsen or Carlsen.

Initially, Ask Your Witnesses to Indicate the Nature of their Testimony

When a witness is called to testify, the jurors, and sometimes the judge, have no idea why the witness is being presented. An effective technique when presenting a witness on direct examination is to ask first, by way of leading question, the topic on which the witness will be testifying; for example: "Are you here to testify about the scene of the accident?" or, "Are you here to present expert testimony?" Then proceed with the necessary questions.

Inquire of Each Witness before Trial Whether There Will Be a Problem with an Oath

Some witnesses will not accept an oath that ends with, "so help you God." Find out in advance what oath or affirmation the court will require of your witnesses. If the court requires only, "Do you swear or affirm under the penalties of perjury?" there should be no problem. If the court typically uses only, "so help you God" and this will be of concern to a witness, alert the court staff or judge in advance to determine whether an affirmation could be used instead. This way, the process will look smooth and should not raise questions in front of the jury. In one action in which an oath was an issue, but not addressed by counsel beforehand, a witness brought a Bible (which, by the way, is strongly discouraged) and a letter from a minister and stated that she would not take an oath. The judge asked her if she would affirm under the penalties of perjury, which she did. Nevertheless, the witness made such an issue of her religion that it affected her credibility.

Have Witnesses Ready to Testify

- When the court says, "Call your next witness." be certain that this witness is available in the courthouse, not in counsel's office or at a hotel.
- If a witness was on the stand at a recess or adjournment, that witness should be on the witness stand ready to proceed when court is resumed.
- If the conclusion of a witness's testimony is followed by a recess or adjournment, the next witness should be ready to take the stand when the trial resumes.
- If a witness's testimony is expected to be brief, have the next witness immediately available.
- Do not run out of witnesses. If there is a substantial delay between witnesses, the court may deem that you have rested. It can difficult to have each witness ready when the prior witness has concluded because you may not know how long the opposing party will take for its case or how long cross-examination will be. Nevertheless, be prepared. My favorite example is an action in which counsel was so organized that as one witness stood up from the witness chair, the next witness entered the courtroom. In another action, the trial reconvened at 1:00 after lunch. The testimony of the first witness was completed at 1:10. When asked to call the next witness, counsel went to the witness

room and came back into the courtroom, stating that the witness was unavailable. When asked where the witness was, counsel said, "At Starbucks." One juror said, "Oh, my God." Jurors do not like to be kept waiting for parties, counsel, or witnesses. Jurors believe that their time is important, too. Going to a Starbucks was considered an insult by the jury.

- Keep court staff informed of potential witness problems in the event that they develop. For example, if your last witness is scheduled to arrive from out of town on Tuesday night for Wednesday testimony, alert court staff of this fact as soon as possible should the testimony of previous witnesses conclude sooner than Tuesday afternoon.
- If you represent a defendant, you must be ready to try your case when plaintiff rests. You must be flexible. A plaintiff may be asked, or will just estimate, how long plaintiff's case will take. This is an estimate only. It could be a poor estimate, or plaintiff may shorten its presentation, or the case just may proceed more swiftly than anticipated. As a defendant, you should not say that plaintiff had said three days for plaintiff's case and that you counted on three days, so you will have no one ready to testify until the fourth day. The jury would have to be sent home, thereby creating a very bad impression for your case. Have a contingency plan to be able to proceed when plaintiff rests. Clear with the court any problems in advance, such as that all your witnesses are coming from out of state and do not work for the party you represent. A plaintiff should have any witnesses ready to proceed on rebuttal as soon as defendant rests. If an opposing party expects to finish on a Friday, but may not, clear with the court in advance as to whether you can wait until Monday to bring witnesses to trial, especially out-of-state witnesses, instead of bringing them in for Friday and then finding that the opposing party does not finish its case.
- Not only should your witnesses be ready when needed but you must be prepared to examine the witnesses. In a preliminary injunction action expected to last two days, one day per side, plaintiff finished prior to the end of the first day. The court directed the responding party to proceed. The responding party had planned to use an easel with its first witness, but the responding party had only witnesses, no easel or pens, available. There had been no earlier request to court staff to supply these

materials. Court staff produced all items within five minutes. If court staff had not been prepared, time would have been wasted and completion of the hearing on the second day would have been jeopardized.

Ask If Witnesses Can Be Called Out of Order

Sometimes, due to other commitments, a witness may be able to testify only on a certain day, or a witness may be scheduled to leave on vacation or business trip on Thursday but scheduled to testify on Wednesday. Due to unavoidable reasons, an earlier witness is still testifying on Wednesday. Ask opposing counsel whether a current witness's testimony can be interrupted to allow another witness to testify, and then make the request to the court, starting with the court staff.

Ascertain whether the court will allow doctors or non-party professional witnesses to testify out of order. Frequently, this is necessary or desirable due to commitments of the professional or the charges being accumulated; it can be expensive to have an expert standing by for three days waiting to testify. Strategically, though, you may want to have a witness standing by so that you can present the witness at the precise time. You do not want to have a break in the trial if you run out of witnesses and are waiting for a witness to appear.

Another issue to consider about order of proof occurs when plaintiff calls in its case-in-chief a witness who resides in another state, but plaintiff covers only part of this witness's testimony. As a defendant, ask opposing counsel and then the court whether you can exceed the scope of the direct examination to complete this witness in one session. This procedure can save time because often when such a witness testifies in a plaintiff's case and then in defendant's case, or in defendant's case and then rebuttal, there is duplicate testimony. This option should be explored anytime a witness will be testifying in both the plaintiff's case and then the defendant's case. This typically is done in bench trials but can also be done in jury trials. For planning purposes, it may be prudent to explore this possibility at the final pretrial conference.

Eliminate Communication/Contact Between Witnesses and Parties

In an age discrimination action, the corporate representative was the regional manager. One witness for defendant was plaintiff's younger replacement. As the replacement employee testified during cross-examination, he kept looking at the corporate representative instead of the jury or the counsel who was asking the question. The jurors commented on this and believed that there was some sort of communication between the witness and the corporate representative, pursuant to which the corporate representative was advising the witness how to answer the question. Defendant lost this case.

In another action, as a female witness, favorable to plaintiff, left the witness chair, she walked by the plaintiff, who was a male; the witness touched the plaintiff on the shoulder. The jury saw this and believed there was some relationship between plaintiff and the witness and gave no credibility to the witness's testimony.

In another action, two witnesses, who were related to the plaintiff, testified and then stopped in front of other witnesses in the trial who were sitting in the gallery and exchanged hugs. The jurors watched this and commented about it negatively after the trial.

Have a List for Each Witness of Exhibits that You Propose to Introduce Through or Use with that Witness

Before you conclude your questioning of each witness, check your list to be certain that all listed exhibits for that witness were admitted or offered and rejected.

Guidance that Should Be Given to Witnesses about Responding to Questions

- Answer firmly and confidently, not hesitatingly. In one action in which the jury found for the defendants, jurors commented that the plaintiffs had "no passion" for their action; plaintiffs showed no emotion and acted as though they were not really interested.
- Respond verbally; a nod or shake of the head is insufficient. There is no better example of this lesson than:

  "Q. No evaluations for tenure, no evaluations for promotion?

  A. (The witness shakes head.)"

  (Note also, this "question" is not only a statement, it is a compound, negative statement.)
- Wait until counsel finishes asking a question before responding. At times, a witness knows, or believes to know, what the question is going to be and will start answering without waiting for the complete question. Two people talking simultaneously can result in an incomplete record. Also, the question ultimately

asked might not be the one the witness expected. Moreover, the question may be compound; and an early answer, interrupting the question, creates an ambiguity as to which part of the question was actually answered. Waiting until the question is completed allows for a timely objection. If the complete question is objectionable and the witness answers before the entire question is asked, the jury may hear an answer it may not otherwise have heard.

- Do not answer if opposing counsel is standing to make or is making an objection.
- Answer the question asked and only the question asked. Going beyond the question asked suggests the witness is trying too hard to win the case. Moreover, when a witness volunteers and goes beyond the question, opposing counsel may object and request that the testimony be stricken. In one instance, a witness was asked if he found the title to a trailer. Instead of answering, "No," the witness tried to describe all the steps he took to find the title. Opposing counsel objected, the objection was sustained, and the witness was instructed to answer only the question asked and not to respond with narratives.

  Another time, an expert testified that her experience was with certain kinds of patients. On cross-examination, she was asked how many of these certain kinds of patients she treated. She answered one per week but went into a long explanation of why there was only one. This explanation was stricken.

  When witnesses go beyond the question asked, it is distinctly possible that the judge will intervene even without objection and tell the witness to confine the answer to the question asked. What is even worse is when, after having been warned, the witness later continues to go beyond the questions asked, the judge asks the witness to stop, the witness continues, and then the judge uses the gavel to silence the witness and orally chastises the witness.

  Even without intervention by a judge, volunteering information can definitely create a total loss of credibility. In one trial, a plaintiff was asked where he lived. He said in Houston, Texas, and without being specifically asked gave the street address. He then added, again without a question being posed, that he also owned a house in Costa Rica; He then volunteered that there was no specific address for the house in Costa Rica. There was no reason to give a specific street address for the

Houston home. There was no reason for this witness to volunteer that he had a house in Costa Rica, and certainly no reason to state that there was no specific address for the Costa Rican property. Similarly, in another action, when asked for an address for his personal residence, the witness said, "Great Eagle Lane." The witness volunteered that because of the area, there was no need for specific numbers at Great Eagle Lane. The witness should not have explained why no numbers were needed in such an exclusive area. In another action, when asked to describe his prior work history, the witness said that he was "illegally" drafted by the Army. There was no reason to mention the Army in the first place, but by claiming that he was illegally drafted by the Army, the witness demonstrated an attitude problem. (Be prepared to intervene with a proper objection when a witness goes beyond the question asked and to move to strike if the volunteered testimony is harmful to your case. An objection alone is not sufficient to keep the testimony out of the record.)

- Do not argue with counsel.
- Answer unequivocally when the answer should be unequivocal. A witness who frequently hedges by saying, "I do not recall at this point in time." or, "Not that I remember at the moment." is not as believable as a witness who is straightforward with a, "Yes," or, "No" answer.

Too many witnesses are afraid to say, "Yes" or, "No." Some witnesses are so afraid of being impeached that they will answer almost every question with, "I don't recall." or, "Not to the best of my knowledge." apparently to leave some room in case there is evidence contradicting them. Saying, "I don't recall." weakens the answer if the answer should be an emphatic, "Yes" or, "No."

One witness was asked, "Did you tell plaintiff he was being discharged because he was too old?" The answer needed to be, "No" if that is, in fact, what happened. The response, "I don't recall," was probably regarded as, "Yes." If one witness says that something happened and another says, "I don't recall" there is no contradiction, the absence of which leads to the conclusion that it probably occurred.

A question asked of an FBI agent was, "Did you tell Mrs. Blake she could not leave?" The agent said, "I cannot recall." If the agent did not tell Mrs. Blake that she could not leave, the agent should have said, "No," as opposed to, "I cannot recall."

When Mrs. Blake testified that she was told she could not leave, the conflict was not between what was said versus what was not said. The conflict was between what was said versus, "I do not recall." This is a big difference.

A plaintiff testified about a conversation with defendant during which, according to plaintiff, defendant agreed to specific terms of a contract. When defendant was asked about the conversation, defendant said, "I do not recall." In ruling for plaintiff, the judge said that it was necessary to credit the testimony of plaintiff. In so ruling, the judge commented that the defendant did not directly contradict plaintiff's testimony of a contract. An answer of, "I don't recall." does not create a contradiction. If the answer should be, "Yes" or, "No," the witness should answer, "Yes" or, "No" in a confident, not reluctant, manner, even if the answer weakens the testimony.

During a deposition, a witness kept answering, "I don't recall," even when asked about his signature on a check. In later proceedings in front of a judge, deposing counsel pointed out that the witness said, "I don't recall," forty times, which was even more incredible considering that the witness could not even identify his own signature.

Discuss with your witnesses the difference between, "yes" and, "no" and, "I do not remember." If the witness truly cannot remember, the answer should be, "I do not remember." If the answer should be, "No," the answer should be, "No." If I were asked whether I had Cheerios for breakfast on February 1, 2007, I would say, "I do not recall." However, if I were asked whether I had steak for breakfast, I would say, "No," because I never have steak for breakfast. If there are a number of questions for which the witness's legitimate answer is, "I don't recall," you may want to provide some explanation. Consider a witness who was in charge of building a power plant and who probably had five meetings every week for five years. At a deposition, two years after the construction was concluded, the witness was asked to identify people attending certain meetings. "I do not recall," is probably the acceptable response; however, at some time, the witness should say something about the lapse of time and the number of meetings the witness attended, with as many as forty people attending each meeting. He also should say that there were minutes available to document who was present at each meeting.

- On cross-examination, a witness should not answer a leading question with a, "Yes, but. . . ." or, "No, but . . . ." A witness should not argue with counsel. Witnesses look evasive if they will not concede what they should concede. A witness who says, "Yes, but. . . ." seems too evasive. Witnesses who straightforwardly answer the questions without argument have more credibility with jurors. Jurors prefer witnesses who answer the questions asked. Jurors do not look favorably on witnesses who hedge or modify every question asked or who argue with counsel. More important, the witnesses will not be well received by the jurors if the judge intervenes and admonishes the witnesses to answer the question without additional comment.

  A witness was asked if he earned a certain sum. The witness said, "No," but then tried to explain why not. The judge interrupted and said, for the record, that the answer to the question was, "No."

  In another action, the following occurred on cross-examination:

  > "Q. Did you think the tariff was violated?
  > A. Yes, but not as much as you do.
  > Q. Did you think it was improper?
  > A. Yes, but not as much as you do."

  At this moment, the judge interrupted the witness and asked the witness to answer the questions and not argue with counsel.

  If the answer on cross-examination needs an explanation, it can be done on redirect examination.

- Avoid responding to questions in a repeatedly similar style such as an emphatic, "Absolutely" time and again. This looks too rehearsed and leads to a loss of credibility when so many items are "absolute."

  When more than one witness used the same words, especially on the same issue, for example, "I don't have enough fingers and toes to tell you how many times the company told us the factory was going to be closed." it certainly appeared that the witnesses were told to say this or were prepared as witnesses together. This quoted statement was used very effectively in closing argument by opposing counsel who used the same words in a different context and without even mentioning the testimony of five witnesses who said they didn't have enough fingers and toes.

In an action in which all six plaintiffs, who were seeking compensation for travel time, each testified that nothing was ever said to them about payment for travel and no plaintiff ever submitted a request for travel time, jurors thought the witnesses lied when each one said she "expected" to be paid.

- Be wary of the witness who frequently responds by saying, "To be honest with you. . . ." First, each witness takes an oath or affirms to tell the truth. Second, if the witness does not say, "to be honest with you," is the answer given not an honest one? As you prepare witnesses for deposition or trial, be sure to point out that the use of "to be honest with you" should be omitted.
- Have witnesses avoid using catch phrases such as "the buzz in the valley."

21

ALTHOUGH THE QUALIFICATIONS, OR LACK THEREOF, OF AN EXPERT ARE CRITICAL, THE CREDIBILITY OF AN EXPERT CAN ALSO BE AFFECTED BY TANGENTIAL MATTERS

Thorough Investigation of an Expert Should Be Conducted Before Hiring an Expert or Examining an Opponent's Expert, Either at Deposition or at Trial

First, determine whether the proposed expert possesses the qualifications to be an "expert" and, if so, if there is any reason why this person should not be an expert in your particular action. Inquire beyond education and work experiences. Browse the Internet, do research at a library, or contact counsel who hired or opposed this person in other cases. Obtain copies of articles and books written, speeches given, depositions given, and trial testimony from prior cases; learn about previous litigation assignments and obtain copies of any reports submitted. This information will assist in making a decision whether the person should be employed or will provide material for cross-examination for an opposing party's expert.

If the expert is employed by the other side, elicit as much of the background information as you can at a deposition to the extent that you were not previously able to obtain it.

If you are searching for an expert to employ, do a thorough interview before employing this person. Emphasize full disclosure before employment. Ask about books and articles written and speeches given. If the proposed expert has been employed in other actions, specifically ask about depositions given and trial testimony, as well as expert reports. Assume that the expert issued a report. Do not take a quick, "No" for an answer if he says he did not write a report. Keep pushing. The failure to discover the existence of a report can be a disaster, resulting in a total loss of credibility for this witness.

An expert witness for plaintiff in an Indiana patent case submitted an earlier written report in a Minnesota patent case, but failed to tell plaintiff's counsel in the Indiana case. At the trial in the Indiana case, the witness was asked if he had issued a written report in the Minnesota case. The witness denied submitting a written report. A lawyer from the Minnesota case, who was in the courtroom during the trial of the Indiana case to observe the expert, gave to the Indiana defense counsel the report written by the expert for the Minnesota case. Thus, the plaintiff had two big problems: The expert lied under oath in front of the jury, and his report in the Minnesota case was inconsistent with his testimony in the Indiana case. The judge set aside a plaintiff's verdict, in part because of the testimony of this expert, and defendant ultimately recovered costs in excess of $100,000.

In another action, an expert testified on direct examination that royalty payments should be ten to fifteen percent. When asked whether she had ever testified that royalty payments should be three to five percent, the witness said she did not remember. Then, counsel produced a copy of a speech delivered by the expert in which she had stated that three to five percent was the proper percentage. She said she had forgotten about her speech. Next, she was asked about another prior speech that was inconsistent with her trial testimony. Again, she said she could not remember. This witness had little credibility with the jury.

Plaintiff's counsel in both of these actions just mentioned failed to investigate properly. Defense counsel, in the second example, did properly investigate and was rewarded for his efforts.

Be certain that your witness is prepared to testify before you list the person as an expert. In one action, thirty days before trial, plaintiff's counsel advised of three newly discovered experts but provided no written reports or disclosure of the opinions of these experts. Over objection, the court ruled that these three experts could testify, but could be deposed. When one of these experts was asked at deposition to state his opinions, he said he had not reached any opinions. When asked why he had not yet reached any opinions, the expert said he had not yet done any work on this case; he had agreed only to be an expert. It is difficult to understand how anyone would agree to be an expert without knowing anything about the case. The court did later rule that this witness could not testify.

Be careful in selecting, as an expert witness, someone who frequently testifies and, thus, appears to be a professional witness. There is a difference between a witness who has a regular profession, such as a doctor, and a witness whose business is being an expert witness. If possible, avoid the witness whose only, or principal, source of income is serving as an expert witness; especially avoid the witness who consistently testifies for the same corporation or insurance company. This raises the question that the expert's continued employment is geared to the testimony and not to the facts. If you decide to utilize the "professional" expert, bring out, on direct examination, how many times the expert has previously testified on the theory that this helps establish the witness's qualifications. Having opposing counsel raise this issue on cross-examination suggests that the witness is not truly independent and testifies solely as a profession. Likewise, if the opposing party's expert appears to be a person whose sole income or majority of income is from serving as an expert, ask the witness whether he is a professional witness.

An expert should be independent from the party who is calling the expert to testify. In a fraud action, the defense called as an expert witness a personal friend of the defendant. The defendant and the expert were not only friends but also fishing buddies and partners who were building a marina in Costa Rica costing several million dollars. Worse yet, the defense on direct examination mentioned only the friendship and fishing. Plaintiff, on cross-examination, established the business venture. The jury gave no weight to this expert's testimony. In fact, a juror's notes were, "Costa Rica, marina venture (no bias!)."

Establishing Qualifications of an Expert

In establishing qualifications of an expert on such things as education, work experience, and articles written, utilize the VEPS either by using a computer feed or the document camera. Do not go overboard in establishing qualifications. When asked to state her qualifications, one witness said she was "uniquely qualified to render an opinion in the action." In a drug action, the witness was asked to describe a study he did for Alcoholics Anonymous. The court interrupted and said to get on with the case.

In establishing credentials, do not have a witness say he attended a course in litigation testimony.

Ascertain Whether the Court Will Declare a Witness to Be an "Expert"

Typically, counsel will elicit the qualifications of an expert. Some lawyers then ask the judge to "accept' the witness as an expert, "declare" the witness to be a expert, or "move" to have the expert declared to be an expert. Some judges will not declare witnesses to be experts, preferring to make a ruling only if there is an objection. Find out beforehand if your particular judge will declare or accept witnesses to be an expert in the event you must do that. If the judge does not declare or accept witnesses to be experts, you will look unqualified in front of the jury if you make such a request during a trial, and the judge says the court will not do so.

Establishing Compensation of Experts May Not Be a Good Idea

Some lawyers insist on asking an expert witness how much he or she charges per hour or in total to show the bias of the witness. Some, but not all, jurors resent this evidence. They say that it has nothing to do with the case or evidence. One juror said that it is ridiculous to ask this question when the jurors receive $40.00 per day and some experts are charging $450.00 per hour. Some jurors also believe it hypocritical for a lawyer to ask how much a witness charges per hour, or in total, when jurors know that lawyers charge high rates themselves or will submit huge bills. In fact, some jurors would like to be told what the hourly rates of, or the total amount billed by, the lawyer asking the questions of the expert. On the other hand, one juror submitted a written question wanting to know how much the expert witness was paid.

A federal judge understands that expert witnesses do get paid. It probably is a waste of time in a bench trial or hearing to establish how much an expert is paid.

But, advise your expert to be ready to disclose hourly rates as well as amounts billed or to be billed firmly and confidently. Experts who testified that they had no recollection of how much they or their company had billed lost credibility.

Be Wary of the Arrogant Expert

Defense counsel called the witness, "Ms. Adams." The witness quickly and sternly said, "Dr. Adams." Counsel probably should have called the witness Dr. Adams. The failure to do so could and should be regarded by the trier of fact as a lack of respect; however, because the witness insisted that she be called, "Doctor," the witness looked arrogant and less likely to impress the jury.

After one witness responded to a question, defense counsel said that he was confused. The expert said that there was no way the lawyer could be confused based on the expert's testimony. Another witness, who was asked whether she was Board certified in family practice, said, "Yes." She was asked whether she was Board certified in internal medicine. Instead of saying, "No," her response was, "Why would I be Board certified in internal medicine?"

One expert, who spent ten minutes with a narrative answer, was arrogant; his lengthy answer was viewed as showing off.

Ensure that the Documents Utilized by Your Expert Are Correct

In one instance, a document prepared by an expert prior to trial, stated that the calculation of damages was line 11 times line *17* times line *19*. At trial, the witness said that the proper calculation was line 11 times line *18* times line *20*. How good was this expert?

An Expert Should Not Only Express an Opinion but Should Also Explain the Bases for the Opinion

In an action involving fingerprints, the witness enlarged both the exemplar and the latent print; the witness then showed the jury why the fingerprints were the same by referring on both enlargements to the composition of the fingerprints.

In another action, involving devices used to intercept TV signals, the jury said that the expert demonstrating the products during the testimony helped explain the expert's opinion.

Some jurors prefer a summary of the expert's opinion at the conclusion of the testimony.

Novel Cross-Examination of an Expert

Counsel started his cross-examination by displaying a posterboard with a column containing various questions written and columns marked, "Y" or, "N." Counsel then started asking the questions listed on the posterboard and tried to have the witness answer yes or no. When the witness answered, counsel checked the appropriate column on the board. This was very impressive. However, the witness then chose to answer many questions with long explanations, thereby weakening the value of the yes or no answer. Nevertheless, by hedging his answers to questions that were fair, the witness looked evasive.

Consider Using a Tutorial Expert

In a technical case, especially in a patent action, consider using an expert at the start of the trial to instruct the jury, or possibly even to instruct the court, on the technical aspects of the action. Clear this with the court to determine whether the court will allow this in a jury trial or would like a technical explanation for a bench trial or hearing.

If a tutorial witness is used, this witness should be neutral and not an advocate. Potentially, permission could be sought, if necessary, to have the witness provide the neutral explanation at the start of the trial and to recall that same witness for the advocacy portion of the trial. However, it is better to use the instructional witness only for tutorial purposes. Contact opposing counsel to attempt to agree on a neutral witness. If agreement is not possible, consider requesting permission for each side to utilize its own expert at the start of the action.

Keep the Expert's Testimony as Simple as Possible

Do not try to impress the jury with your expertise by using technical terms with an expert witness. The jury will not understand. Keep it simple.

22

BE PREPARED TO MAKE SPECIFIC OBJECTIONS AND TO RESPOND TO OBJECTIONS INTERPOSED BY OPPOSING COUNSEL

Rule 103 of the Federal Rules of Evidence states:

> (a) Error may not be predicated upon a ruling which admits or excludes evidence unless a substantial right of the party is affected, and
> (1) Objection. - In case the ruling is one admitting evidence, a timely objection or a motion to strike appears of record, stating the <u>specific</u> ground of objection, if the <u>specific</u> ground was not apparent from the context. . . . (emphasis added.)

Familiarity with the rules of evidence is a necessity so that the specific ground of an objection and, hopefully, the precise rule by number can be stated. Merely stating "objection" runs the risk that the objection will have been waived. Citing the wrong rule may also result in the objection being overruled or waived.

To prepare properly for trial, anticipate what evidence the opposing party may seek to introduce that is considered objectionable and have the precise objection ready to make, by rule number, when that evidence is sought to be introduced. It certainly assists in demonstrating to the judge, and the jury, that you are a competent trial lawyer if you can cite to the appropriate rule by number as well as if your objections are sustained. I kept a list of the most frequently used objections in my trial notebook that I consulted before every day of trial, usually the night before, as well as before every deposition.

Also, anticipate what objections may be interposed by opposing counsel to the evidence you will seek to introduce and be prepared to meet those objections.

Making inappropriate objections or objections to immaterial matters that do not affect the case may cause the jury to believe that counsel is an obstructionist who is trying to prevent the jury from hearing evidence. Likewise, objections in bench trials should be very limited.

The fewer objections made, the better. Having a competent witness who can listen to the questions, understand them, and respond properly is better than having to make technical objections to the questions. I once represented a professional athlete who was intelligent and articulate and whose testimony required almost no objections. For instance, the athlete was asked, "Did Mr. Gray introduce you to Mr. Morgan, an accountant, who was an expert in his field?" The witness answered, "Mr. Gray introduced me to Mr. Morgan. Mr. Morgan was an accountant, but I cannot tell you if Mr. Morgan was an expert in his field."

Other examples of outstanding answers:

- "Q. Did you find that it was normal that when a benefits question arose, you would make some sort of written inquiry?
  A. How do you define normal?"
- "Q. What was your role in employee relations?
  A. Could you be a little more specific?"
- "Q. What exactly is employee relations?
  A. You mean, what were my responsibilities?"

At times, when confronted with a potentially ambiguous question, having the witness re-state the question as the witness understands the question removes the ambiguity. For example:

"A. Maybe I misunderstood your question. If you're asking me whether or not I was aware of any discussions relating to what benefit plans were in force and what have you, the answer is yes."

Miscellaneous Suggestions Regarding Objections

- Stand when making objections. This calls the court's attention to you and allows you to be heard more readily.
- When making an objection, state only that you are objecting and specify the ground, or grounds, for that objection. Do not use objections for the purpose of making a speech, recapitulating testimony, or attempting to guide the witness.
- A court will ordinarily ask for a brief response from opposing counsel. Generally, further argument upon the objection will not be heard until permission is given or argument is requested by the court.

- Where more than one counsel appears for a given party, the attorney who will present the direct examination of a witness is normally the one who should also interpose objections when the witness is being examined by other counsel. The attorney who will cross-examine a witness should be the counsel to interpose any objections during direct testimony.
- If, during a trial, counsel have reason to anticipate that any question of law or evidence is not routine, will provoke an extensive argument, or will require a proffer outside the presence of the jury, counsel should confer among or between themselves and attempt to resolve the matter. If agreement is not possible, give advance notice to the court to allow for appropriate scheduling of any arguments. This allows the court, if the court desires, to address these arguments before the jury returns to open court, during the lunch hour, before the jury reports in the morning, or at the end of the day after the jury has been excused.
- If evidence to which an objection has been sustained needs to be in the record for appeal purposes, an offer of proof is required. Rule 103(a) of the FRE provides that:

> Error may not be predicated upon a ruling which admits or excludes evidence unless a substantial right of the party is affected and. . . .
> 2. Offer of Proof.- In case the ruling is one excluding evidence, the substance of the evidence was made known to the court by offer or was apparent from the context within which questions were asked.

This offer of proof should be made outside the presence of the jury.

23

IMPEACHMENT BY DEPOSITION, IF DONE PROPERLY, CAN SUBSTANTIALLY INFLUENCE THE CREDIBILITY OF A WITNESS

As a courtroom deputy, I have been amazed at the number of lawyers who fail to use to its greatest opportunities impeachment by use of a deposition. Typically, if a witness testifies inconsistently from the witness's deposition, the lawyer will say, "Do you remember me taking your deposition?" The witness typically says, "Yes." Then, the lawyer asks, "Do you remember that I asked this question. . . ?" followed by, "Did you answer. . . ?" Once in a while, the lawyer will ask if the witness was sworn to tell the truth at the time of the deposition. A copy of the transcript is not even given to the witness. This is totally inadequate.

Impeachment by Use of a Deposition Should Include Foundational Questions

Few jurors have the slightest idea of what a deposition is. The notes of one juror referred to a deposition as a "disposition." Second, if you try to impeach by asking only the limited questions described above, your attempt may be met with an objection for failing to lay the proper foundation. A competent lawyer, though, may not object to the failure to lay a foundation, for laying a proper foundation makes the impeaching testimony all the more damaging. Laying a foundation is, nevertheless, a prerequisite to use of a deposition for impeachment, and, if there is an objection, you must be able to lay the proper foundation. As part of the foundation, you must establish such things as the fact that the witness was under oath, answered questions and then read and signed, or at least had the opportunity to read and sign, the transcript.

When I was preparing for trial, I created a folder for each person who might testify at trial. On the left inside of the folder, for adverse witnesses, I taped the foundational questions I would use if impeachment became necessary. To me, it was too important a procedure to do from memory. This technique was based on the story of the admiral who opened a locked drawer in his desk every morning and, after looking at it, locked the drawer. One day, the admiral left the drawer open. The flag lieutenant, who observed this procedure for many months, went over to look. Written on a piece of paper were the words "starboard—right, port—left."

After a witness testifies at trial inconsistently from the deposition, proceed directly to the foundational questions. Do not ask the witness whether he remembers the question and answer. At the appropriate time, after the foundational questions are asked, you should read both the question and answer providing the impeaching material. Your reading of the question and answer can be done with the proper inflection and emphasis.

A proper foundation is required, but a thorough foundation is even more impressive. Consider the following foundational questions:

> Q. Were you at your lawyer's office on February 1, 2007, for the purpose of having your deposition taken?
>
> Q. Was this done in a conference room?
>
> Q. Was your lawyer there?
>
> Q. Was I there?
>
> Q. Was a court reporter also present?
>
> Q. Did the court reporter have a machine similar to the machine the court reporter has here in the courtroom?
>
> Q. Before we started the deposition, did you take an oath to tell the truth?
>
> Q. Was the oath you took on February 1, 2007, like the oath you took today?
>
> Q. On February 1, 2007, did I ask you questions concerning your knowledge of facts relating to this lawsuit?
>
> Q. Did you answer those questions?
>
> Q. Did your lawyer ask you questions (or did your lawyer have an opportunity to ask you questions)?
>
> Q. Did your lawyer decide not to ask you any questions?
>
> Q. Were all of the questions asked by me and by your lawyer taken down by the court reporter using this machine like the machine our court reporter has here?
>
> Q. Were all of your answers to the questions that I asked you (and that your lawyer asked you also) recorded by the court reporter?

Q. After February 1, 2007, were all of the questions you were asked on February 1, 2007, and your answers to those questions, typed or printed on paper and put into a little booklet? (Or, After February 1, 2007, were you given a little booklet containing all of the questions that you were asked on February 1, 2007, and your answers to those questions?)
Q. Let me show you this little booklet. Is this the little booklet you were given? (Leave transcript with witness.)
Q. Is this the transcript of your deposition?
Q. On page 27 of this booklet, there is a signature purporting to be the signature of John Blue. Is that your signature?
Q. Did you, in fact, sign this transcript?
Q. Did you read this transcript before you signed it?
Q. Did you read this at your home or your lawyer's office?
Q. Did anyone tell you there were any limits on how much time you could spend reading the transcript?
Q. Was I present when you read the transcript?
Q. Did you make any changes to your transcript?
Q. Did you have an opportunity to make changes to the transcript?
Q. Is this the sheet listing your changes?
Q. Did you sign this sheet listing changes you thought should be made to the transcript?
Q. Now turn to page 22. On February 1, 2007, did I ask you the following question, "Were you present at the meeting of September 30, 2006?"
Q. Was your answer, "Yes?"

If no changes were made to the transcript, add the following questions:

Q. After you read the transcript, did you make any changes to the answers you gave on February 1, 2007?
Q. At the time you read this transcript, did you confirm the answers you gave on February 1, 2007, by signing this transcript?
Q. Did you ever tell me after February 1, 2007, that any of the answers you gave on February 1, 2007, were incorrect?
Q. Despite your original answers on February 1, 2007, and your confirmation of those answers on March 10, 2007 when you read and signed the transcript, did you wait until this trial to make changes to your answers?

A Copy of the Transcript Should Be Provided to the Witness and the Judge

Any time you seek to impeach by deposition, provide a copy of the transcript to the witness. It is poor trial practice to fail to provide the witness an opportunity to review the actual testimony from the transcript. Too many lawyers remain at the lectern and merely ask whether the witness remembers a certain question and answer and also tend to paraphrase and edit the deposition testimony. It is unfair to expect a witness to remember what was said at a deposition because there could be months or even years between the deposition and the trial. You always want to appear fair, and it is only fair that a witness be shown a copy of the transcript. Showing the witness the transcript can lead to a more effective impeachment because there will be no question as to what the witness said; this will avoid a charge that you have misinterpreted the testimony or incorrectly summarized the testimony or did not read all of the pertinent testimony. If you do not have a separate copy of the transcript for the witness, it is awkward to approach the witness chair and share the one copy you have with the witness. Jurors may think that this is threatening to the witness because you are "in his space."

Make certain that the copy of the transcript is complete. One counsel who sought to impeach was chagrined to learn that the transcript was two sided but the copy given to the witness had only one side copied and was missing the page with the impeaching testimony.

If your witness is being cross-examined, stand up and insist that the witness be provided with a copy of the transcript, even if you have to provide the copy. It is important that the witness review the actual testimony and not accept what might be counsel's interpretation or summary of the deposition testimony. By insisting that the witness be provided with a copy of the transcript, the other side will appear to be unfair and trying to trick the witness.

If you intend to impeach by use of a deposition, or if counsel seeks to impeach your witness, provide a copy of the transcript to the judge to enable the judge to follow the proposed impeaching testimony. This way, the judge can be certain that the alleged impeaching testimony is read correctly, can more easily make a ruling on any objections, or can rule on any request to have additional testimony read from the transcript.

In any event, have at least one copy of the transcript available. Without having a copy, it is unlikely that impeachment can take place unless the witness is inept enough to say that the witness remembers the questions and answers. It is embarrassing if the court insists that a copy of the transcript be shown to the witness and counsel cannot find it. Jurors have commented on this and resent this lack of preparation.

Be Certain that Your Trial Question Matches the Alleged Impeaching Testimony

Asking your trial question using the actual testimony from the deposition is much more effective than formulating a question based on your interpretation or summary of what the witness said at the deposition. You will lose credibility with the court and jury if your trial question does not match the alleged impeaching deposition testimony, and this is especially true if opposing counsel or the judge points out that there is no match. Two examples follow.

Deposition testimony from a police officer was that Mrs. Jones told witness Burns that Mrs. Jones had the gun. The question at trial of the police officer was, "Did Mrs. Jones tell you that she had the gun?" The answer was, "No." Counsel tried to impeach but could not because both the trial testimony and deposition testimony were that Mrs. Jones told witness Burns, not the police officer witness. This was poor impeachment practice. In another case, the witness was asked whether he had ever been involved in the chemical arts. The witness said that he had been. Counsel tried to impeach. When the transcript was reviewed, it was clear that the witness had said that he had been involved in chemical arts. The next question at the deposition sought to determine the witness's experience in the pharmaceutical arts. It was in answer to that question that the witness said he had had no experience. Counsel was using the wrong deposition question and answer to impeach.

Do not expand the trial question beyond what was stated at the deposition. During a deposition, a witness said that he reviewed "some of the reports." At trial, the lawyer asked whether the witness reviewed "all" of the reports. When the witness said, "No," the lawyer tried to impeach using the deposition testimony of "some." This was not impeachment and was noted by everyone in the courtroom, including the jurors.

In another action, which involved a fire in a building, a police officer testified at a deposition that he went into the building but only on the first floor and he saw no fire. At trial, the police officer stated there was a fire in the building. Counsel tried to impeach with the deposition testimony that there was no fire on the first floor. The police officer properly pointed out that there is a difference between a fire in the building, the roof, for instance, and fire on the first floor only.

The above examples demonstrate that it is extremely important that you follow along with the transcript if your witness is sought to be impeached to be certain that there is a match between the deposition testimony and the trial testimony. Frequently, someone, such as a paralegal, summarizes deposition testimony, the summary is inaccurate, and the questioning counsel relies on the summary instead of using the exact words from the transcript.

Do not try to impeach if the deposition and trial testimony are the same. I have seen this happen more than once. For example, the deposition testimony was, "I don't recall if Mrs. Johnson was there." The trial testimony was, "I don't recall if Mrs. Johnson was there." Counsel tried to impeach from the deposition testimony. This was impossible, and counsel looked incompetent.

Do Not Impeach on Irrelevant Matters

Jurors are bright and resent "nitpicking" on impeachment. If a witness at a deposition denied attending a critical meeting, but then said at trial that he did attend the meeting, by all means, the witness needs to be impeached. If, however, the time of a critical meeting is not important, it is not prudent to impeach a witness by establishing that at trial the witness said that the meeting was at 2:00 but at the deposition the witness said the meeting was at 10:00. Likewise, if the date of the meeting is not critical, establishing inconsistency between trial testimony and deposition testimony of the meeting being held on a Tuesday rather than a Wednesday will not be well received by most jurors.

If you are fortunate enough to be able to impeach a witness by use of inconsistent statements, do not ask the witness to explain **why** the witness testified inconsistently. Do not ask whether the deposition testimony is or was accurate.

Have the Impeaching Material Ready

It is essential that the impeaching material be readily available when needed, including page and line. This shows the jury that you are prepared and know what you are doing. It also demonstrates to the witness that you are in charge. If you stumble around looking for the deposition transcript, you lose some of the effectiveness of the impeachment as well as provide the witness with time to think about why the testimony is inconsistent. You also appear disorganized to the jury. In one action, a witness denied having earlier made a statement critical to determining liability. Counsel then tried to locate this statement in the deposition. The whole courtroom was silent as counsel kept looking. Finally, after what seemed like an eternity, counsel found the statement.

Consider Using VEPS for Impeachment

Displaying the deposition testimony on the courtroom monitors may aid jurors in comprehending the impact of the impeaching testimony. Using a computer with software that allows for enlarging, highlighting, and underlining is even better. Using a software program that allows a video deposition where the picture of the witness is displayed along with scrolling testimony and with the document, if the document is being discussed, is outstanding. Ascertain whether the court will allow a VEPS display of impeaching material in the event that an objection is made to its proposed use.

When testimony on direct examination is inconsistent with deposition testimony, consider further the possibility of having the court reporter transcribe testimony on direct at trial that is inconsistent with deposition testimony; then, display both deposition and trial testimony on the monitors, with a split screen if possible.

24

SUGGESTIONS FOR PREPARATION AND USE OF JURY INSTRUCTIONS

Contact Court Staff Sufficiently in Advance of a Trial to Obtain a Copy of the Court's Standard Instructions as well as Preliminary and Substantive Instructions in Similar Cases.

Additional Matters to Ascertain Before Trial Regarding Instructions

1. Preliminary instructions:
   a. Does the court require or allow parties to submit preliminary instructions? If so, when?
   b. Are objections allowed to the opposing party's proposed preliminary instructions? If so, when must they be submitted and how?
   c. When will the court's preliminary instructions be available for review?
   d. Are objections to the court's proposed preliminary instructions allowed? If so, when must they be submitted and how?
   e. Do jurors receive a copy?
2. Final instructions:
   a. Does the court require parties to submit proposed final instructions? If so, when must they be submitted and how?
   b. Must each proposed instruction include a citation to the authority on which counsel relies?
   c. Can objections be submitted to the opposing party's proposed final instructions? If so, when must they be submitted and how?

d. Will the court provide a draft of its final instructions? If so, when?
e. Will there be a conference to address and possibly raise objections to the court's proposed instructions? If so, when and where?
f. Will the instructions conference be on the record? If not, how will any objections to the court's proposed instructions be preserved for appeal?
g. Will instructions be given before or after closing argument?
h. Will each juror be given a copy of the final instructions and verdict form? If so, when?

Providing Each Juror with a Copy of the Final Instructions Is a Good Idea

Almost without exception, jurors appreciate having their own copy of the final instructions. Most important, the jurors say that having a copy of the instructions enables them during deliberations better to understand the law and then to apply the facts to the law.

When jurors have been provided with a copy of final instructions and the verdict form prior to closing arguments, jurors, as the judge reads the final instructions and verdict form or counsel refers to them in closing argument, highlight, underline, or circle words and make notes. If lawyers emphasize words or phrases, these may be highlighted by the jurors during argument and become important during deliberations.

Thus, closing arguments that follow the guidelines/structure of the instructions/verdict form are recommended.

25

DO NOT BE RELUCTANT TO TRY YOUR CASE TO A JURY

Once a complaint and answer are filed, counsel must decide whether to file a demand for a jury, if a jury trial is authorized. Some lawyers, for various reasons, do not believe a jury will reach the right result. Before making a decision on a jury trial, consider the comments in this chapter.

Do Not Underestimate the Intelligence and Attentiveness of Jurors

In one action, the jury, during deliberations, studied and compared x-rays. They found something consistent with defendant's theory of non-liability, but which had never been argued or mentioned by defense counsel or witnesses.

In an action where the physical layout of plaintiff's house was important, plaintiff introduced a picture, taken a week before trial, of her dining room table with a freshly ironed white tablecloth, plates, napkins and napkin holders, and a dozen fresh roses in a vase. The jurors knew this was not realistic and was done for trial purposes only.

During a two hour cross-examination in an action alleging a retaliatory discharge for filing a workman's compensation claim, plaintiff's expert said one time only that plaintiff's disability was a "low level of impairment." In explaining their decision, which was a defense verdict, jurors specifically mentioned these four words. The fact that one or more jurors focused on these four words during a two-hour cross-examination demonstrates that jurors do pay attention.

In an employment discrimination action, plaintiff called as witnesses four people who had similar lawsuits against the same defendant. The jurors, who were not advised of these other lawsuits, later said that they knew there had to be some ulterior motive for these witnesses to be called because these witnesses tried too hard to help the plaintiff and hurt the defendant. This case was a defense verdict.

Many jurors believe that attorneys talk down to them; the attorneys will over and over again make the same statements and ask the same questions; one juror said he felt like shouting, "The horse is dead, please dismount."

Without question, in technical cases, there needs to be some explanation of technical terms and processes, but do not over do it. In an action involving a mechanical device, the first witness explained that there were four chambers to the heart. Subsequent witnesses also told the jury the heart had four chambers. Some jurors were insulted, commenting that the lawyers must have thought the jurors were totally incompetent.

Inquire if the Court Will Allow Jurors to Ask Questions

Find out if the jurors can ask questions of all witnesses, including expert witnesses. One juror actually submitted a relevant question that stumped an expert witness. If questions will be allowed, ascertain:

- Will the jurors submitting the questions be identified?
- Will the court first review the questions?
- Will the court allow counsel first to review and interpose objections? Will this hearing be done outside the presence of the jury?
- Will the court ask the questions of the witnesses?
- Can counsel ask follow up questions?

Notes Made By Jurors Confirm Their Intelligence and Attentiveness

Some judges allow, and even encourage, jurors to take notes during a trial. Ascertain if the jurors will be allowed to take notes. Jurors state they appreciate having the opportunity to take notes during a trial. Examples of these notes are:

- "Cross examination - Reestablishing Already Established Facts (REDUNDANCY!!)."
- "Don't ask a question you don't know the answer to."
- "Witness remembers nothing - convenience, ignorance - man in a technical field cannot remember facts."
- "My thoughts - why not investigate to protect self and company?"
- "Great deal! They paid her more to stay!! She stabbed them in the back and demanded more $."
- "Witness doesn't remember why."
- "He doesn't remember explanation (this guy isn't very believable!)."

- "Expert - good! Conservative."
- "Recalls document, but not time frame."
- "Witness very nervous."
- "Contradicted himself."
- "Not credible."
- "Witness 'Mouthed' I'm sorry when he identified defendant in the courtroom."
- "Defense had no significant questions."
- "Primary argument was to cast doubt on two witnesses; i.e. that they were both lying."
- "Spent practically no time on presenting arguments on telephone calls. Nothing significant toward proving innocence."
- "Long replay of telecom that proved nothing."
- "Lawyer had his documents all fouled up and had to renumber them while the court waited. Documents utterly useless."
- "Whole exercise proved nothing."
- "This witness simply confirmed Baker's testimony."
- "Also found guns that were obviously not for hunting."
- "Counsel presented nothing to refute the fact that defendant got cocaine from Smith."
- "Conclusion: Cross examination changed nothing."
- "Prosecution proved that Alexander dealt in drugs."
- "Questions were useless."
- "Nothing significant."
- "Definitely proved use of code words, which defense tried to stop any of it coming out."
- "Prosecution proved to the point of absurdity that slang use of words referred to drug activity."
- "Objections of defense were ineffective in obviously trying to hold testimony back."
- "Utterly pointless questions that did nothing to refute the records."
- "Completely different stories."
- "Holes in memory."
- "Inconsistencies in memory between deposition and now."
- "More confident when talking about himself."
- "The defense attorney made himself look like the bad guy."
- "Backseat behind passenger (earlier he said behind driver)."
- "Wouldn't answer question about how much it cost."
- "Math doesn't add up."
- "Inconsistencies??"

- "Why is defendant's secretary accepting notes and leaving?"
- "Counsel is grasping for a hole in case."
- "Lied on request for leave."
- "Travel time seems excessive given mileage submitted - average speed for driving would be 5 mph."
- "Do not ask a question that the witness cannot answer."

Perhaps some of these kinds of comments would not be remembered in a long trial. Thus, if you really want the jurors to have a better recollection of what occurs at a trial, as well as their attitudes and impressions, be sure to request that the jurors be allowed to take notes. Even if permitted, some jurors elect not to take notes.

Additional Oral Comments from Jurors

- Do not look at the jurors when asking a question; look at the witness.
- Do not stare at the jurors any time during the trial. Jurors were highly critical of one set of lawyers, one of whom stared or studied the jurors as co-counsel was doing voir dire, conducting an examination of a witness or presenting argument. These jurors said they felt as if they were on trial. On the other hand, during voir dire, opening statements and closing arguments, jurors prefer that the counsel speaking look at them, although not stare.
- Do not ask long questions.
- Time lines are helpful.
- Do not say, "okay,"or "now" between answers and questions.
- Do not lose your temper.
- Do not act or look agitated.
- When the witnesses could not explain how the damages were computed, jurors believed the lawyers solicited the plaintiffs and calculated the damages with limited or no input from plaintiffs.
- When plaintiff's counsel prepared a summary of plaintiff's damages and, with leading questions, attempted to have the plaintiff explain the computations, jurors were lost. They said they wanted to be shown the computations step-by-step and shown the exhibits that documented the computations.
- Jurors had a low opinion of a plaintiff's counsel who, when defense was questioning, would shuffle papers, open a notebook and engage in other distracting conduct. This does not connote a sense of fair play.

- Jurors have also commented negatively about:

  Bodily motions and gestures by counsel or parties during questioning or arguments by opposing counsel.

  Corporate representative scowling in response to testimony.

  Corporate representative nodding in response to the testimony of a witness.

  Parties or corporate representative nodding, scowling, and laughing aloud during closing arguments.

  A lawyer who rolled his eyes as an adverse witness was testifying.

  Communication between a defendant in a criminal action, and his girlfriend as she was approaching the witness stand to testify.

Post-Trial Written Critiques Are Revealing

Some judges contact jurors after the trial is over and ask them to answer certain questions. Examples:

- "Q. What impressed you the most about this lawyer?
  A. Competence and sincerity."
- "Q. What was the weakest evidence this lawyer presented?
  A. Where were the mechanical evidence and the doctor's reports?"
- "Q. How could this lawyer have improved his or her performance?
  A. Stick with factual information and not try to find continuing minor discrepancies in cross-examination."
- "Q. Any comments?
  A. Speed up the trial. Both sides wasted a lot of effort on meaningless information."
- "Q. What impressed you most about this lawyer?
  A. He had a presence. He moved quickly and did not allow you to sleep when he was presenting."
- "Q. What impressed you the least?
  A. I'm not sure he was all that sincere. He came across as a hired gun."
- "Q. Comments
  A. My biggest complaint really involved the attorneys. The constant side bars, and reading of previous testimony. At times they seemed unprepared. I'm really curious how this case got as far as it did. I really felt the plaintiff's case was pretty weak I think the lawyer saw his money and I'm not sure why."

Contact with Jurors After the Trial

If you desire to talk with jurors after a trial, determine if local rules or the judge's own rules or practices permit such contact.

26

PROPER SELECTION, CARE AND FEEDING OF COURT REPORTERS IS PRUDENT

Preparation of an accurate record of what occurs at a deposition is critical for trial; preparation of an accurate record of trial proceedings is critical for appeal. The comments in this chapter should help achieve these objectives.

Selection of a Qualified Court Reporter for Depositions Is Essential

Although there are qualified court reporters that use tape recorders, shorthand, or a mask-like device with which they cover their mouths and repeat everything said into a tape recorder, it is best to use a stenotype-trained court reporter.

Once I scheduled a deposition in a small, county-seat town 125 miles from Indianapolis. The reporter, who was hired by local counsel, was a court reporter from the local state trial court who only used a tape recorder. I should have confirmed the qualifications of the reporter before I went to the deposition, but did not. Nevertheless, I decided to proceed with the deposition rather than reschedule and have to drive another 250-mile round trip, plus run the risk of plaintiff's counsel seeking fees resulting from the cancellation. About an hour into the deposition, the tape recorder jammed and tape was strung out all over the floor. The reporter fixed the machine; however, the transcript was less than acceptable.

I am also familiar with a lawyer being asked if he would accept a reporter using a tape recorder. When he refused, he was asked if he would accept a reporter who was shorthand trained. The lawyer said, "Yes." When the deposition started, a woman with a pen and shorthand pad was introduced as a court reporter. Sometime into the deposition, counsel asked for a question to be re-read. The woman bolted from the chair. She was just a fixture. Behind a screen was a tape recorder that was being utilized to record the deposition.

Establish a relationship with one or two court reporters or court reporting firms for your local depositions. You are more likely to be accommodated when you need a court reporter and perhaps be assisted in other ways. Once I was in the middle of a trial where the courthouse was a three-hour drive from Indianapolis. The court reporter that I used almost exclusively for depositions, and who had taken depositions in the action being tried, located me to advise that he had been subpoenaed to testify in this trial the next day. He did nothing wrong by telling me this, and it certainly helped me to know that he would be testifying the next day.

Information to Supply to the Court Reporter in Advance of the Deposition, Trial, or Hearing

Competent court reporters prefer to be accurate, and to be as accurate as possible the first time they prepare the record of a deposition or court proceeding. Court reporters appreciate receiving, sufficiently in advance of the deposition or court proceeding, the names of witnesses and a list of non-ordinary words, terms, technical terminology, proper names, and acronyms that might be used in the deposition or court proceeding. For court proceedings, one place to start is the word index that is usually included at the end of most depositions. If this system is utilized, select the longest deposition with the most unusual names and terms and supplement as necessary. For oral arguments, court reporters appreciate receiving, prior to or immediately after the argument, a copy of applicable briefs or, at a minimum, a list of the cases cited at the oral argument.

If the courtroom deputy does not circulate an attendance list, it is helpful to the court and court reporter if a list of counsel present is prepared so that the court reporter can properly reflect in the transcript who is present and who will be speaking. Some lawyers do this by giving the court reporter a business card for each lawyer in attendance. One thoughtful lawyer, who was one of six lawyers appearing for an oral argument, copied all six business cards on an 8 1/2-x-11-inch piece of paper and provided that to the court reporter.

Contact the Court Reporter Directly If Real-Time, Daily Copy, or Expedited Transcripts Are Desired

Contact the court reporter for any of these items sufficiently in advance of the trial or proceeding to be sure that the proper arrangements are made. If real-time is desired, determine whether the judge will allow it and ask the court reporter what the costs of this service will be.

Prompt Payment Is Good Practice

At some subsequent date, you may need a transcript or one or two pages, on an expedited basis, of critical testimony. If you have not paid the court reporter, or not paid promptly in the past, the court reporter may remember this and not be eager quickly to assist you.

27

BECAUSE SO MANY ACTIONS ARE SETTLED, LAWYERS NEED TO BE SKILLED IN SETTLEMENT NEGOTIATIONS AND PROCEDURES

Very few actions, probably less than two percent of actions filed, actually go to trial. Because jury verdicts are so unpredictable, most actions are settled. Verdicts from two separate juries, both in employment discrimination actions, tried one week apart before the same federal judge, but with two separate juries, may help explain why so many actions settle. In the first action, the *defendant* offered $100,000 to settle the action. Plaintiff refused the offer and did not even make a counter-offer. The jury returned a verdict for the defendant. In the second action, plaintiff offered to settle for $40,000; defendant countered with $5,000. The jury returned a verdict for $90,000 for plaintiff.

Because so many actions are settled, lawyers need to hone their settlement skills and be aware of the pitfalls of settlement. Issues to consider about settlement are discussed in the following sections.

The Time at Which Settlement Should Be Explored Is Case Sensitive

Although case sensitive, settlement should be considered at the following times:

- After meeting with client.
- After preliminary investigation.
- After paper discovery.
- After depositions.
- At a pretrial/settlement conference.
- After any motions for summary judgment are decided.

The further the action proceeds, the more costly the action becomes to you and your client. An important factor affecting settlements is the existence of fee-shifting provisions contained in various statutes. In employment discrimination actions, it often becomes evident that a plaintiff would be willing to settle for a nominal amount but by the time settlement discussions are held, plaintiff's counsel has invested extensive time on the action and will demand that these fees or a percentage of these fees be paid. For example, one plaintiff settled his claim for $30,000. After a contested hearing on fees, $300,000 was awarded. Thus, realistically addressing settlement early is advisable.

Who Should Participate in Negotiations

Any of the following might participate:

- Counsel.
- Counsel and parties.
- Parties alone.

Use of a Neutral Party Should Be Considered

If a neutral party is involved in the negotiations, this person might be one of the following:

- Presiding judge. Often, judges who will try the action, even with a jury, are reluctant to become involved in settlement.
- Magistrate judge.
- Private mediator. If so, determine in advance how this person will be selected, who will pay any fees, and where the mediation will take place.

All Significant Terms Should Be Agreed and Reduced to Writing Before the Action Is "Settled"

In many settlements, the parties agree upon the monetary terms of the settlement and that the action will be dismissed. However, what then can happen is that one side will draft an agreement, usually a multi-page agreement form that is kept on a computer that contains many terms never previously discussed by the parties. The other side then refuses to settle.

During a fifteen-month period, Judge Hamilton had to address motions to enforce settlement agreements in seven different actions. These motions resulted from the fact that one of the parties in each of the actions stated that there were new or different terms in the "formal" settlement agreement, prepared after the action had supposedly been settled, that had never been discussed and which were unacceptable. Some of these items involved the following issues:

- Whether the employer's records listing the nature of a termination should be a discharge, resignation, or retirement.
- Providing letters of recommendation.
- Vesting in benefit plans.
- Continuation of benefits.
- Confidentiality.
- Amount of compensation to be paid to counsel and how it was to be paid.

If these items are important, they must be addressed at the time that the action is supposedly settled and not inserted into the draft of a settlement agreement subsequently prepared. If the parties agree to settle an action at a conference where the parties and counsel are present, the agreed-upon terms need to be reduced to writing as soon as possible. It is even risky to leave the conference based only on an oral commitment or handshake. Some lawyers have the standard terms of a settlement agreement on their laptop computer. At the time of settlement with all parties present, the lawyer can create an agreement for signature at that time. At a minimum, before leaving the conference, the terms critical to each party should be written in skeleton form and signed by the parties and counsel. For example, in an employment discrimination action, terms such as termination, re-employment (and, if so, terms), money, release, confidentiality, benefits, and fees should be written. If the parties happen to be in a courthouse or court reporter's office, dictating to a court reporter at least the critical terms is recommended. If the action is settled as a result of a series of phone calls, a quick exchange of letters is recommended. If the agreement to settle results from an exchange of letters or e-mails, the terms critical to each party must be summarized in one document and the definitive agreement circulated as quickly as possible.

Any settlement agreement must include the following language:

> This agreement represents the entire agreement between plaintiff and defendant. There are no other written or oral agreements between plaintiff and defendant. This agreement supersedes all prior negotiations, representations, or agreements, whether written or oral, between plaintiff and defendant.

One example demonstrates this point. I represented a company that sold and installed rural telephone systems. After installation, the telephone company complained that the system did not work and filed a lawsuit. The manufacturer believed that the reason for the system failure was the inability of the telephone company to maintain the system. The manufacturer proposed that it be provided the opportunity to restore the system to its proper operational level and, if the manufacturer could not do so, the manufacturer would refund the purchase price. The telephone company refused to accept the manufacturer's proposal. Thereafter, the action was settled. The settlement provided only for the payment of money as well as for mutual releases. The settlement agreement was prepared and signed with the above quoted language included. The nominal amount was paid; the action was dismissed. The telephone company then requested the manufacturer to return to the area and restore the system to its proper operational level, as had previously been proposed. The manufacturer refused; the telephone company filed a new lawsuit. This new lawsuit attached the settlement agreement to the complaint. The result was judgment on the pleadings.

Enforcement of a Settlement Agreement

If, as part of a settlement agreement, an action is going to be dismissed, be aware of the issue of whether or not the court can enforce the settlement agreement if enforcement becomes necessary, or if a new action must be filed. On this issue, see *Pittman v. Dolton Police Dept.*, 2006 WL 2329426 (7th Cir. 2006). There, the 7th Circuit said:

> We have held that when a district court grants a motion to enforce a settlement agreement and dismisses the case with prejudice, any purported retention of jurisdiction to enforce the agreement is ineffective. Lynch, Inc. v. SamataMason Inc., 279 F.3rd 487, 489 (7th Cir.2002). No one disputes that, *prior* to the dismissal, the district court had jurisdiction to decide whether a valid settlement agreement existed. It was only when the district court dismissed the case with prejudice that it lost jurisdiction to do anything further; if it truly wanted to retain jurisdiction, the district court should have dismissed the case without prejudice. See *id.* As it is, the dismissal with prejudice simply means that future disputes over performance of the agreement will not automatically be handled by the district court. (emphasis added).

28

UNDERSTAND ENTITLEMENT TO COSTS AND ATTORNEYS' FEES

Requests for Non-Recoverable and Excessive Costs and Fees Can Result in a Complete Denial or a Substantial Reduction in the Amount Requested

For example, deferring a ruling on a Bill of Costs until after a decision on appeal, one court did note that:

> the bill of costs seeks more than $39,000 and includes costs that clearly are not recoverable under 28 U.S.C. sec.1920, such as expert witness fees and attorney travel expenses. See *Crawford Fitting Co. v. J.T. Gibbons, Inc.*, 482 U.S. 437, 439 (1987)(expert witness fees); *Wahl v. Carrier Mfg. Co.*, 511 F.2d 209, 217 (7th Cir. 1975)(attorney travel expenses).

With respect to attorneys' fees, one court in a Fair Labor Standards Act action that started with fifteen plaintiffs, noted:

> Only six plaintiffs' claims survived for submission to the jury. The jury ruled in favor of defendants on five of those plaintiffs. The one plaintiff who prevailed won a small fraction of the damages she was seeking: $1,172.50, less than four percent of the unpaid overtime wages she sought ($33,359.30 without liquidated damages). In light of these facts, plaintiffs' request for $89,205.00 in attorney fees and $6,727.95 in costs is not reasonable. It is simply absurd.

An example of a fee petition that was substantially reduced can be found in the case of *Eli Lilly v. Zenith Goldline*, 264 F. Supp. 2d 753 (S.D. Ind. 2003). This was a patent case in which Zenith Goldline was sued for challenging Lilly's patent for the antacid product Axid. Finding Zenith Goldline's invalidity defense without merit, the court authorized an award of attorneys' fees and costs. Lilly submitted a petition for fees and costs in the amount of $4,961,969.07 following a three-day bench trial. Describing the fee and cost petition as "exorbitant and unreliable," the court awarded only $1,523,580.85 in fees and $101,576.34 in costs. The opinion discusses such matters as hourly rates, inappropriate charges for time of lawyers and paralegals, as well as expenses for such items as hotel security, court reporters, postage, meals, travel, including renting luxury cars, and a charge of $1,197.55 for what appeared to be a victory celebration dinner after the court ruled for Lilly.

In part, the court stated that, "Lilly's petition is extravagant and inflated" and that, "[c]ase law supports a complete denial of such petitions, at least in extreme cases." Opining that a "substantial disincentive is needed to discourage extravagant and inflated fee petitions" and that "denying this excessive and unreasonable fee petition has considerable appeal," the Court chose "a course less extreme than complete denial."

> That course calls for approval of a reasonable amount of fees and costs rather than complete denial, but with the understanding that doubts about the reasonableness of a request will be resolved by denying or excluding the time or item from the award. In other words, in light of many of the specific excessive and even extravagant requests..., the court has taken a skeptical approach to the entirety of Lilly's petition.

Another informative decision addressing fees and costs is *Simon Property Group, L.P. v. mySimon*, 2001 W.L. 66408(S.D. Ind. 2001), a trademark case. There the court exercised its discretion under 15 U.S.C. Section 1117(a) and denied an attorney fee award. "This is not a case in which such an award is required by equity. Because the court is denying a fee award entirely, the court has not addressed a number of aspects of SPG's fee petition that inflate the requested amount well beyond what would be reasonable even if any award were appropriate."

In the footnote addressing this issue, the court said:

> These features include the use of an extraordinary number of billing timekeepers. During the trial itself, as many as four Jones Day partners, four associates and two legal assistants billed time to the case on the same day, while only

> three attorneys (all partners) played any active role during the trial. Also, for example, Jones Day billed for attendance of three partners, two associates, and a legal assistant to attend one pretrial conference. . . . Another feature is the fact that time was charged at hourly rates well above those that would be reasonable in the Indianapolis market. Partners charged from $330 up to $490 per hour; associates charged from $150 up to $305 per hour; legal assistants charged from $95 up to $120 per hour. (Although the comparison is not legally relevant it is interesting to note, in light of the billed rates for legal assistants, that experienced criminal defense attorneys who handle litigation as complex as any federal courts encounter are reimbursed under the Criminal Justice Act at the rate of $75 per hour.) The fee request also includes sizable expense for travel, some of it necessary because of the national scope of the case and witnesses, and some of it resulting only from SPG's decision to rely primarily on attorneys from other cities. In addition, the court has not tried to unravel the difficult problems imposed by the fact that SPG lost on a number of its separate claims, despite its success in the district court on the central trademark infringement claim. . . .

The Court continued:

> Under Fed.R.Civ.P. 54(d)(1), plaintiff SPG also seeks an award of costs in this matter in the amount of $187,759.14. As the prevailing party, SPG is entitled as a matter of course to an award of costs covered by 28 U.S.C. §1920. MySimon has not raised specific challenges to the cost petition, but the court has undertaken an initial review principally to be sure that the requested items are at least of the right types of expenses. Exhibit 3 to Mr. Murphy's affidavit shows that SPG has distinguished between "costs" and "expenses" for purposes of its petition. From the papers submitted, however, it is not possible to confirm whether the request for costs is limited to those costs properly recoverable under §1920. Exhibit 3 cites specific Jones Day invoices for costs, but for all except the first invoice identified, the court could only guess which items are being treated as costs under §1920 and which are being treated as the broader "expenses" that might be addressed as part of an attorneys' fees award, if at all.

> Moreover, two-thirds of the costs sought are from third-party bills, without any more specific information. Those bills include as costs and expenses (in a way that the court cannot differentiate between the two categories) such obviously non-recoverable items as out-of-pocket expenses for jury consultants and expert witnesses, catered meals for "jurors" in a mock trial, courier services, and the $1,500 per day that SPG paid Mr. Halliday for his travel to Indianapolis to testify at trial. The court will not try on its own to reconstruct from the documentation which costs are properly recoverable under §1920.

Avoid Inappropriate Diary Entries and Billing Statements

To the extent fees and costs may be recovered, submission of diary entries and support for costs will probably be required. Improper submissions can result in a denial of all or a part of the requested amounts as well as raise questions about the entire request.

Examples of diary entries that may raise questions:

- Unusually large number of hours for consecutive days such as 21, 16, 16, 15, or even 21 for one day.
- Excessive time to prepare routine filings such as 14 hours to prepare a Case Management Plan and 21 hours to prepare an Amended Case Management Plan.
- Lawyer time devoted to another file.
- Time for work on motions and briefs never filed.
- Time for work on frivolous motions and briefs.
- Time for work on unsuccessful motions and briefs.
- Time for work on preparing witnesses who never testify.
- Time spent scouting the presiding judge.
- Time spent preparing statements for legal services.
- Time spent on administrative functions such as shopping for supplies and storage cabinets.
- Excessive number of lawyers and paralegals appearing at the same deposition, hearing or trial.
- Inconsistent diary entries such as lawyer Arend recording a meeting with lawyer Booth on February 1, but Lawyer Booth recording the meeting on February 3, or lawyer Arend recording 2.1 hours and lawyer Booth recording 3.1 hours for the same meeting.
- Ambiguous entries such as "trial preparation."

- Duplicative and even triplicate entries for the same lawyer for the same day.
- Billing in large increments of time such as quarter hours.
- Time based on estimates or reconstruction.

. Examples of expense items that may raise questions:

- Purely personal items such as newspapers, books, clothing, movies, and "entertainment service."
- Secretarial overtime.
- Amenities such as first class travel, room service and renting luxury automobiles.
- Duplicate requests.
- Unusually large expenses for unspecified electronic research.
- Charges for items such as electronic research and travel, but with no corresponding time entry.
- Fees and expenses for jury and trial consultants.
- Catered meals and expenses for mock jurors.
- Excessive "express mail" charges.
- Excessive and unspecified copying charges.
- Software purchase.
- Equipment rental and purchase of supplies for a separate "war room."
- Unusually large per page cost for deposition transcripts.
- Costs for expedited deposition transcript.
- Costs for real time or daily copy during trials.
- Extra equipment for the courtroom.

29

FILING UNDER SEAL SHOULD BE USED WHEN REQUIRED AND ONLY SPARINGLY OTHERWISE

The United States Court of Appeals for the Seventh Circuit has insisted:

> that litigation be conducted in public to the maximum extent consistent with respecting trade secrets, the identities of undercover agents, and other facts that should be held in confidence. . . . This means that both judicial opinions and litigants' briefs must be in the public record, if necessary in parallel versions—one full version containing all details, and another redacted version with confidential information omitted. . . .
>
> What happens in the federal courts is presumptively open to public scrutiny. . . . Any step that withdraws an element of the judicial process from public view makes the ensuing decision look more like fiat and requires rigorous justification.

Hicklin Engineering, L.C., v. R. J. Bartell and R. J. Bartell & Assocs. *L.L.C.*, 439 F.3d 346, 348 (7th Cir. 2006).

Typically, filing under seal requires an authorizing statute, court rule, or court order. Unless authorized, the proper procedure is to first request permission from the court.

Be familiar with legal precedents governing what may be and what must not be filed under seal. It is not the purpose of this chapter to discuss what may or may not be protected from public disclosure. See, e.g., *Citizens First National Bank of Princeton v. Cincinnati Insurance Co.*, 178 F.3d 743 (7th Cir. 1999).

Often, prior to the start of discovery, the parties will request the entry of a stipulated protective order but not delineate what information is sought to be maintained under seal. This may result in an order from the court as follows:

> The parties' joint motion for stipulation and protective order is hereby denied. The joint submission fails to show good cause for the court to keep any records in this case under seal.... The parties have not shown what types of information might actually qualify for the protection they seek and the 7th Circuit has instructed district courts not to issue orders sealing court records without a sufficient showing.

Parties to a lawsuit can agree between themselves to keep certain information confidential. Some counsel believe that this agreement grants them the authority to file under seal any document that any party unilaterally believes is entitled to be filed under seal. This will not succeed. The fact that the parties may agree between themselves to keep certain information confidential does not give the parties a license to file that information under seal. What has happened in many instances is that a secretary or paralegal will stamp as "confidential" every document contained in certain files, such as a plaintiff's personnel file. If items from the personnel file are then made exhibits to a pretrial motion, these items often are filed under seal because someone in the discovery process placed a "confidential" stamp on the documents. This has resulted in the absurdity of an empty envelope addressed to a plaintiff and a letter to a plaintiff informing her of a promotion to be filed under seal. This kind of conduct usually results in an order to show cause why any documents should be kept under seal.

If authorized to file certain materials or information under seal, limit your sealed filings only to the protectable information. Too often, the following occurs: There could be certain information on one or more, but not all, pages of a brief that would be entitled to be filed under seal, but counsel files the entire brief under seal. This is wrong. For example, entitlement to protect the rate of return mentioned three different times in a thirty-page brief does not entitle the whole brief to be filed under seal. If only certain words on a page are confidential and protected from disclosure, merely remove those words, include the rest of the page in the brief that is filed with the court, and then file the entire page under seal. The same thing occurs with exhibits in support of motions. One or more, but not all, of the exhibits might be entitled to be filed under seal. Some lawyers elect to file all exhibits under seal. There are situations in which this was done and counsel demonstrated ineptness by including pleadings and published decisions under seal. If only certain exhibits in an appendix containing many exhibits are entitled to be under seal, simply place a blank page in the appendix identifying the exhibit and state that it is filed under seal. Then file the protected documents under seal.

For a non-ECF court, sealed documents should be placed in a sealed envelope with a cover sheet listing the caption and identification of the document. In an ECF district, use the correct prompt for sealed documents, but also file a redacted version.

There is another reason for not over-designating documents as confidential during discovery. Often, when parties designate and stamp all documents and files as confidential, some of these documents, clearly not confidential, become exhibits at the trial. This creates the impression with jurors that one party is trying to withhold certain documents from disclosure.

30

PAY ATTENTION TO DETAIL IN ALL WRITTEN SUBMISSIONS AND ORAL PRESENTATIONS

As a courtroom deputy, I have noticed numerous inaccuracies in documents filed with the court or used during hearings, arguments, and trials. Inaccuracies in documents can result in a lack of confidence in the entire filing or presentation or the loss of credibility of the lawyer who is submitting the erroneous work product. Judges and law clerks do read cases cited in briefs and verify language from deposition transcripts and exhibits used as support for motions. They do not simply rely on what is contained in written submissions of counsel. Judges and clerks expect counsel to cite correctly to the volume, page, and relevant language from cases cited and from testimony or exhibits supporting counsel's position. If the citations are incorrect and cannot be found, the clerks or judges may never read the submissions. For example, during one oral argument, counsel, quoting from his brief, cited a passage from a decision that was 150 pages in length and stated that he was referring to a quotation found at page 65 of the decision. The court stated that it had not been able to find the quotation on page 65 and was not going to read 150 pages to try to locate the quotation.

Errors in documents shown to the jury can raise questions in the jurors' minds about how strong the case is; jurors may wonder whether they can rely on this lawyer to present accurately any of the facts.

Proofread All Documents Filed with the Court or Used in Court Proceedings

Examples of inaccurate work product include:

- Misspellings:
  uin instead of until
  Jude instead of Judge
  simulation instead of stimulation
  infereces instead of inferences
  submission of an "affidavit" stating, ironically, "I slovenly swear. . . ."
- Some lawyers or secretaries believe that relying on computer programs containing a spell checking component is a substitute for proofreading. This is dangerous. Spell checking programs will not alert you to the following errors:
  jury trail (not trial)
  personal (not personnel) file
  Untied (not United) States
  a peel (not appeal)
  latches (not laches)
  principle (not principal)
  council (not counsel)
  179 (not 177) F. 3rd
  220 F. Supp. 240 (not 204)
- Incorrect Caption
  In the United States District Court for the Southern District of Indiana, Indianapolis Division, I have seen the following on court filings:
  Before the Indiana Worker's Compensation Board
  In the Marion Superior Court
  State of Indiana, County of Federal Court
  State of Indiana Southern District
- Incorrect Cause Numbers
- Incorrect Designation of Presiding Judge
  On orders proposed for Judge Hamilton, a United States District Court Judge, I have seen the following descriptions of his position:
  Judge, Hamilton County Superior Court
  Judge, Marion Superior Court
  Judge, Porter County Superior Court
  Richard L. Young (another United States District Court Judge)

- Internal Inconsistencies
  Caption refers to "Amos Brown, Jr." but text refers only to "Amos Brown."
  Caption refers to "Mark David Appleby" but text refers to "Donald Mark Appleby."
  Caption refers to "Victor Electronics" but text refers to "TCS, Inc."
  Text of motion requests a fifteen-day extension of time to file a "complaint"; prayer requests fifteen days to "answer" the complaint.
  Motion requests an enlargement of time of thirty days, but tendered order requests only three days.
  Motion requests an enlargement of time until April 14, 2007, but tendered order requests an extension until March 14, 2007

Some of these errors result from the use of forms on counsels' computers. Although computers are a wonderful time-saving device, documents should be read before they are submitted. Your name is on these documents and you do not want the court, clients, or third parties to conclude that you are careless. Carelessness can result in losing clients and establish malpractice.

Other Examples of Inattention to Details

- Failing to remove "notes" from briefs.

  Available software programs allow counsel to insert electronic comments and notes in drafts of briefs, as opposed to writing in the margins or using sticky notes. If you use this type of computer program, remove any notes before filing the documents with the court. Consider the following example of a brief filed with the court:

  "Mary, the last sentence ('In any event, timely returned the Equipment.') does not seem to fit within this paragraph or even this Section B. Am I missing something? If it does not fit, I would insert the following sentence to conclude Section B. . . ."
  and

  "Mary, why is this last sentence here. I fail to see its relevance. . . . Please advise if you think it should remain in the brief. Thanks."
- Filing documents containing extraneous comments on attachments to a complaint, motion, or brief. Review all documents before filing them with the court and mask any extraneous comments before filing the documents with the court.

- Failing to identify the party being represented when submitting an appearance.
- Failing to know the party that counsel is representing.

  One action started with one defendant, but two additional defendants were added. At trial, one counsel represented all three defendants. At the close of plaintiff's evidence, defense counsel submitted a written Rule 50 motion seeking judgment as a matter of law on behalf of only the original defendant apparently using a signature block from early in the case. The court asked whether the relief was also being sought on behalf of the other two defendants. Counsel sheepishly said, "Yes."
- Attaching an incomplete document to a court filing and then seeking leave of court to substitute the correct attachment.
- Relying on an incorrect rule. Consider this order: "The motion of plaintiff (seeking an order allowing an out-of-state deposition) is hereby denied. There is no 'Federal Rule 28 (E),' although there is an Indiana Rule of Trial Procedure 28(E) that would apply in state court. Movant's request deals with a matter governed by Rule 45 of the Federal Rules of Civil Procedure, which does not require court action before a subpoena is issued."
- Not responding to motions.

  There may be some motions, such as motions for extension of time or the rescheduling of a conference, for which you may not have an objection and, therefore, not bother to file a response. There are other motions, such as motions to dismiss, to compel, or for summary judgment that will, in almost all instances, require a response. Failing to respond within the allotted time can result in the granting of the motion and perhaps also judgment. If you have a valid response and fail in a timely manner to respond or file a motion seeking an enlargement of time to respond, you will certainly establish yourself as incompetent, as well as expose yourself to a malpractice action.

  If the matter covered by a motion has been resolved with opposing counsel so that no response is required, notify the court, preferably in writing, so that the court does not rule on the motion without your response or rule against your client on the motion and contrary to the way the matter was resolved with opposing counsel.

  In one action, plaintiff failed to respond to a motion to compel, believing that the matter had been resolved by agreement with opposing counsel. Neither side notified the court. The court granted defendant's motion to compel and awarded sanctions. Plaintiff then claimed that there was an agreement resolving the issue. Defendant argued that there had been no agreement. If plaintiff had filed a notice with the court claiming that there was an agreement, defendant could have responded by saying there was no agreement. Plaintiff could then have responded to the motion to compel. Because that did not happen in this instance, the court held a hearing to address the amount of the sanctions. Plaintiff tried to argue the merits of the motion to compel but was not successful in this attempt. The court awarded $1,950 in sanctions.

APPENDIX A

NAME AND ADDRESS

Q. Please state your name.

Q. What is your current home address.

Q. How long have you lived there.

(Trace for five years)

Q. What is the date of your birth

EDUCATION

Q. What is the extent of your formal education.

<u>SCHOOL</u>	<u>YEAR OF GRADUATION</u>	<u>COURSE OF STUDY</u>

Q. Have you attended any seminars, training classes or training programs of any kind.

Q. If so,

What type

Who sponsored

When

Any certification received. If so, what.

WORK EXPERIENCE

Q. Please describe your work experience.

For each job:

Name of employer.

When start.

How long stay.

What was your job title when started.

What were your job responsibilities when you started.

Did your job responsibilities ever change.

If so, when.

Describe the change or changes.

Did you ever have a different job

If so,

What.

When.

Why a change.

Was this a promotion or a lateral move.

Responsibilities.

Why leave this employment.

What were the circumstances of leaving.

XYZ RELATIONSHIP

Q. How long has ABC sold products manufactured by XYZ.

Q. How did it come about that ABC started selling products manufactured by XYZ.

Q. Did you have any discussion or negotiation that led to ABC selling products manufactured. by XYZ.

Q. When were these discussions or negotiations.

Q. Were there any others

Q. For each discussion or negotiation,

Q.Where.

Q.Who participated.

Q. Anybody else.

Q. What was said by each person participating in the negotiation or discussion.

Q. Is that all that was said.

Q. Is there any document memoralizing the negotiation or discussion.

> Q. If so, describe each document.
>
> Q. Are there any other documents.
>
> Q. Where is each document located.

XYZ PRODUCTS

Q. What products manufactured by XYZ was ABC to sell when the relationship between ABC and XYZ first started.

Is that all the products.

Q. Was ABC to have responsibility in ABC's territory for all products manufactured and sold by XYZ.

Q. Were any other products added.

If so,

Which ones.

Any more.

For each product added, when was it added.

How did it come about that these products were added

TERRITORY

Q. Was there a territory assigned to ABC for ABC to sell products manufactured by XYZ.

Q. How was the territory defined.

Q. Are there any written documents defining the territory.

If so, describe each document.

Are there any other documents

Where is each document located.

If no writing,

Q. What was your understanding of the territory.

Q. How did you come to believe this was the territory assigned to ABC.

Q. Did you have any discussion with any representative of XYZ as to the territory to be assigned to ABC

When were these discussions.

Have you now identified all these discussions.

If so, for each discussion,

Who participated.

Anybody else.

Was anything else said.

EXCLUSIVE

Q. Did any other person or entity sell products manufactured by XYZ in the same area or areas in which ABC sold products manufactured by XYZ.

Q. If so

Who.

What products.

What locations.

During what years.

Was. ABC aware of this.

When.

How learn.

Did ABC complain to XYZ.

If so, was this done in writing or orally.

When was each oral complaint.

Any others.

For each oral complaint, to whom complain.

Anybody else.

What was said by each person.

Anything else.

Describe all documents in which you complained.

Any other documents.

Q. Could any other person or entity sold products manufactured by XYZ. in the same areas in which ABC was selling products manufactured by XYZ.

PRICE

Q. Who set the prices at which ABC sold products manufactured by XYZ.

QUANTITY

Q.Was ABC required to purchase any specific number of products or dollar amount of products manufactured by XYZ.

If so what was that requirement.

What is the basis for the requirement that ABC purchase that number or dollar amount of products manufactured by XYZ.

FREE TO TERMINATE

Q. Did ABC consider that pursuant to the relationship that existed between ABC and XYZ since 2002 that ABC at any time could stop selling products manufactured by XYZ.

Q. Was there any requirement that ABC tell XYZ that ABC was no longer going to sell products manufactured by XYZ.

Q. What is the basis for that requirement.

If oral, when.

Any other time.

For each discussion,

Who participated in conversation.

Is that all.

What did each person say.

Is that all this person said.

If written, describe all documents.

Any others.

XYZ COMMITMENT

Q. Was there any agreement between ABC and XYZ as to how long XYZ would sell to ABC products manufactured by XYZ.

Q. If so, what is the basis of that agreement.

Q. If oral,

When was each discussion.

Any others

For each discussion,

Who participated.

Any one else.

What said by each person.

Anything else.

Q. Is there any written document memoralizing this agreement as to how long XYZ would sell to ABC. products manufactured by XYZ.

If so, describe each document.

Any others.

Where is each document located.

Q. Did ABC ever ask XYX for a written document memoralizing how long ABC would be entitled to sell products manufactured by XYZ.

If so,

When was each discussion.

Any others.

For each discussion,

Who participated.

Anybody else.

What said by each participant.

Was anything else said.

APPENDIX B

AUGUST 1982 MEETING

Q. ~~Now, when~~ did you first learn that ~~[redacted]~~ Ajax was considering this sale of the ~~[redacted]~~ Southwind plant? in the Fall of 1982?

-33-

WAS THERE A

A. ~~In the fall of '82 they called a~~ meeting ~~and said it was for sale; they was putting it up for sale~~.

Q. ~~Where~~ Was that meeting?

A. ~~I believe~~ in Vincennes.

Q. ~~Do you remember at all when that meeting was held?~~

WAS THE MEETING

A. ~~I'd say~~ in August sometime.

Q. ~~And~~ --

A. ~~Because it was before the fall work~~.

Q. ~~Who all was present~~?

A. ~~I believe just our area. [redacted] was territory -- I think he had sixteen plants I believe under him; and the mix plant up at [redacted]~~.

Q. And ~~what was~~ said ~~at that meeting~~?

WERE YOU TOLD THAT AJAX WAS

A. ~~They told us that they were~~ going to try to get out of the fertilize business. They was putting it up for sale.

WAS IT L. S. AND J.M.

Q. ~~Who is they~~ that told you? THIS

A. L[redacted] S[redacted] and J[redacted] M[redacted].

L.S. AND J M

Q. ~~Again, what~~ Did ~~they~~ say?

AJAX

A. That ~~they~~ was putting it up for sale. ~~Of course, they told us it'd have to be a big outfit to buy it because they was wanting to sell it as a one package deal; their entire fertilize department~~.

Q. ~~Was anything else said at that meeting?~~

-34-

PENGAD CO., BAYONNE, N.J. 07002 FORM IL 24B

A. ~~Well, some of them asked if they could buy their plants and which they said, no.~~

Q. ~~Anything else happen at the meeting?~~

A. ~~They was asked about what kind of an outfit they would sell to and █████ said it would be a good outfit because he was on a negotiating team to do the selling; and his job was at stake the same as ours; and he wouldn't sell to a company that wouldn't take care of its employees.~~

Q. ~~O.K. Was there anything else said at that meeting?~~

A. ~~Not that I can say.~~

Q. Was anything said there about severance?

A. Not that I remember;

AUGUST 3, 1982 LETTER

Q. Would you take a look at Exhibit 2, please. ~~I want to ask if you have~~ ever seen ~~that before~~?

A. ~~I believe I go~~t one of these.

Q. ~~And do you remember when~~ you got it?

A. ~~This says Augus~~t. ~~I guess just~~ a few days after August 3rd, ~~I'd sa~~y.

~~Q. Is that your best recollection?~~

~~A. Yes, recollection.~~

Q. Did you read that exhibit when you received a copy of it?

A. Yes.

Q. ~~And~~ did you understand it when you read it?

A. I thought I did.

Q. Would you take a look at Exhibit 3, please; ~~and I want to ask if you have seen that document before~~?

A. ~~I believe they passed those out to us, or sent them to us.~~

Q. ~~Do~~ you ~~recall~~ receiv~~ing~~ a copy of that Exhibit 3?

A. Yes.

Q. ~~It's dated August 4th. Would your recollection be you received a copy of it sometime in August of 1982?~~

A. ~~I believe they~~ handed ~~this~~ out to ~~us~~ at a meeting in August.

Q. ~~Was that August~~ of 1982?

-38-

A. Yes.

Q. ~~And~~ did you read Exhibit 3 when you received a copy of it?

A. Yes.

Q. ~~And~~ did you understand it?

A. I think so.

QUESTIONS AND ANSWERS

Q. Would you look at Exhibit 6, please; and I would like to ask you if you have ever seen that document before?

A. Uh huh.

Q. ~~Do you recall when?~~

A. WAS THIS ~~They~~ passed ~~this~~ out at a meeting.

Q. ~~Do you remember at which meeting, sir?~~

A. ~~I believe the same as the other exhibit we had two, three?~~

Q. Would that have been in August, 198~~3~~2?

A. Yes, August.

Q. ~~And~~ did you read Exhibit 6 when you --

A. Yes.

Q. --received it? Did you understand it when you read it?

A. Yes.

PRINCETON MEETING

DID YOU ATTEND A

Q. ~~O.K. Can you tell me when this~~ meeting ~~was?~~

~~A. Not the exact date. It was~~ the first of April ~~sometime. I don't know the exact~~ date.

Q. ~~And what year, sir?~~

A. ~~'83.~~ 1983

Q. ~~And where~~ was the meeting?

A. At Princeton, Indiana, Holiday Inn.

Q. ~~Who was there?~~ WERE L.M + L.M THERE

A. [illegible]

Q. [illegible]?

-6-

A. [illegible] from [illegible].

Q. And who else was there besides [illegible] and [illegible]?

A. I don't remember if [illegible] was there or not for sure.

Q. Were there other Amoco employees there?

A. Oh, there was everybody that was in the twenty fertilizer plants and the mix plant at [illegible].

Q. What happened at this meeting?

A. That's when they told us that they'd sold it to [illegible].

Q. What did they say was sold to Triple T?

A. The twenty retail plants and, excuse me, and the mix plant at [illegible].

Q. Who told you that?

A. [illegible].

Q. What else happened?

A. They was a lot of questions put to him about the severance and their jobs and --

Q. O.K. Can you tell me what questions were put to Mr. [illegible] about severance?

A. Well, most of them wanted to know if they would get severance pay.

Q. What did [illegible] say?

A. He told them if they wasn't offered a job with [illegible] or get transferred, TO ANOTHER AJAX JOB that they would be eligible to severance pay.

Q. ~~Get transferred, you mean get transferred to AJAX?~~

A. ~~Yes, stayed with AJAX.~~

Q. ~~Is that all Mr. said about entitlement to severance?~~

A. DID L.M SAY ~~He said~~ if you WERE ~~was~~ offered a job and turned it down, you would not get severance pay.

Q. Did Mr. LM ~~say anything about the same benefits or the same pay?~~

A. With ~~TEMPLE, you mean?~~

~~Q. Yes.~~

A. ~~He said that we'd have to find that out from TEMPLE~~

Q. ~~As to what the benefits would be?~~

A. ~~Yes, he didn't know.~~

Q. ~~But~~ did Mr. LM say that you would get severance pay if the job you were offered at TEMPLE paid less than the job you had at AJAX?

A. No.

Q. Did anybody at AJAX ever tell you that?

A. No.

~~Q. Who was it -- before you told me you think people~~

~~are entitled to severance if the pay was less at~~ [redacted] ~~than at~~ [redacted]

A. ~~Well, some of them was I understood was offered a job for five dollars an hour and no benefits.~~

Q. ~~O.K. But~~ did [redacted] ever say that people would be entitled to severance if the salary or wages or benefits at [redacted] were less than those at [redacted]?

A. No, no.

Q. ~~O.K. Now, getting back to this meeting what else was said~~ at this meeting at Princeton on April 1, 1983?

A. ~~Well, about everybody asked questions about their job; and they was wanting to be assured of a job; and they was~~ told that they would pretty sure that they would keep their job. ~~They couldn't guarantee it because —~~

Q. ~~Who~~ from [redacted] said ~~anything~~ about whether jobs would exist or not exist?

A. Mr. [redacted].

Q. ~~And~~ at the meeting ~~what~~ did Mr. [redacted] say ~~on that subject~~?

A. ~~Well~~, he couldn't guarantee that [redacted] would offer everybody a job; but he thought they would because of their experience of running the plants instead of bringing in new personnel unexperienced.

Q. ~~Is that all that Mr.~~ [redacted] ~~said on the subject of jobs?~~

A. ~~That's all I recall.~~

Q. ~~Now what else happened at this meeting at Princeton on April 1, 1983?~~

A. ~~Well, that's about all I recall we talked about.~~

Q. Now, were there representatives from [redacted] at this meeting?

A. ~~Not at that time.~~ [redacted] ~~had theres; and then when they left~~, then [redacted] came in and ~~the [redacted] personnel left.~~

Q. So were there two parts to the meeting?

A. Yes.

Q. ~~Can you tell me about what happened at the time when the [redacted] people left and [redacted] people came in?~~

A. ~~They came in and said~~ that they had bought out the twenty plants and the mix plant. ~~They said~~ they wanted everybody to stay with them at the same salary that they was a getting with [redacted].

Q. ~~And~~ who said that ~~if you recall?~~

A. Bob -- no, not [redacted]. ~~I can't think of his last name now. [redacted] I believe is his name.~~

Q. ~~Did you interpret that as a job offer by [redacted]?~~

~~A. No.~~

~~Q. What did it mean to you?~~

~~A. Well, they never -- then they expected or hoped;~~

-10-

but they never came out and asked us to work permanent.

Q. Maybe you'd better tell me again. My notes say that you said that Mr. ▇▇▇ said they wanted all of you to stay?

A. They expected all of us to stay at the same salary as with ▇▇▇; but they said that to the group is what I was meaning.

Q. When you say ▇▇▇, you mean ▇▇▇?

A. ▇▇▇, yes.

Q. Did Mr. ▇▇▇ say anything else about jobs at that meeting?

A. I don't know. They talked about the vacation time.

Q. Anything else?

A. Not that I -- nothing I can think of now.

CPSIA information can be obtained at www.ICGtesting.com
Printed in the USA
LVOW082108270213

322005LV00001B/7/P